For Nick,

With best wishes,

Peter

GALDOS'S NOVEL OF THE HISTORICAL IMAGINATION

Grateful acknowledgement is due to the Associate Dean of the School of Graduate Studies and Research, Queen's University, Kingston, Ontario, for a financial contribution towards the publication of this volume.

LIVERPOOL MONOGRAPHS IN HISPANIC STUDIES

2 GALDOS'S NOVEL OF THE HISTORICAL IMAGINATION

PETER A BLY

A STUDY OF THE CONTEMPORARY NOVELS

X
FRANCIS CAIRNS

First published 1983

Liverpool Monographs in Hispanic Studies, 2
General editor: James Higgins
Assistant editors: Ann Mackenzie, Roger Wright

Published by Francis Cairns
The University, P.O. Box 147, Liverpool L69 3BX, Great Britain

British Library Cataloguing in Publication Data
Bly, Peter A
 Galdós's novel of the historical imagination.
 – (Liverpool monographs in Hispanic studies; 2
 ISSN 0261-1538)
 1. Pérez Galdós, Benito – Criticism and inter-
 pretation
 I. Title   II. Series
 863'.5   PG6555.Z5

 ISBN 0-905205-14-6

Printed in Great Britain by Redwood Burn Ltd, Trowbridge, Wiltshire

CONTENTS

FOR MEG

FOREWORD

This book is a revised version of the Ph.D thesis which I completed in 1978 at the University of London under the supervision of Professor J.E. Varey (Westfield College). The inspiration for the thesis was the seminal article by Professor Geoffrey W. Ribbans on *Fortunata y Jacinta* in the 1970 collection of essays, *Galdós Studies*, ed. J.E. Varey (London: Támesis).

For the purposes of my study I have preferred to examine the novels of the *serie contemporánea* in chronological order rather than rearrange them according to the historical period treated. I have also divided them into four distinct groups. Group I comprises eight novels from *La desheredada* (1881) to *Miau* (1888). Group II consists of *La incógnita* (1888-89), *Realidad* (1889), the *Torquemada* tetralogy (1889-95) and *Angel Guerra* (1890-91). Group III embraces *Tristana* (1892), *Nazarín* (1895), *Halma* (1895) and *Misericordia* (1897), and Group IV *Casandra* (1905), *El caballero encantado* (1909) and *La razón de la sinrazón* (1915).

I have omitted discussion of *La loca de la casa* (1892) because, although inserted by Galdós in the *serie contemporánea*, it is sub-titled a play. Relevant material from the novel in dialogue form, *El abuelo* (1907), is treated in the chapter on *Misericordia* in Part IV because it is deliberately not located in Spain.

The text of Galdós's novels used is the *Obras completas* edition by F.C. Sainz de Robles (Madrid: Aguilar), vols I, II, III, VI (1968), IV (1969), V (1961). All quotations are followed by the appropriate volume and page numbers. The volumes of Galdós's unpublished newspaper articles, partially collected by Alberto Ghiraldo as the *Obras inéditas* (*OI*), that I have used include: I. *Fisonomías sociales*; II. *Política española*; III. *Política española*; IV. *Política española* (all Madrid, 1923); VI. *Cronicón* (Madrid, 1924). Relevant material omitted by Ghiraldo is to be found in *Las cartas desconocidas de Galdós en "La*

Prensa" de Buenos Aires, ed. William H. Shoemaker (Madrid, 1973), which will be referred to as Shoemaker.

When citing periodicals, I have used the following abbreviations:

AG	*Anales Galdosianos*
BHS	*Bulletin of Hispanic Studies*
CHA	*Cuadernos Hispanoamericanos*
TLS	*Times Literary Supplement*

In all other cases the full title of the journal is given.

I gratefully acknowledge the generous contribution of Associate Dean John Beal, School of Graduate Studies and Research, Queen's University, towards the publication of this work.

I should also like to thank Mrs Paulette Bark for her prompt and efficient typing of the manuscript.

One final word of thanks is due to my parents, wife and children for their constant encouragement, patience and tolerance during the preparation of this book.

P.A. Bly
Kingston, June-September, 1981

INTRODUCTION

The fictional prose works of Benito Pérez Galdós (1843-1920) are usually divided into two large blocks: the historical novels and the contemporary social novels. The forty-six historical novels or *episodios nacionales* were written in five series of ten interconnected novels each (apart from the unfinished fifth series) and in two distinct periods: the first two series between 1873 and 1879, and the third, fourth, and fifth between 1898 and 1912. They chronicle the major events of Spanish political and military history during the first six decades of the nineteenth century as seen and experienced by a number of fictional and historical characters. Only in the last eight or nine *episodios nacionales* did Galdós come to record events between 1863-1880 which he had personally experienced after he had arrived in Peninsular Spain from his native Canary Islands.

The thirty-one contemporary social novels were published between 1870 and 1915 and were later divided by the author into two separate groups: *Las novelas de la primera época* (1870-1879) and *Las novelas de la serie contemporánea* (1881-1915). The division was in part a matter of chronology. *Las novelas de la primera época* group together his very first attempts at novel-writing: the fantastic short-story *La sombra* (1870) and two early traditional historical novels unconnected with the *episodios nacionales*: *La Fontana de Oro* (1870) and *El audaz* (1871). The remaining novels, *Doña Perfecta* (1876), *Gloria* (1876-1877), *Marianela* (1878) and *La familia de León Roch* (1878-1879), often called thesis novels, deal with contemporary social problems but without being set in a definite time period or in an exact Spanish location.

Las novelas de la serie contemporánea, on the other hand, comprise Galdós's more mature contemporary social novels which were intended, at least initially in 1881, to be different from his earlier *novelas de la primera época*: "Efectivamente, yo he querido en esta obra [*La desheredada*] entrar por nuevo camino o inaugurar mi segunda o tercera *manera*, como se dice de los pintores."[1] One of the principal ingredients of this new "manera" is undoubtedly the precise use of references, whether in single words, sentences or paragraphs, to events and leading characters of contemporary Spanish political and military history. Despite all the attention Galdós's use of history in the *episodios nacionales* has received,[2] the topic in the *serie contemporánea* has been only partially treated. There are occasional passing comments in general studies to the effect that Galdós wrote "history" in both sub-genres, but no serious comparisons are made.[3] Where more specialized and searching monographs do exist, the focus tends to be disappointingly reduced to one or two novels of the *serie contemporánea*, with the result that for some critics Galdós's use of history in this series is considered only as a convenient shorthand device for rapid characterization and realistic background authentication.[4] Clearly the first important step in redressing this serious imbalance in Galdós criticism is to conduct an examination of all the contemporary historical material in the *serie contemporánea*. Secondly, it will be important to determine whether this material is given any special function in the narrative. These are the principal aims of my study. The results will show not only that Galdós consistently employed history throughout the whole series but that he did so in a way that gives the novels an extra dimension of meaning enabling them to be viewed as special kinds of historical novels as well as social or psychological studies. More important still, through

---

[1] In a letter that Galdós wrote in 1882 to Francisco Giner de los Ríos, reproduced in Manuel B. Cossío [M.B.C.], "Galdós y Giner: una carta de Galdós", *La Lectura*, 20 (1920), 254-58.
[2] The major studies are: Hans Hinterhäuser, *Los "Episodios nacionales" de Benito Pérez Galdós*, trans. José Escobar (Madrid, 1963); Antonio Regalado García, *Benito Pérez Galdós y la novela histórica 1868-1912* (Madrid, 1966); and Alfred Rodríguez, *An Introduction to the "Episodios nacionales" of Galdós* (New York, 1967).
[3] See Amado Alonso, "Lo español y lo universal en la obra de Galdós", in his *Materia y forma en poesía*, 3rd ed. (Madrid, 1965), p.209; Joaquín Casalduero, *Vida y obra de Galdós (1843-1920)*, 3rd ed. (Madrid, 1970), p.43; and Eleazar Huerta, "Galdós y la novela histórica", *Atenea*, 72 (May 1943), pp.101, 104.
[4] See Carlos Blanco Aguinaga, "Entrar por el aro: restauración del 'orden' y educación de Fortunata", in his *La historia y el texto literario: tres novelas de Galdós* (Madrid, 1978), pp.49-94; "Five years in Madrid", *TLS*, 12 October, 1973, pp.1227-28; Ricardo Gullón, "Cuestiones galdosianas", *CHA*, 34 (1958), 237-54; Geoffrey Ribbans, "Contemporary history in the structure and characterization of *Fortunata y Jacinta*", in *Galdós Studies*, ed. J.E. Varey (London, 1970), pp.90-113, and "*Historia novelada* and *novela histórica*: the use of historical incidents from the reign of Isabella II in Galdós's *episodios* and *novelas contemporáneas*", in *Hispanic Studies in Honour of Frank Pierce*, ed. John England (Sheffield, 1980), pp.133-47; Antonio Ruiz Salvador, "La función del trasfondo histórico en *La desheredada*", *AG*, 1 (1966), 53-62.

his use of contemporary political material, Galdós conducts a debate on the question of man's fundamental relation to history which has to be duly weighed in any balanced assessment of his historical writing, discussion of which has always hitherto been confined to the *episodios nacionales*.

First, however, it is imperative to define what we mean or do not mean by the terms "historical novel" and "contemporary political history", since we are not as convinced as Fleishman that "everyone knows what a historical novel is".[5] The events of national and international political and military history used by Galdós in the *serie contemporánea* cover the period 1860-1910 (see Appendix for a survey) and obviously do not conform to the usual Medieval or Renaissance components of the traditional historical novel, as developed by Scott and Hugo in the nineteenth century. Nor do our "historical" novels of the *serie contemporánea* resemble Galdós's own special brand of traditional historical novel already formulated in the *episodios nacionales*, which, situated in the nineteenth century, narrate events from the early decades or the intermediate past.[6] In the *serie contemporánea* Galdós uses a much shorter time frame, twenty years or less, between events and his chronicling of them: the immediate or more recent past is his quarry. Paradoxically, for some critics like J.B. Matthews, this is the most accurate type of historical novel.[7]

A further point to bear in mind is the amount of historical material to be found in the novels of the *serie contemporánea*. The eternal problem faced by all historical novelists from Manzoni and Scott onwards has been how to determine the correct balance between the fictional and historical components at their disposal.[8] To what extent can events of public history be pared down before the novel ceases to be "historical"? More dogmatically-minded theorists and readers would probably agree with Fleishman when he states that the historical novel is distinguished from the social or dramatic novel by the "*balanced* weight it attaches to the personal and the collective experience of men in history" [my italics].[9] Yet Azorín sensibly noted

[5] Avrom Fleishman, *The English Historical Novel: Walter Scott to Virginia Woolf* (Baltimore, 1971), p.3.
[6] See Madeleine de Gogorza Fletcher, *The Spanish Historical Novel: 1870-1970* (London, 1974), pp.1-2.
[7] See James Brander Matthews, *The Historical Novel and Other Essays* (New York, 1901), p.18.
[8] As Azorín acutely pointed out in "La novela histórica", in his *Clásicos y modernos* (Madrid, 1919), p.192.
[9] Fleishman, p.10.

that "dentro del género caben muchas variantes".[10] The basic blend of
history and fiction is constant but the proportions of the constituent
parts can vary to a great degree. Butterfield has persuasively argued that
even extremely light doses of historical fact are sufficient for a work to
qualify as an historical novel:

> Many historical novels are stories of ordinary everyday issues in
> the lives of people, and deal with some personal concerns of
> fictitious characters, and with the things that make up the ordi-
> nary kind of novel; but these novels become "historical" ones by
> the fact that their drama is played out as it were in the shadow of
> great public events. Some well-known, historic character looms in
> the background, larger historical issues cast their shadow at times
> and perhaps at some point the narrow concerns of the individuals
> whose fate makes up the story, cross the path of these, and be-
> come interlocked for a moment with some piece of history.[11]

For Thomas Deegan this is precisely the way in which contemporary
historical events are presented in the novels of George Eliot, which he
prefers to call "novels of the historical imagination".[12] It is not that,
again in Butterfield's colourful phrase, "the sending of a few pistol-
shots of actual episode into a piece of work" suddenly transforms a
social novel into an historical one,[13] but rather that the meaningful use
of these historical elements within the fiction adds to the latter a
wholly new dimension that implies a coherent, rational attitude by the
narrator-author towards the historical period and material selected. The
lack of this intertwining of fiction and history was indeed signalled out
by Lukács as an important symptom in the decline of the nineteenth-
century Realist novel, legitimate off-spring of the Romantic historical
novel.[14]

Consequently, if Galdós's *novelas de la serie contemporánea* are
to qualify even as this special type of historical novel, if they are to be
called "novels of the historical imagination", it has to be proved that
they incorporate the events of the past (in their case, very recent) in a
manner that adds a coherent dimension of historical meaning.

[10] Azorín, p.189.
[11] Herbert Butterfield, *The Historical Novel: An Essay* (Cambridge, 1924), p.79.
[12] See Thomas Deegan, "George Eliot's novels of the historical imagination", *Clio*, 1, No. 3 (1972), 21-33.
[13] Butterfield, p.56.
[14] Georg Lukács, *The Historical Novel*, trans. Hannah and Stanley Mitchell, (Harmondsworth, 1976), p.239.

PART ONE
FICTION AS ALLEGORY
OF HISTORY

CHAPTER 1

THE NEW NOVEL OF THE HISTORICAL IMAGINATION: *LA DESHEREDADA* (1881)

The whole question of Galdós's use of history in the *serie contemporánea* is thrust upon the reader by the very first lines of the opening novel, *La desheredada*. Without giving any indication of the speaker's identity or location, Galdós launches into the direct reproduction of a frenzied political speech. As we read the largely disconnected phrases, we slowly deduce that the speaker must be an unnamed nineteenth-century Prime Minister delivering a strenuous rebuttal to a possible Opposition censure motion in the Spanish Cortes:

> Permítame su señoría que me admire de la despreocupación con que su señoría y los amigos de su señoría confiesan haber infringido la Constitución ... No me importan los murmullos. Mandaré despejar las tribunas ... ¡A votar, a votar! ¿Votos a mí? ¿Queréis saber con qué poderes gobierno? Ahí lo tenéis: se cargan por la culata. He aquí mis votos: me los ha fabricado Krupp.

(IV, 985)

Only as we move further into the chapter do we realize that the speaker is no historical figure of turbulent nineteenth-century Spanish parliamentary history, but a madman, Tomás Rufete, who is soliloquizing in the recreation yard of Leganés, the mental asylum on the outskirts of Madrid. This momentary illusion is important because through it Galdós is able to suggest that his new type of novel has an important political dimension. For the moment that dimension is presented in very vague terms because the nature of Tomás's political role here is entirely imaginary. Nevertheless, the reader's attention has been caught and he will read the ensuing fiction with one eye ready to light on further historical allusions, whether they be vague or precise. One could almost say that the reader of the new Galdós novel has now been "programmed" to read not only *La desheredada* but also the other seven novels in our Group I of the *serie contemporánea.*

Tomás's tirade also establishes two other points. First, the violent and unbalanced nature of the individual's relation to the larger political entity. Galdós will build on this dissociation when he later shows the reaction of other individuals to more concrete historical events. Secondly, if Tomás is only a madman and imagining this Cortes scene, there might be an inverse suggestion that the Spanish parliamentary system contains a number of cranks like him who engage in such rhetorical, emotional scenes. This suggestion could be extended to the country at large if we take into account the evidence of the map of Spain in Canencia's office.

While there is no evidence in Tomás's speech to suggest that he is not thinking of himself as a Prime Minister ("Los funcionarios eran para él la oposición, la minoría, la Prensa; eran también el país que le vigilaba, le pedía cuentas" [IV, 988]), a regal comparison is not to be excluded either. Isidora, who later in prison compares herself to Queen Marie Antoinette (IV, 1148), reports to Canencia that her father would always be drawing up all sorts of decrees, laws and royal charters. The corner he occupies in the Leganés courtyard is described as the throne of his power. Are there, though, any grounds for considering Tomás Rufete as the representation of a particular historical figure such as the hapless Amadeo I, scorned by practically all of his subjects and in whose short-lived reign the action of Part I of *La desheredada* is situated? The phrase used by Rufete to describe his supposed ascent to power ("Subí al Poder empujado por el país que me llamaba, que me necesitaba" [IV, 989]) certainly recalls the processes that had brought Amadeo to the Spanish throne. In *Amadeo I* (1910), an *episodio nacional* of the fifth series, Galdós writes that Prim's friends and emissaries "le habían buscado y traído [a Amadeo] para felicidad de estos abatidos reinos" (III, 1009). Later in the same novel the respected journalist, Pepe Ferreras, is moved to say of Amadeo's abdication: "Don Amadeo se va; don Amadeo vuelve la espalda a este pueblo de orates y nos deja entregados a nuestras propias locuras" (III, 1108-09). If Spain is to be viewed as a madhouse in *La desheredada,* as Canencia's map suggests, then Tomás Rufete could well be the fictional counterpart to King Amadeo. It is a tempting hypothesis, which Galdós encourages the reader to explore with this arresting allusion to the country's political forum.

Certainly when Galdós does include concrete historical events – in Part I, Chapter IV – this twinning of fictional and historical characters becomes somewhat more explicit. As Isidora and her Manchegan friend, Miquis, stroll down the Paseo de la Castellana, they become spectators of the famous anti-Amadeo protest by aristocratic Bourbon sympathisers in March 1871. If we overlook Galdós's inaccuracy in changing the event to an undisclosed time between April and the Autumn of 1872, we can say that the historical episode fulfils an important role in the development of Isidora's character: the coaches and fashions of the female protesters are a visual stimulus for her pretensions of nobility; they are the first confirmation in the short time since her arrival in Madrid from La Mancha that her dream-world of luxury and nobility can be a reality. The narrator wryly observes: "Era la realización súbita de un presentimiento. Tanta grandeza no le era desconocida. Había soñado, la había visto, como ven los místicos el cielo antes de morirse" (IV, 1014). The strong implication is that Isidora's hold on reality, even when it is before her eyes, is suspiciously precarious, that her vivid imagination dangerously misrepresents that reality: "Así la realidad se fantaseaba a sus ojos maravillados ... La hermosura de los caballos y su grave paso y gallardas cabezadas eran a sus ojos como a los del artista, la inverosímil figura del hipogrifo" (IV, 1014). This *mantillas* protest corroborates, then, Ribbans's theory that historical detail in the *serie contemporánea* is used for deepening characterization.[1] For it clearly reveals a defect that has hitherto been only hinted at: Isidora's propensity to superimpose her own imaginings on the reality (on this and other occasions, a political reality) that she is observing, just as her father had done in the novel's initial chapter.

Moreover, the historical episode is the cause of that character change or at least the catalyst which spurs it on. History, Galdós is trying to show us in the new type of novel he is attempting in 1881, intervenes decisively in the lives of fictional characters; history and fiction intertwine in a meaningful way that Butterfield would have considered sufficient for *La desheredada* to be called an historical novel.

Yet Galdós goes one step further than character illustration or development in his rich use of this incident. Structurally it serves to anticipate a later and important development in the novel: Isidora's descent into prostitution. As his readers would quickly remember (the incident had occurred only ten years before), the most memorable part of the demonstration was the unscheduled appearance of a rival

---

[1] Ribbans, *"Historia novelada ...",* p.143.

counter-demonstration of prostitutes organized by the *demócrata* deputy, Felipe Ducazcal.[2] The only allusion to this turn of events in *La desheredada* – and it is only a very veiled allusion – is the mention that "de cuando en cuando la presencia de un ridículo simón lo descomponía [el hermoso tumulto]" (IV, 1014), their occupants, Miquis suggests, being money-lenders and not prostitutes. If they had been the latter, there would certainly have been a great deal of irony, only appreciable at the end of the novel, in Isidora's indignant outburst: "Debían prohibir . . . que vinieran aquí esos horribles coches de peseta" (IV, 1014).

The deliberate reticence or minor falsification on Galdós's part, far from diverting attention from the historical truth of the political episode, encourages the reader to establish parallels between it and the fictional thread of Isidora's life. Like Amadeo, Isidora is newly arrived in Madrid and eager to impress people in her attempts to assert the legal rights to her inheritance from the aristocratic Aransis family. Just as Amadeo is encountering stiff opposition, Isidora will soon be defeated by the family she desperately wants to join. Her failure will eventually lead to prostitution whilst the *mantillas* protest will be the beginning of five turbulent years in Spain's political system.

As Hans Hinterhäuser has pointed out, the twinning of "la historia grande" or public history and "la historia chica" or fiction is a constant feature of the *episodios nacionales*.[3] Hence its employment in *La desheredada* and throughout our Group I novels in the *serie contemporánea*, if not original, does serve to link this new type of novel of the historical imagination with the more traditional historical novels that Galdós had been cultivating in the previous decade. There is, however, one fundamental difference between the usages of this similar technique in the two sub-genres. In the *episodios nacionales* it is only one ingredient amongst many joining history and fiction. The *episodios nacionales* would still be historical novels even if there were no coincidences of major fictional and historical events to underline the obvious. In the novels of our Group I of the *serie contemporánea* the device assumes a greater importance simply because a great deal of the rest of the material in these eight novels is not immediately connected with the historical matter. The historical episodes stand out in the text, exposed and open for all to see, stepping-stones of historical data which lead to the novel's overall historical dimension. To label these historical

[2] See Melchor Fernández Almagro, *Historia política de la España contemporánea*, 3 vols. (Madrid, 1969), I, p.114.
[3] Hinterhäuser, pp.236-44.

details as the pillars of an underlying historical allegory might initially
appear unwarranted, but the reiterated and careful use of the method
depends for maximum effect on continuing the associations suggested
beyond the initial mention and into the subsequent development of the
fictional matter.

By the same token, the historical events included in this way
suffer from contamination, as it were, by the fictional developments.
The distanced presentation of the political protest by these Bourbon
sympathisers, amidst fashion commentary and amorous banter between
Isidora and Miquis, distorts the historical event so that it appears no
more than a fashion parade dictated by motives of female vanity similar
to those displayed by Isidora. The chaotic physical movement of the
carriages and horses and Isidora's sensorial excitement underline the
hollowness of the occasion, the lack of good political reason behind the
demonstration: Amadeo had just arrived in a foreign land and his good
intentions and honest character were now deliberately being ignored
and spurned by such factions as the *alfonsistas*, anxious only that their
own candidate, the young son of Queen Isabel II, should ascend the
Spanish throne. By incorporating this historical episode into the fiction
in the manner that he has chosen, Galdós shows that he has a comment
(negative) to make on its significance in the march of Spanish history.
History is not ignored in these predominantly social novels, as has often
been suggested; on the contrary, Galdós's interest in history is still
insatiable. No mere backdrop, history is being reinterpreted for the
reader. Adapting a colourful phrase coined by Michael Nimetz, one
might say that if in these novels history upgrades fiction, fiction also
downgrades history.[4]

The *mantillas* protest also allows Galdós to introduce a theme
that he will treat continuously in all the novels of the *serie contemporánea*: the fictional characters' ignorance or awareness of public
affairs. As an eye-witness of the demonstration, Isidora is too bedazzled
by the physical sensations of the scene to absorb Miquis's correct
analysis of its political meaning: "Esto de las mantillas blancas es una
manifestación, una protesta contra el rey extranjero" (IV, 1015). She is
carried away by the externals: if at first she is prepared to curtsey to
Amadeo who is, after all, the King, as her uncle the Canon had told her,
when the procession moves away she is ready to don a white *mantilla*
and join the *alfonsistas*. Isidora has no political scruples or indeed

---

[4] Michael Nimetz, *Humor in Galdós: A Study of the "Novelas contemporáneas"*
(New Haven, Connecticut, 1968), p.112.

interest in politics, and it is on this point that Galdós is criticizing her most sharply. He is not asking her to predict the outcome of Amadeo's reign, to foresee how this protest by the one class in Spanish society that might have ensured Amadeo's success as monarch led to his abdication. Even the wise Miquis is not accorded such an historical foresight. All Galdós is asking Isidora to do is to evaluate what she sees happening in front of her. This she cannot do because of her greater obsession with the externals of the public event. If Isidora cannot absorb the political lesson, then there can be no excuse for the contemporary reader of 1881, the principal object of Galdós's attention in all the novels of our Group I.

The next mention of contemporary or recent historical events — in Part I, Chapter VI — is also relatively brief, but for the first time, precise: the assassination of Juan Prim in the Calle del Turco, near the Parliament buildings, on the night of December 27, 1870. It comes in a paragraph of authorial comment on a street game of soldiers played by Isidora's brother, Mariano, and his friends. Mariano has donned a *ros*, the famous flat-topped military cap that Prim had worn so often, and struts around the street with a toy sword in his hand shouting, " ¡Soy *Plim!*":

> ¡Ser Prim! ¡Ilusión de los hijos del pueblo en los primeros albores de la ambición, cuando los instintos de gloria comienzan a despuntar en el alma . . . Esta ilusión, que era entonces común en las turbas infantiles, *a pesar de la reciente trágica muerte del héroe, se va extinguiendo ya conforme se desvanece aquella enérgica figura. Pero aún hoy persiste algo de tan bella ilusión*; aún se ven zamacucos de cinco años, con un palo al hombro y una gorra de papel en la cabeza, que quieren ser Prim o ser O'Donnell.
> (my italics; IV, 1020)

The emotional tone of this political gloss indicates the deep significance that Galdós attaches to Prim's tragic assassination in *La desheredada*. This example is not an isolated reference: the memory of that 1870 tragedy permeates the whole novel, providing the chronological and thematic reference point for the other historical allusions. Moreover, the fictional episode of the boys' game can be interpreted as a general parable on the political events of 1868-1870 in which Prim was the principal actor. All the boys want to be Prim and wear the *ros*. In the same way the various factions in the 1868 Revolutionary coalition wanted to assume power for themselves once they had toppled Isabel from her throne, and squabbles and arguments ensued. The development of this factional in-fighting is vividly reflected in the dramatic change in the boys' behaviour once they have crossed the railway track after the passage of a goods train. The order and military discipline of their earlier marching are now replaced by disputes and arguments as to who shall wear the *ros*. As Galdós was later to record in the companion *episodio nacional*, *La de los tristes destinos* (1909), the definitive collapse of the Isabelline regime was visually emphasized for everyone in Spain in September 1868 by the train journey of the Queen and her family from San Sebastián to the French border. The passage of the goods train in the story of Mariano's exploits could thus represent the passage of the September Revolution: before its arrival, all is order and discipline in the revolutionaries' ranks; after it has passed by, anarchy and chaos take over. Moreover, in both the fictional and historical episodes there are tragic victims: Prim, the leading supporter of Amadeo's candidacy for the Spanish throne, was assassinated in the street, supposedly by supporters of his great opponent, the fanatical Republican, Paúl y Angulo. In the boys' game, *Zarapicos* – a regular recipient, it should be noted, of food left-overs from the kitchens of Amadeo's Royal Palace – is knifed to death in the street by his arch-rival, the later anarchist bomb-thrower, Mariano Rufete.

This parallelism of the fictional and historical episodes is re-inforced by the description of the manoeuvres of "el menudo ejército" (IV, 1021) of boys who are really playing a dangerous game of civil war: "En aquel murmullo se concentraban los chillidos para decir: 'Somos granujas; no somos aún la Humanidad, pero sí un croquis de ella. España, somos tus polluelos, y, cansados de jugar a los toros, jugamos a la guerra civil' " (IV, 1022). Within the chronology of the fiction Galdós could be referring to the forthcoming disorders of the Second Carlist War and the First Republic that are presented in blunt form at the beginning of Chapter I, Part II; but armed conflict had already occurred earlier, soon after the success of September 1868 and before Prim's death: in September 1869, Federalist revolts had taken place in Ampurdán, Valencia and Zaragoza. The illusion of reality becomes so complete that at one point Galdós emphatically remarks: "*Era una página de la historia contemporánea*, puesta en aleluyas en un olvidado rincón de la capital. Fueran los niños hombres y las calles provincias, y *la aleluya habría sido una página seria, demasiado seria*" (my italics; IV, 1021).[5] The whole sequence of the boys' game and

---

[5] Carmen Bravo Villasante, "El naturalismo de Galdós y el mundo de *La desheredada*", *CHA*, 77 (1969), 479-86, maintains that the whole episode is a literary re-working of a very popular nineteenth-century *pliego de aleluya* called *La pedrea*.

subsequent fight is in fact an "episodio nacional" in its own right, a piece of contemporary history. Not only does it resume in general outline the development of the main events during the 1868-1870 interregnum, but it also illustrates how history can decisively intervene in the life of a fictional individual. In *La desheredada* the memory of Prim's valiant achievements leads youngsters to argue, fight and ultimately kill.

In Mariano's second act of physical aggression at the end of the novel his aim is now directed at the new ruler of Spanish society: the young Alfonso XII, ironically the one candidate for the Spanish throne whom Prim had strenuously rejected. If Prim's end was a tragic crime, Mariano's final execution is a just punishment for the attempted assassination. Galdós's clever interweaving of history and fiction leads to some surprising and tragically ironic twists. One can also say that just as the *mantillas* protest decisively propelled Isidora along a path of ultimately tragic destiny, the memory of Prim's life and death is the catalyst which triggers off a cardinally important development in the life of her brother Mariano.

As if Galdós's own remarks on Prim's death and the parody of the course of *La Gloriosa* were not sufficient layers of political commentary at this point, another is added with the personification of the strutting turkey-cock who appears on the scene as the boys fight over the *ros*, which, it is to be noted, has a turkey-feather affixed to it:

A cada voz respondía [el pavo] con sus estornudos y su carcajada. Parecían aclamaciones a la patria, *vivas* contestados con *hurras* . . . El viento le despeinaba las plumas, y al arrastrar las alas y dar el estornudo, *era el puro emblema de la vanidad* [my italics]. No le faltaban más que las cruces, la palabra y la edad provecta para ser quien yo me sé.

(IV, 1022)

The animal indeed shows a remarkable likeness to history's strutting military heroes.

All that remains of Prim's noble service to Spain is the memory of the superficial trappings of his authority, his *ros*. Deprived of any moral guidance from adults, as the ridiculous comments of the public officials who arrive on the murder scene make very clear, Mariano and his playmates suffer a tragic dissociation from contemporary history. Mariano cannot read or interpret the meaning of political events because he has no teacher to guide him . Hence the appropriateness of the dedication of *La desheredada* to the country's teachers. Significantly, Galdós considers, but then rejects, dedicating the novel to politicians: ". . . convendría dedicar estas páginas . . . ¿a quién? ¿Al infeliz paciente, a los curanderos y droguistas que, llamándose filósofos y políticos, le recetan uno y otro día? ... No" (IV, 985). As in the *mantillas* scene, he is unequivocally pointing his historical lesson at the readers of 1881, for Mariano's band of unruly ragamuffins, or at least those who have survived, are today's adults: "Eran la discordia del porvenir, una parte crecida de la España futura, tal que si no le quitaran el sarampión, las viruelas, las fiebres y el raquitismo, nos daría una estadística considerable dentro de pocos años" (IV, 1021). Not that 1881 was a particularly violent year in Spanish history; Spain was after all embarked on the relative peace and prosperity of the Restoration. No, Galdós's aim in reinterpreting the events of recent history is to encourage his contemporary readers to understand the underlying spiritual-cum-moral reasons which led to those events and which persisted within the Spanish character: the personal egotism of individual Spaniards. The description of the boys' drilling makes this point clearly: "¡Allí la envidia, aquí la generosidad, no lejos el mando, más allá el servilismo, *claros embriones de egoísmo en todas partes!*" (my italics; IV, 1022).

To guide his readers in this historical reinterpretation Galdós introduces two chapters later an important secondary character, José de Relimpio, who, unlike his wards, the Rufete children, does possess a keen feeling for contemporary history. In his youth Relimpio had served in the militia, and now his patriotism is translated into a voracious appetite for contemporary political events. He religiously scans the evening newspapers for the latest details: "Echóse al cuerpo el periódico, *leyendo con extremada atención* las conferencias de hombres políticos y pasando al fin los muertos y los anuncios. Luego, mientras atarugaba la máquina de pitillos, *meditaba sobre los sucesos del día y sobre política general*" (my italics; IV, 1038). He is in communion with what he perceives as the historical spirit of the country. Unfortunately, these noble feelings ("Sentía por las glorias de su patria un entusiasmo ardiente" [IV, 1038]) are not matched by a practical sense of what can realistically be achieved in Spanish politics: he is opposed to all political parties and thinks that when Spaniards join together for the common good all the revolutionary plotting will stop. Even his more concrete proposals (the return of Gibraltar to Spain, the abolition of ex-ministers' salaries and the erection of a statue to Méndez Núñez[6]) also reveal his political naïveté. The clear implication, then, is that the latest addition to his repertoire of set conversation topics – the merits of King Amadeo[7]

---

[6] The famous commander of the frigate *Numancia* who in the Pacific War against Chile and Peru won the decisive battle of El Callao in 1866.
[7] His cries for a revolution a short while later (IV, 1049) detract from this support of Amadeo.

— represents another worthy cause which has no likelihood of success in the harshly egotistical and immoral world of contemporary Spanish politics, and it is significant that people will not listen to his comments. In the same way his efforts to instruct Isidora in domestic book-keeping fail to take into account the moral realities of the young girl's character. Relimpio is, in part, a reproduction of a fictional type that Galdós had introduced in the first *episodio nacional* he wrote, *Trafalgar* (1873), in the figure of Don Alonso de Cisniega: the well-intentioned old soldier or amateur political commentator who is inspired by a strong and noble sense of patriotism, but whose sense of what is practical in national politics is unrealistic. The continuation of this voice of national consciousness in *La desheredada* and most of the other novels of our Group I of the *serie contemporánea* is, thus, an important confirmation of Galdós's continuing interest in public history in the so-called social novels.

However, even Relimpio's noble patriotism can become subordinated to a more dominant interest: his fascination for Isidora's physical charms. After reading the political news one evening, he retires to bed; as he undresses he is forced to defend the ways of Isidora, who is living in his house, against the sharp criticisms of his wife, Laura, who is very eager that she move out. José's outburst of praise for the girl's beauty is quickly and conveniently excused by a sudden reference to King Amadeo. It is clear that at this moment lascivious thoughts of Isidora's body take precedence over any political concern in this the most politically aware of the fictional characters. His stature as a model voice of national consciousness is accordingly diminished.

This conversation between Relimpio and his wife also cements the parallelism between the stories of Amadeo and Isidora. José had entered the bedroom muttering about the politicians' harassment of Amadeo. Laura had retorted immediately that she was more interested in Isidora's actions and attitudes than in what was happening to the King. The fusion of the two worlds becomes even more intimate when in the same sentence she predicts: "Vamos, que si ésta [Isidora] tuviera dinero gastaría un lujo asiático y tendría lacayos colorados como ese rey [Amadeo]" (IV, 1038). We can now see that Galdós's earlier identification of Monarch and fictional heroine in the *mantillas* scene is not an isolated point. He is now building upon that initial correspondence and forwarding the action of the novel, even pointing towards a future development: just as Laura's surveillance of Isidora will produce the desired result of her removal from the Relimpio home and eventually her ruin, so the growing harassment of Amadeo by the squabbling, selfish politicians will lead to his final abdication and departure from Spain in February 1873, and the consequent chaos of the First Republic.

The two major political events Galdós has chosen to incorporate in the fiction of Part I of *La desheredada* — Prim's tragic death and Amadeo's gradual slide to abdication — are skilfully brought together in the penultimate chapter of Part I, significantly entitled "Igualdad-suicidio de Isidora".

Rufete's daughter has just seen her claims to be an Aransis heiress cruelly rejected by the old Marquesa, and the chapter opens with her frantic wanderings across Madrid followed by the solicitous Relimpio. As we saw in the *mantillas* episode, Isidora's interest in politics has been minimal; but now everything changes and her absorption in the news of Amadeo's abdication is total. She can perceive an opportunity to reverse her fortunes because of the sudden and traumatic changes due to take place on the political scene: "Isidora pensaba que aquello de ser todos iguales y marcharse el rey a su casa, indicaba un acontecimiento excepcional de esos que hacen época en la vida de los pueblos, y *se alegró en lo íntimo de su alma*, considerando que habría cataclismo, hundimiento de cosas venerables, terremoto social y desplome de antiguos colosos" (my italics; IV, 1077). This sudden Republicanism is aroused on a chaotic journey that takes her right across Madrid to the outskirts and back again to the political nerve-centre of the Parliament buildings, the Congreso, in the Carrera de San Jerónimo. As in the *mantillas* scene, physical sensations are responsible for her new-found interest in politics:

> A Isidora le gustaba aquella noche, sin saber por qué, el choque de las multitudes y aquel frotamiento de codos. *Sus nervios saltaban, heridos por las mil impresiones repetidas del roce, del empujón, de las cosas vistas y deseadas.*
> (my italics; IV, 1078)

The corollary of this ridiculing of Isidora's newly acquired political conscience is that the political events themselves, the details of Amadeo's abdication, are also played down and ridiculed. The signs which might be expected to accompany such a momentous political event as the change in a country's political regime from monarchical to republican are noticeably absent. The shouts of tavern patrons, blood dripping from animal carcasses being transported through the streets in wagons, and the masks, disguises and costumes displayed everywhere (it is, coincidentally, Carnival time) deflate the potential seriousness of the moment, and Galdós reinforces his fictional devices with direct political commentary from the narrator:

No había entusiasmo, ni embriaguez revolucionaria, ni amenazas. La República entraba para cubrir la vacante del Trono, como por disposición testamentaria. No la acompañaron las brutalidades, pero tampoco las victorias. Diríase que había venido de la botica tras la receta del médico. Se le aceptaba como un brebaje de ignorado sabor, del cual no se espera ni salud ni muerte . . . Eran turbas comedidas que no daban vivas ni mueras. Se hablaba de la llovida República como se habría hablado de un chubasco que acabara de caer. Nada de lo que dentro de las Cortes pasaba se traslucía fuera.   (IV, 1078-9)

This is not an inconsiderable political gloss for a supposedly social novel and points to a serious interest in the accompanying political developments.

Galdós has streamlined the succession of events somewhat: he does not mention, as he does in *Amadeo I* twenty-nine years later, and as the deputy Gallego Díaz recalled in his memoirs, the fact that on the night of February 10 and the morning of February 11, 1873, Republican agitators were milling threateningly around the Congreso building.[8] Nor does he delve into the precise reasons for Amadeo's abdication (the Monarch's final disagreement with the Radical Government of Ruiz Zorrilla over the question of the abolition of the artillery corps); he prefers to lay bare the individual moral defects behind the political actions. Once more fiction comes to the aid of history. If, as Isidora believes, the political crisis will enable her to take energetic action to assert her family claims, or to "dethrone" her grandmother (and her use of political vocabulary in the social context is symptomatic of the confusion of the two worlds), then her egotistical fantasies or delusions of grandeur will help explain the deeper reasons for the fall of Amadeo and of the subsequent chaos of the First Republic: the Republican politicians and the *alfonsistas* are more interested in carving up power in the country for themselves than in letting a decent monarch continue with his honest task of binding the country together.

Again Galdós resumes this direction in his argument in a vividly emblematic scene. Isidora, now determined to take advantage of her friendship with Joaquín Pez, waits for him outside the Congreso, where he is a deputy: ". . . no apartaba sus ojos de aquella puerta pequeña por donde entre y sale toda la política de España" (IV, 1079).[9] As soon as

[8] See Fernández Almagro, I, p.157.
[9] It is to be noted that Galdós clearly still associates political developments with people and not with impersonal laws, decrees or debates. Political history is made and written by people and, therefore, has every right to figure in the lives of fictional characters.

he emerges with some friends, she sets off after him. Politics, the future of the country, do not occupy her mind: the abdication of Amadeo has only fleetingly attracted her attention because she sees that it provides her with a chance to pursue her desire for aristocratic splendour and high-living.

More seriously, while she was standing at the corner of the Calle del Turco, Isidora had remained totally deaf to Relimpio's laments on the assassination of Prim at this same spot over two years previously. Her dissociation from an awareness of recent national history is exquisitely expressed in a single sentence which again binds fiction and history in one indissoluble unit. Isidora chases after her prospective "saviour" the moment he turns the famous street corner: "Cuando el señor del gabán claro [i.e. Joaquín] pasó por la trágica esquina, Isidora echó a correr, llegóse a él, se le colgó del brazo" (IV, 1079). This is the spot "donde a balazos estaba escrita la página más deshonrosa de la historia contemporánea" (IV, 1080), for the assassination of the charismatic Prim had abruptly destroyed the chances of a new Liberal Spain emerging from the 1868 Revolution and had been the source of all the subsequent troubles and disorders. By the same token Isidora's chasing after Joaquín Pez will be equally disastrous for her: it is the beginning of her slow slide into prostitution. Isidora is indeed the symbol of her epoch: so far, of the Spain of 1868-1872; but by the novel's end, of the whole decade, 1868-1878.[10] By making parallels at this and other structurally important points Galdós can afford to let the rest of the fiction carry the historical allegory along in subterranean silence, or to allow the reader's imagination to make the necessary links until another vantage point is reached.

What of José de Relimpio, the voice of national consciousness, in this crucial penultimate chapter of Part I? His role is important as he tries to indicate to Isidora the significance of events: ". . . don José dejaba oír . . . consideraciones prudentes y juiciosas sobre el suceso del día" (IV, 1077). Yet in spite of his superb political insight, Relimpio is still an impotent bystander, unable to affect the course of national history, or to inculcate its lessons in his pupil. In part Galdós chides him for this impotence: the old man simply does not have the force of character to impose his political vision on Isidora, just as he is unable to prevent male passers-by from offering her questionable compliments. José's failure on both fronts could be interpreted in terms of our

[10] See Antonio Ruiz Salvador; also Chad C. Wright, "The representational qualities of Isidora Rufete's house and her son Riquín in Benito Pérez Galdós's novel *La desheredada*", *Romanische Forschungen*, 83 (1971), 230-45.

political allegory as the failure of nineteenth-century Spanish Liberalism to realize its ideals or control the destiny of Spanish politics as it
should and could have done. Hence, it is appropriate that his last act in
this chapter is to shed tears at a street corner of such great importance
in recent Spanish history.

The intimate bond between history and fiction is once more
very evident in the opening sentence of the first chapter ("Efemérides")
of Part II, where substantial reference is made to the major political
events of the period 1873-1875 and to the whereabouts of the Rufetes
during this period. Now, instead of the tantalizingly vague or partial
references of Part I, a plethora of exact historical data is served up
"como las páginas de un manual de Historia" (IV, 1083). The accuracy
and extent of these references, which cover three pages at the core of
the novel, might now satisfy Fleishman's requirements for the standard
historical novel. Perhaps for the less demanding Butterfield the careful
manner in which Galdós inserts this information would have been
adequate proof.

The historical events rarely occupy more than one line whereas
the single episode of the *mantillas* protest in Part I had taken up a page.
Moreover, they are just name entries in a diary drawn up by the
narrator, not as an eye-witness or participant, but as the grateful recipient of information supplied by Relimpio. In the same way, this
apparently simple-minded narrator had relied on a chance visit to
Miquis's surgery for the continuation of the Rufetes' story. There are,
therefore, three barriers separating the reader from a depiction of the
historical events: José's reading of developments in the newspaper; his
relation to the narrator; and the latter's intertwining of history, fiction
and the allegory of Spanish bureaucracy involving the Pez and Pájaro
factions that he had initiated in Part I, Chapter XII.[11] Furthermore the
narrator now pretends at times to be indifferent to the march of public
events, "tantas formas políticas, sucediéndose con rapidez, como las
páginas de un manual de Historia recorridas por el fastidio" (IV, 1083).

The interleaving of the Rufete family history provides sudden di-
gressions from the historical material. The following example is typical:
"San Pedro Abanto.[12] Inmenso interés despiertan en toda España el

---

[11] By a coincidence, the first fully Republican Cabinet after Amadeo's abdication and before the *Cortes Constituyentes* of June 1873 was called "el Ministerio de los Pájaros" because of the euphony of the names of its leading members:
Pi, Chao, Sorní, Tutau! Galdós may be playing at ironic inversions in this instance.
[12] A fierce battle fought on the banks of the Somorrostro river on February
25, 1874 which the forces of the Madrid Government under General Moriones
lost to the Carlists, thereby delaying the final capture of Bilbao.

estado de la guerra y el sitio de Bilbao.[13] Tristeza del marqués viudo de Saldeoro [Joaquín]" (IV, 1086). Such an abbreviated, compressed style only generates confusion as the reader is propelled from one sphere to another without warning. The multiplicity of events, the kaleidoscope of scenes, the terseness of phrases, the inequality of lapsed time between the respective diary entries (those for 1874 are January, March, May, June and December respectively) disorientate the reader. If the dislocation of the temporal sequence of these entries is unmatched in the rest of the novel (Part I covers events over a period of about ten months: April 1872 to February 1873; Part II, after Chapter I, includes events between December 1875 and January 1877), equally distorted is the spatial perspective as the narration moves to various points around the country, abandoning the confines of Madrid in which most of the novel has been hitherto, and will afterwards be, located.

   This juxtaposition of private and public contexts produces varying effects. Often there is a close similarity between the respective actions. For example, when, on the first of March, 1873, Isidora and Joaquín's recent cohabitation in the Calle de Hortaleza arouses the moral indignation of Doña Laura and *La Sanguijuelera*, there are outbreaks of armed revolt in Barcelona by soldiers in favour of a separate Catalan state in opposition to the preferences of their officers. Isidora and Joaquín's dispute over the use of the inheritance money coincides with the episode in which the rebellious Madrid militia units of General Pavía and the Radical leader Martos are disarmed by the loyalist militia of the Civil Governor, Estévanez. Pi y Margall's famous speech in the Congreso against the rebel deputies, the so-called *asambleístas*, parallels the complaints of the baker and coal merchant about Isidora's failure to pay the bills. As the Second Carlist War spreads to regions beyond the northern provinces, Isidora loses contact with Mariano. Later when the Carlists are pushed back from Bilbao and their rebellion is all but over, Mariano returns to the family fold, more knowledgeable in certain aspects of life, if not in social decorum. Isidora's difficulties with her lawsuit, the deterioration of her financial position and her relations with Joaquín had earlier coincided with the intensification of the siege of Bilbao. Joaquín is compared to the country's Exchequer. With the restoration of the Bourbon monarch in 1875, the Pez faction have to surrender their position to the Pájaros and Isidora's affairs get out of

---

[13] January-May, 1874. General Concha's troops finally managed to break the Carlists' siege of the Vizcayan capital and relieve the encircled supporters of the Madrid Government.

hand: Joaquín is philandering, Mariano has absconded again, she cannot find a cure for *Riquín*'s macrocephaly and her lawsuit is once more floundering. She has lost control of her Republic just as Castelar and Salmerón and the other Republican leaders were finally deserted by their own political families.

Other characters now join Isidora and Joaquín in their symbolic function. Melchor, as a provincial governor, becomes part of the political machine, epitomizing its corruption and self-centredness. Doña Laura, who is tentatively presented as a symbol of the unity and honour of all Spain, falls ill in July 1873 when Alcoy, Seville and Montilla revolt against the Madrid Republican Government. Her death occurs in September of the same year, when Cartagena declares its independence. In the failure of her two daughters to achieve her ideal of a good (i.e. wealthy) marriage (Emilia marries the son of an orthopaedist, Leonor elopes with an army sergeant), Galdós seems to be representing the divisions in the Spanish family at this time. Relimpio, naturally, is engrossed in the different actions and movements of the Carlist War in the north and goes so far as to buy a map of Vizcaya to plot all the operations: "... clavando sobre él alfileres, *sigue y escudriña y estudia con sublime anhelo* los movimientos militares" (my italics; IV, 1087). It is over this map that José again sheds tears when recalling the unrealized matrimonial aspirations of his wife for their two daughters. Thus, another very effective emblematic scene joins fiction and history in intimate embrace.

The cumulative effect of this constant intertwining in the initial chapter of Part II is a part-comic, part-tragic appreciation of the historical events, an impression of black humour which is reinforced by the recurrent animal imagery:[14] the Carlist War grows a new head and tail every day; the country has the seven lives of a cat; opposing bureaucrats are divided into the Pez and Pájaro factions and Isidora's son, born on December 24, 1873, almost simultaneously with Pavía's coup d'état of January 3, 1874, is a macrocephalic.[15] Personification also increases the note of comedy, with the Restoration likened to a stranger knocking at the front door: "La Restauración toca a las puertas de la patria con el aldabón de Sagunto. Asombro. La Restauración viene sin batalla, como había venido la República" (IV, 1087). Yet, in the next sentence Galdós

---

[14] In the opening chapter of Part I Tomás Rufete had visualized Spain as a monster "con cabeza de barbarie y cola de ingratitud, ... país de las monas" (IV, 985).
[15] Wright, p.231, goes further and sees the house that Isidora inhabits during this period as a symbol of the chaotic First Republic.

invents an original image which, in its controlled economy of expression, conveys the great depth of anguish he obviously felt at Spain's proneness to civil war: "La Providencia y el Acaso juegan al ajedrez sobre España, que siempre ha sido un tablero con cuarteles de sangre y plata" (IV, 1087). Not only is he anxious to make comments for the reader of 1881 on the political events through his various techniques of representation, but also his opinions are shot through with deep feelings of despair and anger.

The intense precision of detail in this initial chapter will not be repeated again in *La desheredada*. Hereafter Galdós will revert to the more nebulous format, the more imprecise focus of the earlier sections of the novel. By so doing, he is able to draw the reader's attention to this important centre of the novel, the penultimate chapter of Part I and the initial chapter of Part II, where, through the precision of detail, Isidora's story is firmly rooted in national history in such a way that it is illuminated by it and in turn illuminates it.

We can see the change in style when we note the political allusions made during Isidora's relationship with another politician, Sánchez Botín. We do not see Botín in the midst of important historical developments. Only general indirect references to his parliamentary manners or speech remind us of his political position, as, for example, when he addresses Isidora "mirándose su pie pequeño, como hacía en el Congreso" (IV, 1115). His dictatorial control of Isidora and her activities might possibly reflect Spain's oppressive attitude to the colony of Cuba. Just as the latter had tried to revolt against Restoration Spain in 1875, Isidora tries to assert her independence of Botín, furtively visiting the popular San Isidro fair. Galdós's language at this moment is pertinently political: "Para fundar este imperio convenía un golpe de Estado" (IV, 1112). Botín (the name is not accidentally suggestive) had purchased the Government promissory notes made out to the Spanish soldiers fighting in Cuba, and at one point, without realizing the full meaning of her words, she shouts to him: "Soy la vengadora de los licenciados de Cuba" (IV, 1115). Clearly, then, he does exemplify metropolitan exploitation of Cuba, while Isidora symbolizes suffering Spain in the colony. Such brief allusions are sufficient to maintain the outline of the political allegory as the story of Isidora's personal degradation unfolds.

If Isidora represents the national history of Spain during the period 1868-1878, characters like Botín, Joaquín, Relimpio, her string of admirers and lovers, could represent the various political parties and attitudes which had seduced and debased Spain in these years. Juan

Bou is another symbolic figure who, with his anarchist rhetoric, re-presents the left in the political spectrum. Surprisingly, though, Galdós does not go into details when recording his activities during the 1868 Revolution. Particular references are reserved only for spiteful con-demnation of political personalities: "Pero no envidies a los personajes del día, a esas sanguijuelas del pueblo. Mira tú qué tipos. ¿Prim? Un tunante. ¿O'Donnell? Un pillo. Tiranos todos y verdugos. Olózaga,[16] Castelar, Sagasta, Cánovas. Parlanchines todos" (IV, 1103). Possessed by ideological dogma, Bou cannot appreciate the historical reality that is occurring before his eyes and prophesies a new type of history "en que no figuren más que los que han inventado una máquina o per-feccionado la herramienta *A* o *B*. Esos sí, esos sí que tendrán estatuas" (IV, 1103). This rejection of national politics, so opposed to the attitude of Relimpio, might be tenable (as Galdós was seriously to pro-pose in the last two series of the *episodios nacionales*) if Bou's concerns were genuinely disinterested; but we know that he is a successful capitalist whose anarchist ideals are a sublimation of an underlying egotism. His belief in the complete upheaval of society to create a new order is clearly ridiculous and has to be evaluated in the light of the excessive violence experienced during the chaotic First Republic and which had been minutely catalogued in the opening chapter of Part II. As a lover Bou is really no better for Isidora than the others, and in terms of the political allegory, the appeal for Spain of such extremist organizations as the Anarchists and Republicans is a dangerous rhe-torical illusion that only brings more damage and trouble to the nation.

Gaitica, Isidora's final identified mate before her plunge into prostitution, associates himself with the political system, if not with the specific events of history; he considers himself a loyal subject and tax-payer who will sell mules to the army and cannot bear any mention of a revolution. However, in his personal behaviour, *Gaitica* is the complete antithesis of human decency and, like Botín, Pez and Bou, uses public life and political affiliations for his own selfish ends.[17] It is Isidora's misfortune that these men of some position within the political system should be so unprincipled as to deny her a privileged insight into the true meaning of contemporary Spanish history, which in their small way they are helping to create. They cannot rise to such an

[16] Salustiano de Olózaga (1805-1873) was *progresista* leader in 1848.
[17] Brian J. Dendle, *Galdós: The Mature Thought* (Lexington, Kentucky, 1980), p.7, is decidedly mistaken when he claims that in *La desheredada* Galdós was defending the values of the Restoration, urging a commonsense need for sur-vival and a distrust of solutions based on fantasy.

occasion, for they have no interest in the true meaning of recent public events.

It is the tragedy of *La desheredada* that even Relimpio becomes estranged from the contemporary political reality and lapses into a dream-world of medieval romance in which he is the knight errant chosen to defend Isidora. His growing reliance on drink leads eventually to his death after a fall to the floor. This almost suicidal death follows closely on the metaphorical suicide of Isidora when she abandons him for a life of prostitution. Despite the note of levity sounded by the narrator's closing comment on Relimpio's character ("José, eres un ángel" [IV, 1181]), there is much for Galdós to lament in the loss of this voice of national consciousness, whatever his shortcomings. Isidora has lost her only source of reasonable counsel and if she is now to represent the political world of Restoration Spain, then Galdós's political message is bleak indeed: the *turno pacífico* is no more than a prostitution of the political system, a deal struck up between two partners bent on their own respective gain. Relimpio's semi-suicide may have been a welcome release from the ordeal of witnessing such degradation. This response of the sensitive individual to the political tragicomedy antedates a similar solution which later emerges with greater precision in the fourth and fifth series of the *episodios nacionales*. The fate of Relimpio and what he stands for in *La desheredada* is, therefore, an important anticipation of Galdós's later attitudes to contemporary Spanish history and further proof that the *serie contemporánea* cannot be totally divorced from the *episodios nacionales* in any discussion of his treatment of history or of his attitudes towards it.

The title of the last chapter of *La desheredada* ("Muerte de Isidora – Conclusión de los Rufetes") indicates that Galdós wishes to relate Mariano's tragic ending to that of his sister. In Part I Mariano's association with Prim's assassination had appeared to presage an important development in his growth to adulthood. The full logic of that earlier experience is now realized in the closing chapters of Part II. Galdós again chooses to connect this climactic development with a public happening, which, on this occasion, he cloaks in a veil of semi-imprecision. Mariano's assassination attempt on the King (it must be Alfonso XII, although we are never told) is a compression of the two abortive historical attempts on Alfonso's life made on October 25, 1878 and December 30, 1879 into a fictional assault in the Calle Mayor near the Plaza de la Villa some time in January 1877. Galdós seems to have chosen the setting of the first assassination attempt by Juan Oliva, and Ruiz Salvador reckons that Mariano is a synthesis of the latter and

Francisco Otero, the would-be assassin of 1879.[18] On both occasions Alfonso went the following day in public procession to the Basílica de Atocha to give thanks for his escape. In *La desheredada* there is, then, some irony in Galdós's use of a procession to Atocha as the occasion for Mariano's attempt and in his refusal to specify the reasons for the procession. In the public's memory of recent events, a visit to Atocha would be automatically associated with the historical attempts at regicide during Alfonso XII's reign.

Ruiz Salvador's surprise at this telescoping of historical truth reveals a failure to grasp the deeper artistic purpose behind Galdós's use of historical material in *La desheredada* and the *serie contemporánea* as a whole. Galdós is not trying to be the historian stating the facts as they happened. He is more anxious to show Mariano's tragic unawareness of the import of his actions for the nation. In many ways Mariano's involvement with contemporary history is from an angle opposite to that taken by his sister. For her, historical events like the *mantillas* protest or Amadeo's abdication serve as confirmation of the legitimacy of her noble aspirations. For Mariano, the public event of Alfonso's procession is the confirmation of society's injustice to him, the individual. His appreciation of the royal procession forms a grotesque counterpoint to Isidora's romanticization of the *alfonsista* ladies' protest: "¡Puño, vienen más coches, todos con tías brujas o con mozas guapas muy tiesas!" (IV, 1157). Yet Mariano's resentment against society is very similar to Isidora's underlying attitude, which finally manifests itself in a rebellious self-imposed exile from normal society. In his desire to compensate for his inadequacy, Mariano tries to exaggerate his importance by reversing the positions of society and individual: "La nación en masa, ¿qué nación?, la sociedad entera estaba confabulada contra él. ¿Qué tenía que hacer, pues? *Crecerse, crecerse hasta llegar a ser, por la fuerza sola de su voluntad, tan considerable que pudiera él solo castigar a la sociedad, o al menos vengarse de ella*" (my italics; IV, 1167). Isidora, in jail, as we noted at the beginning of this chapter, compares herself to a queen. The curious aspect about these feelings of injustice and their compensation is that the events of public history are the means by which the fictional characters achieve, or are encouraged to achieve, that compensation. More particularly, these events are of real or potential significance in the history of the country. Thus, the consequence of Mariano's killing of the King would have been to throw the whole country into turmoil, as had the earlier abdication of Amadeo.

[18] Ruiz Salvador, p.55.

Furthermore, all of these three incidents – the *mantillas* protest, the crowd congregations on the day of Amadeo's abdication and the attempted assassination of Alfonso XII – are street happenings involving processions of varying kinds. They are all put into wider historical perspective by the presence at the last-named event of Mariano's aunt, Encarnación Guillén, the embodiment of "la novelería, la bullanga y el entusiasmo monárquico del antiguo pueblo de Madrid" (IV, 1165). *La Sanguijuelera* has been a passionate spectator at many historical processions and parades "desde la entrada de María Cristina hasta la de don Juan Prim, desde ésta hasta las festividades del actual reinado" (IV, 1165).[19] Mariano's historically-based, though fictitious, attempt on Alfonso XII's life is thus part of a long line of similar street events that Encarnación has witnessed over the years.

To a certain extent *La Sanguijuelera* is the Conservative counterpart of the Liberal Relimpio, since, unlike other characters, both take an intense delight in public events: " . . . hallaba en aquel espectáculo *desinteresados placeres*" (my italics; IV, 1165). If Relimpio likes to ponder the inner meaning of these events, *La Sanguijuelera* mainly adores the external trappings, the uniforms of the servants or the appearance of the coaches. She does have some old-fashioned political views, though: she looks back nostalgically to the good old days of Isabel II's reign when bread was cheaper and there was "más religión, más aquél, más principios, . . . los grandes eran grandes y los chicos chicos, y había más respeto a todo" (IV, 1165). Is not this traditionalism (ironic in view of her nephew's distortion of normal social relationships) as outdated and inappropriate as Relimpio's hankering after the return of Gibraltar to Spain? Certainly her faith in the mercy and benevolence of the Monarch is as misplaced as Relimpio's hope that Isidora will take note of his political commentaries. Her written appeal for clemency, tossed, significantly, into the royal carriage "con la presteza del asesino que alarga el puñal" (IV, 1176), fails to save Mariano from the gallows. A more realistic, more effective attitude to national events is called for, an attitude which will recognize the importance of the inevitable interaction of public and private spheres. Is Galdós suggesting, then, that the contemporary reader of 1881 may well be the sole individual to have the chance to formulate that correct response, benefiting as he does from the mistakes and omissions of the fictional

---

[19] Again the mention of Juan Prim's name serves to remind the reader of the concrete historical event that has given rise to this murder attempt by Mariano. The memory of Prim haunts *La desheredada*, as all the tragi-comic developments of 1870-1878 have stemmed from that senseless act.

and historical actors? The care with which he selects his historical period and incidents, the manner in which he varies their presentation (from the vaguely imprecise to the minutely accurate) and gives them important positions in the novel's structure and character development so that the fictional plot becomes an illustrative allegory of the historical events of the period 1868-1878, appear to indicate that his use of contemporary history in *La desheredada* reflects a deep concern and didactic mission on his part. Our examination of this topic in the initial novel of the *serie contemporánea* has been necessarily extensive and detailed, since we have been concerned to establish the exact nature and function of these historical references. The style will be repeated in varying degrees in the other seven novels of our Group I, works which we might term novels of the historical imagination or even historical allegories.

CHAPTER 2

THE PHILOSOPHER OF HISTORY: *EL AMIGO MANSO* (1882)

Despite the almost complete absence of minutely detailed historical passages of the type found in *La desheredada*, the second novel in our Group I continues and develops Galdós's interest in the relevance of history for his contemporaries. Muted, but suggestive, parallels of characterization and incidents are once more employed but a new device is introduced: the discussion of the philosophy of history at a somewhat abstract level. *El amigo Manso* contains Galdós's first sustained treatment of this matter in the *serie contemporánea*, anticipating the more substantial exposition in the later *episodios nacionales*. Máximo Manso is the first professional philosopher of history in his work, more analytical than the earlier Gabriel Araceli, but perhaps not so consistent as the later Marqués de Beramendi or *Confusio*.

The difficulties surrounding any interpretation of the role of contemporary history in *El amigo Manso* derive in great measure from the deliberate paradox of the initial sentence and chapter. Having declared that he does not exist but is only a spirit, Máximo goes on to wonder whether he is really Everyman instead, the representative of all humanity on earth. The reader then discovers that in his supposedly spiritual world there exist all the social hierarchies and conflicts usually associated with organized societies on earth, with their "antagonismos tradicionales, privilegios, rebeldías, sopa boba y pronunciamientos" (IV, 1185). So, from the novel's outset the reader is confronted by the integral role that public, historical events play in the life of an individual who claims to belong to the realm of pure spirit, and yet who at the same time represents all humanity. In the circumstances, it is perhaps only to be expected that political references will not be of a precise nature.

Since Máximo is in essence a spirit who becomes incarnate, there is some reason for considering him as being not only the philosopher of history he reveals himself to be in the novel, but also an embryonic Spirit of Spanish History, slightly comparable to the Mariclío of the later *episodios nacionales* or to La Madre of *El caballero encantado*. In the account of his earthly origins Máximo makes pointed reference to his birth close to the fountain of Spanish nationalism: "Nací en Cangas de Onís, en la puerta de Covadonga y del monte de Auseba. *La nacionalidad española y yo somos hermanos, pues ambos nacimos al amparo de aquellas eminentes montañas . . . constantemente noto en mí algo que procede de la melancolía y amenidad de aquellos valles, de la grandeza de aquellas moles y cavidades, cuyos ecos repiten el primer balbucir de la historia patria*" (my italics; IV, 1187-8). Máximo's inability to see the full implications of this assimilation with the granite masses of Covadonga does not detract from Galdós's allegorical intentions, also discernible in the nightmares Máximo suffers after once seeing the bear and king story depicted on the capitals of the monastery of San Pedro de Villanueva. The consequence of this latter experience is that "aun hoy siempre que veo un oso me figuro por breve instante que soy rey; y también si acierto a ver a un rey, me parece que hay en mí algo de oso" (IV, 1188). If we recall that the bear is part of the crest of Madrid and that Madrid is so often a cipher in Galdós's work for all of Spain (which was once again a monarchy in 1882), then perhaps one can interpret the medieval story in the nightmare as an allegory of contemporary Spanish political life in which the country devours its rulers, and Máximo's humorous identification with both royal victim and beast as indicative of his projected role as the Spirit of Spanish History, both regal and popular. Doña Javiera's description of Máximo as the fifth *padrote*, companion to the four bust figures in his study, reinforces this role as an historical conscience or instructor in national history, especially when the professional politicians who like to regard themselves as *padres de la patria* are so patently corrupt and negligent of their duty to their ward and charge, the Spanish nation.[1]

---

[1] In many ways *El amigo Manso* is a novel about fatherhood. Máximo becomes a fatherly adviser to Irene, Manuel, Javiera and José María's family. In this surrogate role — underlined by his task of selecting a wet-nurse for Lica's new-born child — Máximo performs better than the natural father (e.g. José María), or fills a vacuum for those like Manuel and Irene whose fathers have died. Yet, this spiritual parenthood does not end with success. Likewise, his political fatherhood as instructor in history is much more valuable for the country than the self-seeking manipulations and shallow ideas of the country's ruling fathers epitomized by José María or Cimarra. However, in the final analysis, this political parenthood proves sterile because of his refusal to dirty his principles in politics.

If Máximo is the unwitting Spirit of Spanish History, there is some justification for seeing the members of his immediate family and his friends as representatives of the Spanish nation whom he is to instruct, though their symbolic characterization is not made explicit because of his limited awareness of the full importance of some of his words. Using a familiar technique, he records the Peña family history in dynastic terms, so that Manuel Peña's love affair with Irene and the difficulties in the way of their marriage might well reflect the matrimonial circumstances of Alfonso XII in the years immediately prior to the publication of *El amigo Manso* in 1882.[2] Irene, it is to be noted, associates herself with the Royal Palace in Madrid when she recounts her childhood to Máximo during the performance of the Christmas play.

With Manuel and Irene as the sovereigns of Spain's restored order, José María, Máximo's brother, is the personification of the Restoration parliamentary system, despoiler of colonial Cuba. After his election victory, the assimilation is complete: "Desde entonces tomó el sarao [of José María] un aspecto político que le daba extraordinario brillo. Había tres ex-ministros y muchos diputados y periodistas, que hablaban por los codos. La sala del tresillo parecía un rinconcito del Salón de Conferencias" (IV, 1229). Within this microcosm of the Spanish Parliament, another absurd microcosm, that of the Spanish Cabinet, is formed: La Sociedad general para Socorro de los Inválidos de la Industria, with its rigid hierarchy of portfolios and positions. Máximo's appointment as "consiliario" of this Society completes the parody of the national entity. The rapacious Cándida appropriately plays the role of "Consejo de Estado" to Lica and Chita, representatives themselves of a once-more subjugated Cuba.[3] Galdós adroitly suggests this political role of his Cuban characters, the in-laws of José María Manso, through their reluctant conformity to Madrid's social customs, their speech and their longing to return to their homeland.

---

[2] Fernández Almagro, I, p.288, notes: "muy ardua cuestión era la del matrimonio de don Alfonso." Máximo's reference to Peña as "algún Coburgo Gotha" (IV, 1299) may be an allusion to the diplomatic activity undertaken in Germany and other European capitals by Cánovas's government to secure a second wife for Alfonso after the death of María de las Mercedes. It is also interesting to note here that Manuel shares some character traits with Alfonso XII. The King was very popular with all groups in the country, while Máximo notes in Peña "un don de gentes cual no le he visto semejante en ningún chico de su edad" (IV, 1201). Alfonso was also a splendid orator and Manuel likewise makes an impressive display of oratory in the *velada* scene. In Javiera's opposition to her son's marriage to Irene there may be echoes of Isabel II's reaction to Alfonso's first marriage with Mercedes.

[3] In 1877 Martínez Campos successfully terminated the ten-year Cuban insurrection with the peace treaty of Zanjón. See Fernández Almagro, I, pp.313-29.

Máximo has suggested through his circle of acquaintances the general outlines of the contemporary political frame in Spain; but Galdós's real innovation in *El amigo Manso* is to relate that picture of symbols to an expression of a rational philosophical attitude (as opposed to the emotionalism of a José Relimpio) towards contemporary history. In the interaction of Máximo and the other characters Galdós is conducting a debate on two different approaches to public events: the rational, distanced political analysis which tries to determine the general principles at work beneath the surface ephemera, and the obsessive egotism which seeks to profit from those ephemeral political events in some way.

The debate is, of course, integral to the wider discussion, noted by critics, on the merits and demerits of the *krausista* system of individual education. The *krausistas* had also expounded a philosophy of history according to which mankind was progressing through successive stages towards reunion with God. It was the task of the philosopher of history to study the "idea de Dios" in the three successive stages of humanity's development (infancy, youth, maturity) and to discover this divine essence beneath the multiple layers of historical occurrences. The historian who chooses merely to chronicle the latter would show "una noción torcida de su misión, porque lo particular, lo *positivo* histórico es inteligible sólo como manifestación limitada y parcial de la divina esencia".[4] This search for the true, inner, divine meaning of history had been energetically propounded over twenty years before the publication of *El amigo Manso* by Francisco Giner de los Ríos, Sanz del Río's most brilliant pupil, founder in 1876 of the Escuela Libre de Enseñanza and, importantly, a great friend and adviser of Galdós at this time.[5] Hence it is not surprising that Máximo Manso, a *krausista* philosopher, should echo this *krausista* emphasis on the more authentic kind of history when advising his politician brother:

> Al oír esto del país, díjele que debía empezar por conocer bien al
> sujeto de quien tan ardientemente se había enamorado, pues
> existe un país convencional, puramente hipotético, a quien se refieren todas nuestras campañas y todas nuestras retóricas políticas,

---

[4] Juan López-Morillas, *El krausismo español: perfil de una aventura intelectual* (Mexico, 1956), p.40.

[5] In an essay "Consideraciones sobre el desarrollo de la literatura moderna", reproduced in Juan López-Morillas's *Krausismo: estética y literatura* (Barcelona, 1973), pp.111-61. Stephen Gilman, "Novel and society: *Doña Perfecta*", *AG*, 11 (1976), pp.21-22, maintains that it was Galdós's intimate contact with *krausismo* and *krausistas* at the University of Madrid which was "primarily responsible for the allegorical structure of his novelistic art".

ente cuya realidad sólo está en los temperamentos ávidos y en las cabezas ligeras de nuestras eminencias. *Era necesario distinguir la patria apócrifa de la auténtica, buscando ésta en su realidad palpitante*, para lo cual convenía, en mi sentir, hacer abstracción completa de los mil engaños que nos rodean, cerrar los oídos al bullicio de la Prensa y de la tribuna, cerrar los ojos a todo este aparato decorativo y teatral y *luego darse con alma y cuerpo a la reflexión asidua y a la tenaz observación. Era preciso echar por tierra este vano catafalco de pintado lienzo y abrir cimientos nuevos en las firmes entrañas del verdadero país, para que sobre ellos se asentara la construcción de un nuevo y sólido Estado.*

(my italics; IV, 1208)[6]

Máximo even defines his methodology: "... estudiar la filosofía de la Historia en el individuo, en el corpúsculo, en la célula. Como las ciencias naturales, aquélla exige también el uso del microscopio" (IV, 1223). The particular individual who will lead him to his general theory will be his brother José María; but it is really in his teaching of Manuel Peña that his philosophy of history is put to the test. Initially Peña responds with encouraging diligence: he is delighted by his readings and by his ability to discover the beautiful synthesis of history. However, two years later his commitment to this rational analysis of history has given way, under the effects of his love for the Vendesol heiress, to the diametrically opposite interest in the minutiae of the present's public events: "Manuel se enzarzaba más de día en día en sus amores, escatimando tiempo y atenciones al estudio ... Nos veíamos diariamente, charlábamos de diversas cosas, *y mientras yo procuraba llevar su espíritu a las leyes generales, él no gustaba sino de los hechos y de las particularidades, prefiriendo siempre todo lo reciente y visible*" (my italics; IV, 1203). This transformation is decisively consolidated by the arrival of José María and his family from Cuba and his involvement in the hurly-burly of Restoration politics. The antithesis between the attitudes of Máximo and his pupil is fully exposed in the famous *buñolería* scene of Chapter XX. Thereafter, especially with his *velada* success, Manuel's upward ascent is never in doubt as he becomes the youngest deputy in the Congreso and is then destined for entry into the Cabinet. The defeat of Máximo's system of inner history seems complete.

As the "mujer-mujer" that she eventually reveals herself to be, and not the "mujer-razón" that Máximo had falsely believed her to be

---

[6] In view of Máximo's origins in the mountains around Covadonga, it is appropriate that his vision of a new Spain should be expressed in an image of petrification (IV, 1208). He also embarks on his instruction of Manuel with the joy of a sculptor ready to shape a statue from a perfect piece of matter (IV, 1193).

from earlier encounters, Irene shows a similar aversion to the history of the national life of past ages: "¡Qué cosa más aburrida! ... Es tremendo. Le soy a usted franca. Si yo fuera el Gobierno, suprimiría todo eso" (IV, 1239). Confused by the welter of figures, places and events, she flippantly dismisses medieval history as a succession of wars and marriages:

> Aquellas guerras de moros, siempre lo mismo, y luego los casamientos del de acá con la de allí, y reinos que se juntan, y reinos que se separan, y tanto Alfonso para arriba y para abajo.
>
> (IV, 1239)

In so doing, Irene shows herself ironically unaware of the relevance of her remarks for contemporary national history or for her own situation some time later. By specifically referring to only the eleven medieval Alfonsos, she invites a parallel to be drawn with the current monarch, Alfonso XII, whose marriage plans created a constitutional problem. Although Spain was not fighting a war in Africa, it was only twenty-one years since O'Donnell's capture of Tetuán, so that "aquellas guerras de moros" were not limited to the medieval period. Closer to home, Doña Javiera's family has built up dynastic alliances and Manuel's intended marriage will be opposed by his mother as an unsuitable union. The pattern of medieval Spanish history as defined by Irene herself, therefore, shows remarkable duplication in the lives of nineteenth-century citizens, be they royalty or commoners. Her unawareness of the relevance of the past for the present is in fact typical of the times, as Máximo bemoans: "La Historia tiene cada día entre nosotros menos valor de aplicación y está toda ella en las frías manos del arqueólogo, del curioso, del coleccionista y del erudito seco y monomaníaco" (IV, 1202). The living, progressive, inner history, the "intrahistoria" of the *krausistas* is not to be found in Restoration Spain which regards itself as cut off from the past, and living only on the hectic superficial flow of the here and now.

It is also clear, however, that Máximo's performance as a philosopher of history is not presented without indirect criticism. His ready use of erudite references (highly comical in the classical descriptions of the ubiquitous Cándida or of Ramón María Pez) is symptomatic of his indiscriminate method of absorbing knowledge and forming his opinions on the reality of life. Moreover, in fulminating against the shallowness of the parliamentary system, Máximo does not support his general conclusions with precise detail, but studiously avoids all mention of the particular:

Hacía [José María] frecuentes viajes al Congreso, y me admiró verle buscar sus amistades entre diputados, periodistas y políticos, aunque fueran de quinta o sexta fila. Sus conversaciones empezaron a girar sobre el gastado eje de los asuntos públicos, y especialmente de los ultramarinos, que son los más embrollados y sutiles que han fatigado el humano entendimiento.

(IV, 1208)

This imprecision may be suitable for a nonchalant ahistorical narrator, as we shall see in our discussion of *Lo prohibido*, but for a supposed *krausista* philosopher of history, Máximo's reluctance to go into details is serious. The only precise historical references in his analysis (to the elections of 1881 and to the Partido Democrático[7]) are of the most fleeting kind. Surprisingly, more detail is presented in his account of Cándida's glorious past during the rule of the Unión Liberal government. It is surprising both because Máximo would have been only a youth at that time, and also because he reproduces the general outline of events not hitherto studied in Galdós's work, events which are not contemporaneous with the main period covered in *El amigo Manso* (1878-1881): "... los días, no sé si dichosos o adversos, del consolidado a 50, de la guerra de Africa, del *no* de Negrete, de las millonadas por venta de bienes nacionales, del ensanche de la Puerta del Sol, de Marió y la Grissi, de la omnipotencia de O'Donnell y del Ministerio largo" (IV, 1195-6). It is also the only passage in the novel in which Máximo, the potential Spirit of Spanish History, takes a retrospective look at the past. Yet he fails to link immediate past and present in any pattern of cause and effect, his roll-call of social and political developments being a sufficient indication of his inability to evaluate any of the particular events. His opening words ("los días, no sé si dichosos o adversos") admit this surprising inability in our professional philosopher of history. It is, thus, ironic and also paradoxical that when Máximo does bring himself to be factually precise, he cannot add the layer of general synthesis that the facts call for. Politics in *El amigo Manso* may be "only the sound of surf on an unseen beach",[8] but Máximo's distanced view, whilst constituting an effective criticism of the hollowness of the Restoration system, also betrays the inauthenticity of his philosophy of history: precise factual details must accompany

---

[7] No doubt Galdós is referring to the Partido Democrático-Monárquico founded by Beranger and Moret to contest the 1881 elections, only to be superseded by Serrano's Izquierda Dinástica a year later. See Fernández Almagro, I, p.374.
    [8] G.A. Davies, "Galdós' *El amigo Manso*: an experiment in didactic method", *BHS*, 39 (1962), p.26.

the abstract commentary and vice-versa. Because he gives such little space to the daily ephemera of history, Máximo's tutoring of Peña proves ultimately to be a failure and he finally admits:

De conocimientos experimentales he hallado grandísima copia en Manuel Peña. Lo que yo le enseñé apenas se distingue bajo el espeso fárrago de adquisiciones tan luminosas como prácticas obtenidas en el Congreso y en los combates de *la vida política, que es la vida de la acción pura y de la gimnástica volitiva*.

(my italics; IV, 1309)

Máximo the analyst has to acknowledge the supremacy of the actors of history: his brother and his pupil. His failure is particularly lamentable because his awareness of the prevalent corruption of Spanish politics, far superior to the opportunism of others, could have received the necessary leaven of practical relevance if he had presented himself as a candidate in the elections. He could then have been in an ideal position to influence its direction in a way José de Relimpio and *La Sanguijuelera* in *La desheredada* had never been able to do.

Máximo's failure to harmonize his philosophy with practical action is all the more reprehensible because he rejects the exercise aprioristically. Or is it that he foresees the futility of involving his principles in the world of political action? Is it that he already knows that the two opposites are irreconcilable? If he does foresee all this (and we have no way of knowing because of his elliptical first person narrative), then his final return to the nebulous existence that he enjoyed at the novel's beginning can be construed not as an act of defeatism but rather as a realistic awareness of the impossibility of inculcating a sense of Spanish history in even such a gifted and receptive future politician as Manuel Peña. Montesinos correctly glimpses this pessimistic conclusion to *El amigo Manso* and appropriately expresses his view in national terms: "España necesita ciertamente educadores, pero ¿qué suerte de educadores? El encuentra aquella España ineducable, y por ello es ingobernable".[9] One of those educators whom the country so badly needed was the philosopher of history who could point out the meaning of contemporary history for present and future generations. The country loses Máximo just as it had lost José de Relimpio in *La desheredada*, not only because it was indifferent to his message, but also because the educator was himself imperfect.

One important reason for the non-realization of the potential in Máximo's philosophy of history is clearly the increasing influence

[9] José F. Montesinos, *Galdós*, 3 vols. (Madrid, 1968-1973), II, p.60.

that his love for Irene exerts over him. It is not without significance that he represents this important change in a passage of sustained political language, thereby once more fusing the fictional and historical aspects of the novel into an indissoluble union:

> ... La determinación de sentimiento iba tomando tal fuerza en mí de día en día, que andaba la razón algo desconcertada, como autoridad que pierde su prestigio ante la insolencia popular. Y doy por buena esta figura porque el sentimiento se expansionaba en mí al modo de un plebeyo instinto pidiendo libertad, vida, reformas y mostrándome la conciencia de su valer y las muestras de su pujanza, mientras la rutinaria y glacial razón hacía débiles concesiones, evocaba el pasado a cada instante, y no soltaba el códice de sus rancias pragmáticas. Yo estaba, pues, en plena revolución, motivada por ley fatal de mi historia íntima, por la tiranía de mí propio y por aquella manera especial de absolutismo o inquisición filosófica con que me había venido gobernando desde la niñez.
>
> Aquel día, pues, el brío popular era terrible, se habían desbordado las masas, como suele decirse en lenguaje revolucionario, y la Bastilla de mis planes había sido tomada con estruendo y bullanga.

(IV, 1243)

Irene, of course, is responsible for seducing Peña away from his interest in history and, as Eamonn Rodgers has shown, her love is dictated by a strong desire for material comforts.[10] As with Isidora Rufete, true romantic love has no place in this world of corrupt national politics. Thus José María Manso soon discovers the political advantages of having attractive female friends in high places, and his long-suffering Cuban wife, Lica, makes a perceptive comment: "Faldicas, ¿eh? ... José María es como todos. Esta vida de Madrid ... Tenemos calaveradas ... Ya se ve, un hombre que va a ser diputado y ministro ... Hay en Madrid cada gancho ... ¡Ay!, qué mujeres las de esta tierra; son capaces de pervertir al cordero de San Juan" (IV, 1229).

In *El amigo Manso* Galdós has continued the debate he had initiated in *La desheredada*: how far can the events of contemporary history form an integral and meaningful part of an individual's existence? In the case of Máximo Manso, the question is even more pertinent, because he is suggestively presented at the beginning as some materialized Spirit of Spanish History and then appears at times in his earthly form as a philosopher of history. Although the creation of

[10] See Eamonn Rodgers, "Realismo y mito en *El amigo Manso*", *CHA*, 84 (1970-1971), pp.430-44.

Manso as the autonomous narrator of his own story enables Galdós to expound the argument as he had not been able to do before in the *serie contemporánea*, Máximo's own methodological shortcomings as a philosopher, his refusal to participate in practical politics and his gradual submission to the rule of sexual love, all combine to negate that positive potential. His return to Limbo is an admission of this inadequacy. Kirsner was, thus, partly incorrect when he said that *El amigo Manso* "es una novela más bien que una composición histórica sobre triunfos o desastres nacionales; que su objeto es la vida de un individuo imaginario, y no hechos o personas históricas".[11] *El amigo Manso* is, in truth, as much about nineteenth-century Spain and Spanish history as are *La desheredada* or any of the *episodios nacionales*.

[11] Robert Kirsner, "Sobre *El amigo Manso* de Galdós", *Cuadernos de Literatura*, 8 (1950), p.196.

CHAPTER 3

THE PUPIL OF HISTORY ABANDONED:
EL DOCTOR CENTENO (1883)

Montesinos labelled *La desheredada*, *El amigo Manso*, and *El doctor Centeno* "novelas pedagógicas"[1] because of the serious attention they gave to the question of the formal instruction of Spanish youth. If *La desheredada* was dedicated to the country's teachers and showed the appalling effects of the lack of education on young boys, *El amigo Manso* offered a view of private, individualized tuition of the university-level student. *El doctor Centeno* now widens the treatment of formal pedagogy with a detailed description of Pedro Polo's school and teaching methods, Ido del Sagrario's instruction and Felipe Centeno's attempts to absorb it and other types of instruction, and finally Jesús Delgado's far-sighted plans for the reform of the country's whole educational system. Yet in all three novels the frame of formal learning is used to put into relief the greater instruction offered by life's experiences, in particular by the events of contemporary history. At this level, Isidora, Mariano and Peña were all pupils of history under the tutorship of their respective teachers, Relimpio, Bou and Máximo Manso. In *El doctor Centeno* the interrelation of the two worlds of learning is comically represented in Ido's absurd claim that he has personally taught a number of ministers and deputies in the current parliament to write properly. On the other hand, Jesús Delgado holds that there must be a complete change in the political structures of the country if his educational reform programme is to have any chance of being implemented.

Moreover, the lessons of history are directed at the contemporary reader. In *La desheredada* and *El amigo Manso* the relevance of

[1] Montesinos, II, p.61.

the narration was assured by the contemporaneity of the stories' chronologies: 1868-1878 and 1877-1881 respectively. In *El doctor Centeno*, on the other hand, Galdós is not reviewing events of the last five to ten years but jumping back almost twenty years to 1863. None the less, he is still determined to indicate the relevance of his novel for the reader of 1883, making a direct address to him at the beginning of Part II: "Acuérdate, lectorcillo, de cuando tú y yo y otras personas de cuenta vivíamos en casa de doña Virginia" (IV, 1383).[2] Clearly separating and contrasting the two time periods evoked in the novel (1863-1864 and 1883), this allusion serves to warn the reader of the significance of Doña Virginia's establishment for the Spain of 1883, which for the people of 1863 was the Spain of the future. Forewarned about the fate of some of these boarders and their contributions to national life before they appear in the novel in their own right, the reader has to view their subsequent remarks and actions with some degree of tragic irony:

> . . . considera cómo el rodar de los tiempos, dando la vuelta de veinte años, ha cambiado cosas y personas. La casa ya no existe: doña Virginia y su marido, o lo que fuera, Dios sabe dónde andan. Ni he vuelto a verlos, ni tengo ganas de encontrármelos por ahí. Aquellos guapos chicos, aquellos otros señores de diversa condición, que allí vimos entrar, permanecer y salir, en un período de dos años, ¿qué se hicieron? ¿Qué fue de tanto bullicioso estudiante, ¿qué de tan variada gente?
> En la marejada de estos veinte años, muchos se han ido al fondo, ahogados en el olvido o muertos de veras . . . Estos y otros que no nombro, ¿dó están? ¿Viven? ¿Se salvaron, o se sumergieron para siempre?
>
> (IV, 1383)

This inversion of the normal chronological sequence allows the reader to learn, for example, of Sánchez de Guevara's death fighting rebels in Valencia when he is a *comandante* (this could be after the 1868 Revolution or during the 1873 disorders) before we ever see him as a young military cadet in Virginia's *pensión* sitting in bed at night with his *ros* pulled over his head and using his sword to snuff the candle. Clearly the 1883 reader is being asked by the narrator to compare and contrast the two periods, and to determine whether there have, in fact, been any real changes in the lapse of time between the two.

The same request is indirectly made in the humorous letter the prankster students send to their eccentric fellow boarder, Jesús Delgado,

---

[2] The reader's involvement is not as far-fetched as it first appears if we consider Doña Virginia's *pensión* as a symbol of pre-1868 Spain.

a letter in which they jestingly claim that they are really living in the year 1883 and that Spanish society, now drastically changed by recent political events, is ready at last to accept his marvellous ideas on educational reform:

> En este lapso, ¿no sabe usted que . . . ha sido derrocado el trono secular, y con él han desaparecido las prácticas añosas y las ideas rancias? Cual generosa espada cubierta de orín, que en un momento es limpiada y recobra su hermosura, temple y brillo, así la nación se ha limpiado su mugre. Nuevas instituciones tenemos ya, ¡oh!, y nuevos caracteres y principios.
>
> (IV, 1405)

Once again the public events of history have a direct bearing on the immediate fictional context; but of greater importance here is the game of chronological juggling that Galdós is now playing. Of course, the first laugh is at the expense of Delgado, but the second laugh is on the student pranksters who cannot know that their fictional creator is making them predict in general format the sequence of political events as they did in fact occur after 1863. However, there is even a third level of irony, directed this time at the reader who may believe that the shining new order of reason and law envisaged by the students has actually been realized. By cleverly dating their letter November 8, 1883, just a short time into the future beyond the period of the novel's composition, Galdós is clearly suggesting that the reader of 1883 should ask himself whether the 1868 Revolution or the 1875 Restoration have produced any notable changes in Spanish life or educational methods, or whether all that has been achieved in those twenty years is only more death and poverty. On this last point Galdós is specifically gloomy: "En la marejada de estos veinte años, *muchos se han ido al fondo, ahogados en el olvido o muertos de veras*" (my italics; IV, 1383). Of the lucky few who do survive and prosper, two are, not surprisingly, servants of the State: Zalamero is a Cabinet minister and Poleró, who studied to be a civil engineer, has attained a high position in the navy. The 1883 reader of *El doctor Centeno* is, thus, encouraged to reflect critically on the events of 1863-1864 and to relate them to the Spain of his own day.

Does Galdós flesh out his argument with specific details as he did in *La desheredada*? For Montesinos, the most important historical event recorded in *El doctor Centeno* is the burial of Calvo Asensio on September 18, 1863, an event that Galdós could himself have witnessed soon after his arrival in Madrid from the Canary Islands. The other historical details to be found in the novel are considered by Montesinos as not being "de primer orden",[3] a view that fails to take note not only of the seriousness of Galdós's wish to address the lessons of recent history to his contemporary readers, but also of the care with which the historical data is dispersed amongst the conversations of his characters for the possible instruction of Felipe Centeno, its features distorted in various ways but always bound to the fictional components.

The description of Calvo Asensio's funeral cortège as witnessed by young Felipe permits Galdós to create an atmosphere of foreboding for the future political stability of the country:

> Vió Felipe el carro mortuorio, tirado por caballos negros y flacos, con penachos que parecían haber servido para limpiar el polvo de los cementerios; vió el armatoste donde el difunto venía, balanceándose como una lancha negra en medio de las olas de un mar de sombreros de copa ... ¡Cómo serpenteaba la fatídica procesión, cómo se detenía de trecho en trecho, cómo empujaba! Era cuña que en las plazas abría la masa de curiosos, y en las calles se dejaba oprimir a su vez por aquélla.
>
> (IV, 1364)[4]

The narrator's own introductory comments emphasize the tremendous importance of the journalist's death for the political situation of the country:

> En tal día enterraban con gran aparato de gente y público luto al atleta de las rudas polémicas, al luchador que había caído en lo más recio del combate, herido de mortal cansancio y de fiebre ... Reventó como culebrina atacada con excesiva carga, y su muerte fue una prórroga de las catástrofes que la Historia preparaba.
>
> (IV, 1363)

The funeral is thus truly an event of national significance because it signals the postponement of the revolution against the Bourbons. Galdós is more than justified in including the procession in his fiction: even the tawdry appearance and the slow, twisting passage of the cortège are a reflection of the growing turmoil on the political scene as the country slithers and slides to revolution. There can be no doubt of Galdós's serious intent in commenting on the relevance of this ceremony nor of the depth of his emotions when making that judgement.

A distanced viewing point and childish eyes and ears are again

[3] Montesinos, II, p.78. Pedro Calvo Asensio (1821-1863) was the fiery political columnist of the Madrid newspaper, *La Iberia*.
[4] Felipe's elongated perspective of events due to his position atop a lamppost is an example of Galdós's skilful use of distance in this novel to underline the deformed vision of Spanish reality that he is presenting. This distortion is also present in the protagonist's initial view of Madrid from a hilltop.

the media used by Galdós to describe the confused bumbling of Queen Isabella II and her advisers during this critical period. As Centeno and his friend Juanito gaze at the Royal Palace, the latter gives a hilarious report, derived from his parents' acquaintances amongst the royal servants, on the inner workings of palace life. The report effectively ridicules the confused behaviour of the Palace's inhabitants:

> Tiene un salón más grande que Madrid, con alfombras doradas, de tela como las de las casullas, ¿estás? El coche de la reina sube hasta la propia alcoba . . . Yo lo he visto. Aquí todo está lleno de resortes. Calcula tú: tocas un resorte y sale la mesa puesta; tocas otro y salen el altar y el cura que dice la misa a la reina . . .
> (IV, 1353-4)

Felipe listens attentively at first but he eventually realizes that his friend's account of palace life or of preparations for the inevitable revolution that everyone is talking about can be discounted. At this point the childish vision reduces public figures and events to farcical absurdity, as Michael Nimetz has noted.[5] But, as we have seen, we are to be forewarned at the beginning of Part II of more tragic events that might be on the horizon.

Felipe Centeno does not fare much better with his second guide to contemporary history, the venerable Don Florencio Morales, who readily proclaims the superiority of his own learning from life to that derived from books by the students of Doña Virginia's *pensión*. Like Estupiñá and José Izquierdo in *Fortunata y Jacinta*, Don Florencio boasts of his acquaintance with such important public figures as Fermín Caballero, Antonio González and Calvo Asensio.[6] He also attends the *progresista tertulias* which are now plotting in earnest to overthrow the Bourbons. Felipe begins by listening most attentively to this apparent oracle but by the novel's end he derives only amusement from his pompous oratory. Montesinos is partly correct when he states that Morales's function in the novel is to "hacer ver lo que iban a ser los destinos de 'la Gloriosa' con progresistas así".[7] But Galdós is also showing that these so-called participants in recent history or amateur historians make inadequate teachers of the country's youth, the segment of the population in most need of some instruction in the meaning of contemporary history. Like Relimpio, Morales professes some rather naïve political views: he strongly believes that the political and civil liberties demanded

---

[5] Nimetz, p.154.
[6] Fermín Caballero (1800-1876), a radical Liberal, was Minister of Government in 1844. Antonio González (1789? - 1865?) was Prime Minister in 1842.
[7] Montesinos, II, p.91.

by the *progresistas* are not incompatible with the teachings or interests of the Roman Catholic Church: "Póngannos la Milicia, la Constitución del doce [i.e. 1812], y basta. El clero, en su puesto; la Milicia, para defender el orden; el Ejército, para caso de guerra; Cortes todo el año, buenos seminarios, mucha discusión, mucha libertad, mucha religión, y venga paz. ¡Si esto es claro y sencillo . . .!" (IV, 1432). At times the narrator's ridicule almost turns to sarcasm:

> Desde su edición pequeña de *Las Novedades* observaba el movimiento político, *sin comprender de él más que la superficie bullanguera y la palabrería rutinaria*. A veces hallaba en su diario algunas cosas ininteligibles, algo que era como los escalofríos y el amargor de boca del cuerpo social y síntoma de su escondida fiebre. Entonces se llevaba el dedo a la frente, afectaba penetración, y, risueño, borracho de agua, decía a su consorte:
> — Saturna, ¡qué cosas escriben estos haraganes para hacer reír a la gente!
>
> (my italics; IV, 1325)

His patriotism may extend to such mundane aspects as water-drinking habits, but it is also a sentiment which can dictate some wildly contradictory statements. Having told Felipe that there are multitudes of poor people in Spain, he declares a short while later that Castile produces enough corn to supply the whole world! Imperfect imitator of Salustiano de Olózaga and his pompous oratory, Don Florencio is a pathetic dupe of Spanish political life, dazzled by the surface activities into believing that it is a noble profession. Yet, for the reader, if not for Felipe, his extravagant identification with the political system is a timely warning.

Felipe shows no development of concern for these national problems. How can he with such a guide? His role is apparently limited to that of a reliable recorder of political talk upon whom the narrator can call for information. His recollections of the *pensión* after-dinner discussions dwell on the dramatic elements of the scenes, especially the reactions to Basilio Andrés de la Caña's homily on the national debt: "Terror. Doña Virginia oculta la cabeza detrás del hombro de su marido para poder reír a sus anchas. Cáusale más risa que el discurso de don Basilio la seriedad con que le oye Poleró" (IV, 1387-8). Not only does the consequent distortion of the political situation reduce the seriousness and effectiveness of the lesson for Felipe, but the scene is also typical of the way in which politics intervene in the daily lives of ordinary people, whether it be through newspapers, street processions or, as here, dinner-table arguments. What is more important, though, is that this "domestication" of high politics can lead to developments on the political level through something like a reverse process. The narrator's long commentary on the scene manifests the notion that there is an inevitable interaction, mysterious and at times unfathomable, between public and private spheres:

> En pocas épocas históricas se ha hablado tanto de política como en aquélla, y en ninguna con tanta pasión. *Jamás tuvieron parte tan principal en las conversaciones populares los chismes palaciegos y las anécdotas domésticas de altas personas.* No gozando de libertad de Prensa para la controversia, se la tomaba el pueblo para la difamación. No se ponen puertas al campo ni mordazas a la malicia humana. La opinión tiene muchas bocas a cuál más fieras. Cuando se le tapa la del lenguaje impreso, abre la de las hablillas. Si con la primera hiere, con la segunda asesina. Estaba muy en la infancia la política española para conocer que nada adelantaba con suprimir las cortadoras espadas del periodismo, cuyos filos se embotan pronto cuando se les permite el constante uso. En tanto los cuentecillos envenenaban la atmósfera, haciéndola irrespirable, y lo que se quería conservar y defender se moría más pronto. De fuertes y seculares imperios se cuenta que, habiendo podido defenderse de terribles discursos y escritos fogosos, han caído destrozados por los cuchicheos.
>
> (my italics; IV, 1386-7)

No major political event may develop from the conversations of these particular political gossipers, but their activity is representative of the period and has to be considered a part of its national history, another "episodio nacional".

The narrator's direct political commentary jolts the 1883 readers of *El doctor Centeno* into an awareness of history's recent lessons. For their additional benefit, Galdós presents locales in the novel with a certain amount of symbolism. Doña Virginia's *pensión* reproduces the political chatter of the period with the division between the two major parties, the *progresistas* and the *moderados*. With the lodgers coming from all corners of the country, there is even more reason for viewing this establishment as Spain in microcosm. Alejandro Miquis's room becomes a popular meeting place akin to the more usual centres of public gathering in Spanish society: "Era el casino de la casa, el disputadero, Atenas [sic], Bolsa, club, salón de conferencias, el Prado y el Conservatorio, porque allí se charlaba, se fumaba, se discutían cosas hondas, se leían los autores sublimes, se contaban aventuras, se escribían versos, se leían cartas de novias, se tiraba el sable, se hacían contratos y se cantaban óperas" (IV, 1390). Alberique, an accomplished heraldic designer of Moorish descent who is described as a bear (IV, 1384), could symbolize the capital, Madrid, and therefore Spain. Similarly, the corridors of the more populous tenement houses in the Calle de Cervantes to which Miquis moves in Part II are likened to a parliament "en que se ventilaban las cuestiones de aquella federación de familias" (IV, 1422). Through indirect detail the major characters of the novel are related to the current political situation. Miquis's great-aunt, Doña Isabel, is clearly identified with the Bourbon regime. Her full name, Doña Isabel Godoy de la Hinojosa, inevitably associates her with Queen María Luisa's favourite earlier in the century, and Galdós's assertion to the contrary only serves to confirm this impression: "No atendáis al olor de privanza que aquel apellido tiene, para suponer parentesco entre esta familia y el Príncipe de la Paz [i.e. Manuel de Godoy (1767-1851)]. Aunque de procedencia extremeña, estos Godoyes nada tenían que ver con aquel por tantas razones famosísimo y más desgraciado que perverso" (IV, 1369). Depicted as an important pillar of the Spanish State, Isabel's family has supplied "más de un consejero de Indias, muchos guardias de Corps al Ejército, a la Iglesia regular y secular doctos definidores y capellanes de reyes nuevos" (IV, 1369). Whilst her antediluvian red-and-gold painted sofa might be considered a parody of the national flag, she demonstrates a fervent allegiance to Queen Isabel and even hints at a close friendship: "Tengo prometida una visita a su majestad; pero ¿para qué quiere la señora ver vejestorios en su real casa?" (IV, 1373). More importantly, the money that she will give to her greatnephew, Alejandro, is money repaid by the Dirección de la Deuda for loans the Godoys made to the Real Hacienda decades ago. Since its real value has depreciated over the years, the family has in fact made a considerable sacrifice to support the State at times of crisis in the nation's history. There is additional irony in Alejandro's later squandering of this money, for in their futility and wastefulness his escapades parallel the historical campaigns which Isabel Godoy's money had helped to finance. There is thus a close and circuitous relationship between public and private finances, a fact that Basilio Andrés de la Caña cannot appreciate in his otherwise estimable analysis of the ailing national economy.

Pedro Polo y Cortés, the priest-cum-schoolmaster, is another central character identified with the Bourbon monarchy. Again, the narrator's half-hearted, jocular denial of the connections with his historical namesake, the famous *conquistador* from the same home town of Medellín ("¿Había parentesco? Dice Clío que no sabe jota de esto." [IV, 1329]), only serves to solidify the association. According to Don Florencio Morales, Polo is to be named an honorary chaplain to

Queen Isabel, seemingly at the insistence of such powerful court figures as the writer and politician, Nicomedes Pastor Díaz (1812-1863) and Father Cirilo, Cardinal-Archbishop of Toledo and spiritual adviser to the Royal Consort, Francisco de Asís. Through his mother's contacts with the palace servants, he is appointed chaplain to the nuns of San Fernando, despite his well-known sexual proclivities. Coming to possess the gluttony of a courtier, he also has the elegant appearance of a papal envoy accustomed to the diplomatic activity of the Court. Appropriately, when he goes for an afternoon stroll in the Retiro with a friend from the Finance Ministry, he is more concerned about the recognition of the new kingdom of Italy and the war in Santo Domingo than about any economic talk.[8] With sexual promiscuity and religious fanaticism the dominant notes of the Spanish Court during these years, Polo can be regarded as an embodiment of this particular aspect of national life. The point is underlined for the reader in two important scenes. Felipe is terrified by Polo's pale, dishevelled appearance one morning after some nocturnal adventures with Amparo Sánchez Emperador, the embodiment of ideal Spain; his master's eyes, with their "matices amarillos y ráfagas rojas" (IV, 1351), remind him of the Spanish flag, whilst his lips are the colour of a bishop's robe. Later the boy's marionettish account of the priest's surprising generosity to him after he had mentioned Amparo's name recalls the earlier description of palace life given by his friend Juanito:

> Es que el señor don Pedro ... tiene dentro una lucecita que se enciende en cuanto le tocan un botón, como el de las campanillas eléctricas que se usan ahora. El que acierta con el botón y enciende la luz, hace de él lo que quiere. El que no, se *amuela*.
>
> (IV, 1430)

From this moment onwards the signs of degeneration in Polo's appearance, his house and his family become increasingly obvious, paralleling the slide to complete disorder and collapse which characterized Isabel's rule from 1863 to 1868. And Polo's identification with traditional Spain is reinforced by some small touches: comparisons with Julius Caesar, Napoleon, Cromwell and Moses, as well as with the

---

[8] The Italian references in the novel are not without significance. Alejandro's play, *El duque de Osuna*, deals with Osuna's alleged plan to take over the kingdom of Italy in the seventeenth century. Ruiz sees the play as a falsification of the historical truth in an attempt by Miquis to represent the contemporary situation in Italy: "El duque para este niño es un precursor de Víctor Manuel y un émulo de Garibaldi" (IV, 1456). Interestingly, Felipe celebrates his master's receipt of a gift of money from Doña Isabel by singing "el himno de Garibaldi" (IV, 1380).

conquistador Hernán Cortés; his preference for fictionalized historical readings, especially those in the Old Testament; his historical consciousness; the narrator's many invocations to Clío, the muse of history, when talking of Polo or his relatives; and finally, Polo's pedagogical methods, likened to the warfare of his historical namesake. Through Polo's liaison with the virginal Amparo (*La Emperadora*, for Felipe) Galdós may be suggesting that the Spain of the past, the Spain of the Cross and the Sword, will strongly affect that of the future. It is as if Galdós were already anticipating in his fictional thread the disillusionment which followed the 1868 Revolution and which he will soon chronicle in *La de Bringas*.

Felipe Centeno's other master, the quixotic Alejandro, is the character most removed from the contemporary world, absorbed as he is by the fantasy of the historical drama that he is writing. Yet we have already seen how his spendthrift ways could reflect the irresponsible financial attitudes of this critical period. Alejandro is indeed integrated into the structure of Galdós's political picture. His *demócrata-progresista* ideas provoke strong discussion in Virginia's house; he is also reported to have had political discussions with Florencio Morales and with Ido. The historical drama that he is writing is judged by Ruiz to be a political tract for the contemporary period, while for the superpatriot Don Florencio it will be the source of a nefarious atheism spreading over the holy land of Spain. Alejandro's political-cum-literary representativeness is stressed by the parallel which is drawn between the two funeral processions recorded in the novel: Alejandro's at the end of Part II and that of Calvo Asensio in Part I. The tawdry appearance of the funeral appurtenances for Alejandro's corpse and the slow, twisting march of the cortège are almost a repetition of the earlier description:

> Veterano corcel tira con trabajo de la escena, a la cual preceden otros cinco vehículos de igual aspecto mísero, con sus cortinillas, su dormilón cochero y su caballo claudicante. La fila marcha, perezosa, por calles y caminos, siguiendo a otro armatoste poco agradable de ver, cosa negra y desapacible, sobrecargada de tristeza y de duelo.
>
> (IV, 1464)

Political and literary Romanticism appear to have been buried in this period 1863-1864 with the respective interment of these two characters, one historical, the other fictional. However, as the reader knows from historical hindsight and is reminded by Galdós's careful dovetailing of the two periods of 1883 and 1863, not much has changed in the intervening years, despite appearances. Unlike the *pícaro* Felipe Centeno, now only concerned for his future material well-being, or the undiscriminating, if noble-hearted, Morales and Isabel Godoy, the reader of 1883 must discover the intimate bonds that tie him and all Spaniards to both the past and present. To facilitate this study, Galdós tells a story with important touches of historical colouring that enables the whole novel to be read in part as a political allegory of the period 1863-1864. Montesinos makes another typically pertinent summation: "La primera sorpresa que *El doctor Centeno* nos depara es que, más aún que en *La desheredada*, pues la peripecia está más remota en el tiempo, *Galdós hace algo muy análogo al 'episodio nacional'. En mayor y en menor medida*" (my italics).[9]

[9] Montesinos, II, p.78. Geraldine M. Scanlon, "*El doctor Centeno*: a study in obsolescent values", *BHS*, 55 (1978), 245-53, considers Galdós's use of a relatively distant time period as a means of criticizing the survival of anachronistic social and literary values in modern Spain.

CHAPTER 4

MINOR SHIFTS OF DIRECTION:
TORMENTO (1884)

Tormento reveals some changes in Galdós's fictional use of recent Spanish history: there is now a much shorter time-span – three months (November 1867-February 1868); the historical guide-figure and even the prospective pupil of history have disappeared; and the fictional characters are closer to the sources of political action. On the other hand, character symbolism, parallel plots and explicit commentary by the narrator are techniques which are still employed to develop the historical dimension of the story. At the same time, we now have very important outside evidence to corroborate some of the political views and interpretations of history which Galdós advances in this and subsequent novels of our Group I: the newspaper articles which he started writing in 1884 for the Buenos Aires newspaper, *La Prensa*.

As in *El doctor Centeno*, Galdós deliberately chooses a period of recent Spanish history that is more distant than those selected in *La desheredada* or *El amigo Manso*. Through the narrator, he reiterates his view that the Spain of 1884 is the same as that of 1867-1868 in spite of the momentous political developments of the intervening years: "En una sociedad como aquélla, o como ésta, pues la variación en diez y seis años no ha sido muy grande . . ." (IV, 1480). This sense of two time periods joined together by the narrator is strengthened by the latter's identification with the fictional world through his publicized friendship with some of the main characters: Agustín Caballero, Muñoz y Nones and especially Francisco Bringas. In a manner similar to the presentation of the occupants of Doña Virginia's *pensión* in the previous novel, the narrator gives us, right at the beginning and before we

actually see the character in action, a portrait of the decrepit Francisco
Bringas whom we will later meet in the closing pages of *La de Bringas*:

> ... era en 1867 un excelente sujeto que confesaba cincuenta
> años. Todavía goza de días, que el Señor le conserve. Pero ya no
> es aquel hombre ágil y fuerte, aquel temperamento sociable, aquel
> decir ameno, aquella voluntad obsequiosa, aquella cortesanía
> servicial. Los que le tratamos entonces, apenas le reconocemos
> hoy cuando en la calle se nos aparece, dando el brazo a un criado,
> arrastrando los pies, hecho una curva, con media cara dentro de
> una bufanda, casi sin vista, tembloroso, baboso, y tan torpe de
> palabra como de andadura. ¡Pobre señor! Diez y seis años ha se
> jactaba de poseer la mejor salud de su tiempo.
>
> (IV, 1474)

As in *El doctor Centeno* the lack of genuine political change between
1867 and 1884 can be put into significant relief by very real changes
(often deteriorations) affecting individual human beings.

Having recorded the political temper of the period 1863-1864
in *El doctor Centeno*, Galdós now chooses to omit such important
historical events as the *Noche de San Daniel* riot of April 8, 1865, or
the mutiny and subsequent execution of sixty-six sergeants of the San
Gil barracks in June 1866. Instead, he prefers to concentrate on shading
in the trend of the times, the drift to the inevitable revolution. To
achieve this, he again adopts a distanced perspective, echoes of developments being sounded in conversations between the fictional characters.
Thus, the general anarchy of the palace administration, the fondness of
the Queen for dances, her readiness to listen to petitioners, are inserted
through the reports of Francisco Bringas. The continuous plotting in
the country and abroad by opponents of the Queen is briefly captured
in the news of Prim's skirmishes in Aragon, now moved from the
summer months to November 1867.[1] The death of Leopoldo O'Donnell,
the stalwart of the Isabelline regime, on November 5, 1867 is likewise
indirectly suggested. When the Bringas couple are arranging furniture in
their new house at the beginning of November, there is a slight disagreement over the best positions for the portraits they have in the drawing
room, specifically compared here to the famous Sala Gasparini in the
Madrid Royal Palace:

> — Rosalía ... ven acá, hija ... A ver dónde te parece que coloque
> estos cuadros. Creo que el Cristo de la Caña debe de ir al centro.
> — Poco a poco. Al centro va el retrato de su majestad ...

---

[1] See Rafael Olivar Bertrand, *Así cayó Isabel II; siglo de pasión política* (Barcelona, 1955), pp.182-84.

— Es verdad. Vamos a ello.
— Se me figura que su majestad está muy caída. Levántala un poquito, un par de dedos.
— ¿Así?
— Bien.
— ¿En dónde pongo a O'Donnell?
— A ése le pondría yo en otra parte . . . por indecente.
— ¡Mujer . . .!
— Ponlo donde quieras.
— Ahora colgaremos a Narváez.

(IV, 1478)

The totteriness of Isabel II's regime is well expressed by the sloping picture of the Monarch, but of greater importance here is the dispute over the placing of O'Donnell's portrait: a few days later the real existence, not the portrait, of O'Donnell did go "a otra parte". The implications for the Bringas couple are obvious: just as the Isabelline regime is entering a critical and decisive stage of its existence after the loss of one of its most faithful supporters, so Rosalía and Francisco Bringas, clear representatives of the reigning monarchs, as we shall see shortly, are entering upon a new and dangerous period in their lives with this move to a new residence. It is hardly fortuitous that Galdós should have commenced his novel at this point in November of 1867 or that he should have initially presented the Bringas couple in the middle of moving house. For this association invites us to read the subsequent narration not only as a personal story but also as a subtly suggested historical allegory of the drift of Spanish politics in this period. The reader's imagination has been sparked by this initial coincidence of circumstances between the thread of fiction and that of history, and by pencilling in the odd subsequent allusion Galdós is able to maintain the skeleton of the historical period under review.

To a greater degree even than in *La desheredada*, Galdós positions some of his characters close to the sources of contemporary history. The Bringas family do not yet live in the Royal Palace, but their new house in the Costanilla de los Angeles is close enough to the centre of old Madrid, the Royal Palace, the Ministry of State and the Royal Chapel. Rosalía Bringas visits the Palace from time to time to see the Queen and Francisco works in a near-by State office, the Real Comisaría de los Santos Lugares. Even so, despite this promise of a real "close-up" of public events in the making, Galdós provides very few glimpses of proceedings in these public areas. When we are taken to the Royal Palace, on the occasion of a gala ball, the feature highlighted is Francisco Bringas's loss of his new overcoat. Despite being so close to the seat of power and its occupant, we are not given any view of the Queen, her ministers or what they are doing at this ball. This tantalizing omission is deliberate on Galdós's part. In his indirect, allegorical style, the "represented" or "symbolized", that is to say, the figures of history, have to be left off stage. The effectiveness of this technique of twinning or paralleling history and fiction depends upon subtle hints and suggestions.

It is the fictional Francisco who is charged with the function of reflecting the sad distortion of human values which characterized Isabel II and her Court. Couched in reactionary generalities, his diatribe against the coming revolution is juxtaposed to his anguished lament for the loss of his overcoat:

> ... En su desesperación, el digno funcionario pensó dar parte a los Tribunales, contar el caso a su majestad, llevar el asunto a la Prensa; pero el decoro de Palacio le detenía ... ¡Si cogiera al pícaro, canalla, que ...! Parece mentira que cierta clase de gente se meta en esas solemnidades augustas ...! Un país donde tales cosas pasan, donde se cometen tales desmanes junto a las gradas del trono, era un país perdido. Por distraerse, cogió don Francisco un periódico.
> — Ya no puede quedar duda — dijo con fúnebre acento después de leer —: la revolución viene; viene la revolución.
>
> (IV, 1578)

Elsewhere we have seen him avidly gather up any left-over materials he can find in the offices of the royal craftsmen and pilfer office note-paper for his own domestic account-book. As a servant of the Crown, Francisco should have been primarily preoccupied with the threat against his Sovereign; he is not, because personal interests assume greater prominence in his life. What this twinning of public and private spheres achieves is to raise strong suspicion that the parasitism of Bringas and other royal servants is as important a cause of the imminent revolution as the Queen's own personal weaknesses or the Government's ineptitude, and that, inversely, the Queen is also guilty of the same egotistical, materialistic attitudes in her own actions, public or private.[2]

Tormento also differs from its three predecessors in that for the first time we have another source to verify what we are suggesting is Galdós's contemporary political concern in these novels: the one

---

[2] In his proclamation to the country in August 1867 Prim spoke of "la inmoralidad en las altas esferas". See Tristán La Rosa, *España contemporánea: siglo XIX* (Barcelona, 1972), p.206.

hundred and seventy-six articles that he wrote regularly for *La Prensa* of Buenos Aires between December 1883 and 1901.[3] We must also remember that from 1885 to 1890, the period of Sagasta's *Parlamento largo*, Galdós, under the gentle persuasion of the Liberal leader, served as a government-sponsored deputy for Puerto Rico in the Spanish Cortes. Therefore, he had a grandstand seat from which to observe the major political developments of the second half of the decade, to see for himself the true worth of a parliamentary democracy at work. In his at times cryptic, heavily-fictionalized, autobiography, *Memorias de un desmemoriado*, written in 1916 when he was already ailing and four years from his death, Galdós recalls with some clarity how he attended the parliamentary sessions faithfully every day "sin despegar los labios. Oía, sí, con profunda atención cuanto allí se hablaba" (VI, 1679). In the absence of any recorded speeches in the Congreso during this period (because of his notorious shyness) these articles in *La Prensa* are, as Peter Goldman has aptly reminded us, an important body of evidence for the elaboration of Galdós's views as a political commentator of recent national history.[4] Of greater importance for our study, however, is the confirmation these articles offer of Galdós's continuous interest in politics at a time when he was also busily engaged in writing most of the important novels in the *serie contemporánea*. Consequently, the carefully suggested frames of political allegory with which he endowed these novels are not so difficult to accept, given this abiding interest in the written commentary of recent Spanish political history.

Notwithstanding the occasional ironic tones or the subtle glosses demanded by the special nature of his Argentinian public, the *La Prensa* articles can be profitably used to elucidate the hidden messages contained in the novels of the *serie contemporánea*. As we have seen above, *Tormento* chronicles a period of increasing political instability, and internal conflict is also the chief characteristic of the time when Galdós was writing the novel, although not to such a serious degree. The resignation of the first Liberal government of Sagasta in October 1883 over the question of King Alfonso's welcome in France, and the instability of the subsequent Posada Herrera government, composed of dissident Liberal *izquierdistas* and opposed by Sagasta's *fusionistas*, created a crisis in the Restoration political system. When Sagasta's party defeated the new government's plans for electoral reform, Posada

3 See the "Estudio preliminar" to Shoemaker's edition of the articles, pp.9-35.
4 See Peter Goldman, "Galdós and the nineteenth-century novel; the need for an interdisciplinary approach", *AG*, 10 (1975), 5-18.

resigned in January 1884 and the indispensable Cánovas returned as Prime Minister. Fernández Almagro observes: "Por vez primera, a partir de Sagunto [i.e. 1875], daba la política una penosa impresión de incertidumbre, hasta el punto de producirse cuantiosa baja en las cotizaciones de Bolsa, haciendo cundir el desconcierto y la alarma".[5] In his first letter for *La Prensa*, dated December 20, 1883, Galdós gives full details of these events for his Argentinian readers and it is very important to note that he places them in the repetitive cycle of recent Spanish history: "... es el [vicio] que trajo las catástrofes de 1823, del 53, del 57 y del 72 ... El fenómeno [the division of the Liberal party into factions once it has attained power] es tan viejo y se ha repetido tanto, *que al leer la historia parécenos ver lo que ahora pasa*" (my italics; *OI*, III, 7-8). A similarly jaundiced view of the constant instability of Spanish politics, expressed in an article of January 19, 1884 – the same month that *Tormento* was published –, evokes the successive *déménagements* of the Bringas family, first to the Costanilla de los Angeles and later, in *La de Bringas*, to the Madrid Royal Palace: "Nuestra política tiene siempre algo de nómade y errante. No parece que vivimos en casas, sino en movibles y frágiles tiendas, y, lanzados de aventura en aventura, no sabemos nunca dónde dormiremos mañana" (*OI*, IV, 16).[6] Even more significantly, the same overriding personal interest that Galdós diagnoses in the fictional and historical characters of *Tormento* appears in his newspaper articles as the principal cause of the 1883 crisis in Sagasta's Liberal party: "... los verdaderos *obstáculos tradicionales* están hoy en la indisciplina de la familia liberal y en las ambiciones de sus díscolos individuos" (*OI*, III, 17); "La virtud del perdón es muy difícil en política, sobre todo tratándose de *estos temperamentos hechos a la rivalidad y a las ásperas emulaciones del amor propio*" (my italics; *OI*, III, 14).

By far the most important means by which Galdós overlays his political message in *Tormento* is the symbolism which he establishes when introducing his characters and the general direction of their actions in the fiction. Alfredo Rodríguez's observation ("A nadie se le oculta, además, el paralelo físico [Rosalía] y el sicológico [Bringas] con

---

[5] Fernández Almagro, I, pp.403-4.

[6] With its narrow corridors, the Bringas house in the Costanilla de los Angeles could well represent the Spanish Congreso building. Describing the equally narrow passageways of the Congreso in an article for *La Prensa* of January 19, 1884, Galdós noted that they seemed symbolic of "nuestro estado social y político" (*OI*, IV, 9). The empty rhetoric of parliamentary debates, also mentioned in this particular article, is echoed in *Tormento* in the sessions of Paquito and friends in the Bringas house.

los monarcas españoles."[7]) is, of course, true, although in *Tormento* Galdós does not make the parallel conform in all respects. The Queen's sexual immorality is not repeated by Rosalía at this stage although, as Robert Ricard has suggested,[8] there are warning signals in the references to her honour: "Era hermosa, y le gustaba ser admirada. Era honrada, y le gustaba que esto también se supiera" (IV, 1490). Nor does Francisco display the effeminateness for which his royal namesake, Francisco de Asís, was renowned.[9] However, with his Christian name, his generally ineffectual relationship with his wife (more pronounced in *La de Bringas*), his position in the royal service and his passion for domestic and economic order, Francisco Bringas could well represent Isabel's consort whose subservient tolerance of his immoral wife was accompanied by hypochondria and religious fanaticism.[10] Indeed, Bringas's opportunistic protectiveness towards Amparo (the enemy of Rosalía), once Agustín's marriage plans are made known, could mirror Francisco de Asís's support for the fusion through marriage of the two rival Bourbon branches to settle the dynastic dispute that had racked Spain since the death of Fernando VII in 1833.[11] In his extreme thriftiness and cautious control of the domestic budget, which, according to the narrator, should be copied by the Treasury,[12] Bringas might again be sketching in traits of the Royal Consort.

The parallel assumes an even greater degree of caricature when Francisco is also compared to Adolphe Thiers (1797-1877), the great French nineteenth-century statesman and historian, for the Spanish fictional character is, in mind and intelligence, the antithesis of the French politician whom he resembles so much physically: "No faltaba en Bringas más que el mirar profundo y todo lo que es de la peculiar fisonomía del espíritu; *faltábale lo que distingue al hombre superior, que sabe hacer la historia y escribirla*, del hombre común que ha nacido

---

[7] Alfredo Rodríguez, *Aspectos de la novela de Galdós* (Almería, 1967), p.78. See also Alison Sinclair, *Valle-Inclán's "Ruedo ibérico": a Popular View of Revolution* (London, 1977), pp.29-30.

[8] Robert Ricard, *Aspects de Galdós* (Paris, 1963), pp.49-50.

[9] See Francis Gribble, *The Tragedy of Isabella II* (London, 1913), p.139, and also Sinclair, pp.31-34.

[10] Francisco Bringas is called a saint and "the angelic Thiers", but only in contexts which emphasize his domestic thriftiness. Although he has a Bible in the house, Francisco also possesses (his only other book) *El Diccionario* of Pascual Madoz, a most suitable book for an accountant whose work deals with ecclesiastical property. Bringas is never presented as a practising Catholic; he is never seen at prayers or in church.

[11] See Raymond Carr, *Spain 1808-1939* (Oxford, 1966), p.193.

[12] The desk in whose many compartments he keeps his various piles of cash is a so-called Minister's desk.

para componer una cerradura y clavar una alfombra" (my italics; IV, 1477). The first occasion we see our historical caricature, the narrator shamefacedly regrets, is in the middle of the prosaic occupation of house-moving: Francisco clambers over the piles of furniture dressed in work clothes, hardly the activity or apparel associated with the real Thiers, actor and analyst of great events in nineteenth-century European history. Later, when Francisco, holding a candle aloft, conducts his cousin Agustín Caballero through the dark corridor to his office at the back of the family home, Galdós describes him almost maliciously as "el faro de la Historia derramando claridad sobre los sucesos" (IV, 1488). Francisco Bringas with his obsession for the petty material things of life is the complete antithesis of Thiers the professional historian, politician and economic theorist. This ironical comparison, first perceptively noted by Varey,[13] turns Bringas into a patently absurd character whose comic outline may also extend to his royal counterpart. Galdós may be not so direct as Valle-Inclán in his *Ruedo ibérico* but the satirical attack on public figures is clearly evident in those features of the fictional character that are highlighted; the parody will be even more evident in *La de Bringas*.

Not content with these two historical comparisons, Galdós adds others which, paradoxically, put into relief the fundamental ahistorical mould of this bureaucrat. In the midst of the bustle of house-moving, Francisco reproduces Napoleon's famous phrase after he had heard of the loss of his fleet at Trafalgar: "Yo no puedo estar en todas partes" (IV, 1478). Moreover, Bringas has a namesake in early nineteenth-century Spanish history: the Liberal conspirator and martyr whom Galdós had already presented in the *episodio nacional* of the second series, *Los apostólicos* (1879).[14] Galdós's denial in *Tormento* of any relationship between fictional and historical characters, similar to that noted in *El doctor Centeno*, only produces the opposite effect of underlining the historical parallel.

The first two series of the *episodios nacionales* are also evoked in the account given of Rosalía's family. Her grandfather, Juan de Pipaón, whose portrait, beside that of the Queen, adorns the Bringas's parlour, was an ubiquitous opportunistic Conservative reactionary in the Spain of 1815-1832. Consequently, the respective surnames of

---

[13] See J.E. Varey, "Francisco Bringas: nuestro buen Thiers", *AG*, 1 (1966), 63-69.
[14] For an examination of Galdós's use of the Bringas surname, see Pedro Ortiz Armengol, "Tres apuntes hacia temas de *Fortunata y Jacinta*", *Letras de Deusto*, 4 (1974), 241-59.

Francisco and Rosalía resume the ideological clash between Liberals and Conservatives from the ending of the War of Spanish Independence in 1815. Rosalía's matronymic (Calderón de la Barca) is delightfully ironic: it suggests the possibility of long and noble service of a distinguished literary and political nature to the Crown. In reality, however, the service of her forebears has been limited to more menial tasks, as servants, pages and footmen. Our first view of Rosalía in the novel, like that of her husband, is distinctly unflattering: she is cleaning their new house helped by her distant cousin, Amparo Sánchez Emperador. She looks far from aristocratic in her old clothes, resembling rather a typical landlady of a *pensión*! Only cosmetics and clothes supply the aristocratic veneer. With the history of her family and her aspirations for the future centred on the Madrid Royal Palace – she is anxious that Francisco be promoted to a position in the royal household –, Rosalía is an apt person to convey the coarseness and vulgarity of the Queen. The physical similarity, of course, is strikingly obvious for all to note: "Era Rosalía ... una de esas hermosuras gordas, con su semblante animado y facciones menudas, labradas y graciosas, que prevalecen contra el tiempo y las penas de la vida" (IV, 1476). In spite of this parallel with the Monarch, Rosalía is not a person with an historical conscience. She completely lacks any sense of public duty and the national interest. Loyalty to the Crown does not involve any more obligations than attention to her own personal well-being. She abuses her friendship with the Queen to ask for left-over dresses or other favours, and although she is aware of the country's economic plight, she remains unaffected by the news of imminent revolution until the moment she realizes that it might affect her life-style. In *Tormento* the Bringas couple are on stage only as secondary characters; but their turn as principals will come in the sequel where the implications of the caricaturesque parallel with the Monarchs will be fully developed.

The trio of principal characters in *Tormento* – Amparo, Polo and Agustín – are not as closely connected with the Palace world as the Bringas couple and, therefore, are unable to act as potential witnesses to national events. None the less, Galdós does present them in general outline as important representatives of certain political groupings in pre-revolutionary Spain and notes their attitude to the political developments.

In *El doctor Centeno* Pedro Polo had been described as a symbol of the degeneracy of the Isabelline Court. In *Tormento* this symbolism is continued and adapted. The physical and moral disorder which he suffers as a result of his attempts to seduce Amparo and which is reflected in the anarchical state of his living quarters is an illustrative example, full of salutary warnings: "¡Enseñánza triste que debieran tener muy en cuenta *los que han subido prontamente al catafalco de la fortuna!*" (my italics; IV, 1510). His generosity to his poor neighbours and to the dying Celedonia, a redeeming feature shared by the Queen and her Court, does not absolve his lust, just as Isabel's munificence did not excuse her sexual immorality nor save her throne.

In *Tormento*, however, Polo also undergoes a form of hesitant self-reassessment and penitence that will lead, finally, under the firm guidance of Nones, to his departure as a missionary for the Philippines. If we recall that in *El doctor Centeno* he had been described as a military leader of a bygone era and note that this military air is continued in *Tormento* to qualify his decadence, it may be possible to conclude that Galdós is characterizing a segment of the military Establishment which had previously condoned, even encouraged, Isabel's ruinous behaviour and which was now prepared to remove her from power; one thinks instantly of her former favourite, General Serrano, who was to be exiled from Spain to the Canary Islands in July 1868. Polo's departure for the Philippines, originally his own idea, is eventually transformed into a kind of exile imposed by Nones and which for the calculating Amparo will signify freedom to marry Agustín Caballero. Polo's revolt against his former role and identity is expressed in suitably political language: "Era un hombre que no podía prolongar más tiempo la falsificación de su ser, y que corría derecho a reconstituirse en su natural forma y sentido, *a restablecer su propio imperio personal, a efectuar la revolución de sí mismo, y derrocar y destruir todo lo que en sí hallara de artificial y postizo*" (my italics; IV, 1511).[15] His condemnation of the Spanish institutions he formerly represented is complemented by frequent dreams of emigration to Australia, and of the fall of the Bourbons. Reflecting perhaps the bitter mood of those generals who were now turning against the Queen, his desire is to see the total destruction of the old order: ". . . se encantaba con la idea de un cataclismo que volviera la cosa del revés. Si él pudiese arrimar el hombro a obra tan grande, ¡con qué gusto lo haría!" (IV, 1519). The greatest threat to the Isabelline regime was to come, in fact, from its former supporters.

It is perhaps significant that Polo's spiritual adviser, Father Nones, has participated directly in important military events of national

---

[15] By a curious coincidence, one of the few Opposition deputies in the Government-dominated Congreso who spoke out against the policies of Narváez in January 1868 was a José Polo, a respected voice of order. See Olivar Bertrand, p.192.

history before he changed professions to become a priest. He was a
soldier in the Seville garrison at the time of Riego's uprising and was
also part of the firing squad which executed Torrijos, so that he seems
to have been in both the Liberal and *absolutista* camps in his military
life.[16] For the first time in the *serie contemporánea* a fictional character
is made to participate authentically in national historical episodes. Even
in his second vocation Nones continues to take an important part in
national events through his ministrations to criminals who have been
condemned to death: "El cura Merino, los carboneros de la calle de la
Esperancilla, la Bernaola, Montero, Vicenta Sobrino y otros criminales
pasaron de sus manos a las del verdugo" (IV, 1519).[17] Polo, the occasional criminal, is now joined, by the common denominator of
Nones's role as spiritual adviser, to celebrated figures in recent Spanish
criminal as well as political history, and his case is thus part of a series
of recent national events in which Nones has intervened. Therefore, by
assimilation, his problem and its resolution can be considered a comparable "episodio nacional". Moreover, if Polo represents a group
within the Revolutionary coalition, the success and then failure of *La
Septembrina* may well be anticipated by his association with Nones's
career: the 1868 Revolution will be just another part of an interminable
cycle of political advances and setbacks in the fortunes of the Liberal
cause, a cycle illustrated by the histories of Riego and Torrijos. One
final contrast confirms this interpretation. Nones is a soldier associated
with the failure of military attempts at Liberal revolution, who then
becomes involved with what might be termed spiritual failures. Polo
seems to be on the same path, but heading in the reverse direction: a
failed priest, he now dreams of fighting for the Revolutionary cause.
Forced to go to the Philippines as a missionary, he can also be called a
failed military man who will take no part in the 1868 Revolution . . .
that is, if it is ever determined that he leaves the country.

    Counterbalancing the character of Polo is Agustín Caballero,
who, although similar in fiery temperament and Herculean physique, is
trying to progress in the opposite direction: from the real disorders
of Texan border-life during the American Civil War to the order of

[16] Rafael del Riego (1785-1823) led the famous uprising in 1820 in Cádiz
against the absolutist tyranny of Fernando VII and in the name of the Liberal
Constitution of 1812. When French intervention restored total power to Fernando in 1823, Riego was captured and executed. José María Torrijos (1791-
1831), another famous Liberal general, was executed in 1831 after an abortive
pronunciamiento against the King.
[17] The inclusion of Merino in this list of common criminals reinforces the
fiction-history parallel. The priest had tried to assassinate Isabel II early in 1852.

centuries-old Madrid: "Por lo mismo que había pasado lo mejor de su vida en medio del desorden, sentía al llegar a la edad madura, vehemente anhelo de rodearse de paz y *de asegurarla arrimándose a las instituciones y a las ideas que la llevan consigo* . . . le mortificaba . . . todo lo que anunciara discordia y violencia, *lo mismo en la esfera privada que en la pública*" (my italics; IV, 1528). This desire for order at all costs misleads him into believing that Spain is a country of order, a view that becomes increasingly unrealistic with the announcement of the Aragonese disturbances. Like Don Florencio Morales in *El doctor Centeno*, he is in error when he believes that opposing ideologies in the Spanish political scene can be reconciled, or that "los obstáculos tradicionales" can be overcome by peaceful means.

The inherent contradiction in his political beliefs also appears in other details. In the evening *tertulias* with his business associates he criticizes the government of the day: although a Unión Liberal supporter who has made extensive loans to the Government, he agrees with the moderate *progresistas* Arnáiz and Trujillo that the current government of Narváez is leading the country towards revolution (IV, 1531). It should be remembered, however, that Agustín is primarily a business man. The discussion in the *tertulia* held in his house only becomes animated when commercial policies are the topic, the free-traders (Agustín, Arnáiz and Trujillo) clashing vehemently with the Catalan protectionist, Mompous. Besides faithfully capturing the important economic polemic of the times,[18] Galdós is also pointing out that Agustín's interest in the political situation conceals a greater interest in Spain's commercial policies. He made his fortune as gun-runner and merchant out of the tragic conflict of the American Civil War and his public commitment to Isabel does not prevent him from investing his capital abroad. If Felipe Centeno is to be believed, it would seem that Caballero's only financial activity in Spain was to lend money to the Government for personal propaganda reasons. Using Madrid merely as a convenient correspondence centre, he avoids investing in the local money market or establishing industries or businesses to help solve the country's economic woes. His patriotism, therefore, does not overcome his good business sense and takes second place to financial profit. And if self-interest is the motivation behind his political affiliations, it is not surprising that, once that interest is endangered, he abandons the side of order to ally himself with the forces of revolution.

Agustín's public attitudes are paralleled in his private life. There,

---

[18] See Jaime Vicens Vives, *Manual de historia económica de España*, 3rd ed. (Barcelona, 1959), p.643.

too, he seeks order through marriage to Amparo, for "no podía, en manera alguna, ir a la posesión de su amoroso bien por caminos que no fueran derechos" (IV, 1536). Yet when he learns of her sexual indiscretions with Polo he quickly abandons Establishment virtues: "Orden, política, Religión, moral, familia, monsergas, me fastidiáis" (IV, 1578). His commitment to Spain is subordinate to his passion, for for her he is prepared to settle anywhere: "Le dejo a usted la elección de patria pues hoy por hoy me considero desterrado" (IV, 1495). And when the two set off for cohabitational bliss in Bordeaux, his repressed sexuality plays as great a part as true romantic love, as Rodgers has pointed out.[19] As ever, his point of reference is himself, and given these inner inconsistencies in Caballero's character, Montesinos's view of the *indiano* as a positive incarnation of Galdós's own ideas on social, economic and political reform seems rather inaccurate.[20] If Caballero does represent a certain sector of the Spanish business community which eventually welcomed the Revolution of 1868, then some of its spiritual weaknesses do not augur well for the post-revolutionary period.

As the principal point in the love triangle, Amparo is the main protagonist and also stands as a symbol of a virginal, ideal Spain trying to emerge from the emotional conflicts of the past (Polo) in order to establish a new life (Caballero). Will she be tortured by the Spain of the past (although it is Polo who calls her his torment) or will she inhabit Caballero's palace, the new Royal Palace, as Empress, *La Emperadora*? Galdós clearly establishes Amparo's regal status in a number of ways apart from her surname. For Nicanora and her husband, she is nothing less than a princess or the daughter of a very high noble. The talk of marriage to Agustín, the crown which she does not want to refuse,[21] immediately prompts Rosalía and Refugio to imagine her already inhabiting her palace (IV, 1543). Only a royal mansion would indeed be suitable for Amparo, for she is a daughter of Madrid's Royal Palace, sharing with Rosalía Bringas an ancestor who was a palace servant in the employ of La Vallabriga and the Infante Luis.[22]

[19] See Eamonn Rodgers, "The appearance-reality contrast in Galdós' *Tormento*", *Forum for Modern Language Studies*, 6 (1970), 382-98.

[20] See Montesinos, II, p.110.

[21] Early in the Spring of 1868 the dissident Unión Liberal generals had offered the Spanish Crown to Isabel II's brother-in-law, the shrewd, thrifty Duque de Montpensier. See La Rosa, p.206.

[22] The Infante Don Luis de Borbón (1727-1785) had angered his brother, King Carlos III, when in 1776 he married a young Aragonese girl, María Teresa de Vallabriga; for this he was banished from Court. It is typical of Galdós that even this minor historical detail is full of meaning for the main story of Agustín and Amparo's affair; the similarity of some points between the two cases again serves to join the fictional and historical threads. Galdós's selection of the most minor details is always relevant.

As the Spain of the future, Amparo wants to forget her contact with the past. Her journey to Polo's ramshackle apartment to make the final break is appropriately initiated with political language: "... se echó a la calle, digámoslo en términos revolucionarios" (IV, 1507). Putting distance between herself and Madrid, moving away from the scene of her earlier liaison with Polo, Amparo hopes, unrealistically, to avoid and to forget the pull of the past, a desire that is superbly captured by the narrator when he shows her impatiently looking out of the train window in the Estación del Norte, located just by the side of the Madrid Royal Palace. Amparo and Agustín represent the new-Spain-that-might-have-been, but which preferred self-imposed exile and individual happiness to the stultifying confines of traditionalist Spain. This potential association of the couple with the impending revolution, discernible throughout *Tormento*, is confirmed by Rosalía Bringas's reaction to their elopement in the novel's closing scene, a reaction which is dutifully echoed by her husband: "... ¡faltar así a los buenos principios, dando un puntapié a la sociedad, a la religión, a la familia, a todo lo venerando ...! Si es lo que te digo: el desquiciamiento se aproxima. La revolución no tarda; vendrá el despojo de los ricos, el ateísmo, el amor libre ..." (IV, 1583). Her references to the Caballeros' disloyalty could be a reminder to the reader of González Bravo's similar charges in his letter to the Duque de Montpensier notifying him of his banishment to Portugal on July 7, 1868.[23] If Amparo and Agustín eventually become rebels against Spanish society, it is only their own salvation that preoccupies them as they abandon Spain. Is Galdós implying that punishment of similar motives or attitudes also lay behind the exile meted out to the disaffected generals and the Duque de Montpensier, and that when they returned to Spain after the triumph of *La Gloriosa* they set about feathering their own nests at the expense of the nation? His gloomy asides on the similarity of pre- and post-revolutionary Spain in *Tormento*, noted at the beginning of this chapter, his more explicit comments on the 1883 political crisis in his articles for *La Prensa* and the bitter description of the hollowness of the victory of *La Septembrina* at the end of *La de los tristes destinos* (1909) ("¡Inmensa y ruidosa mentira! La misma *Gaceta* con emblemas distintos ... Palabras van, palabras vienen. Los españoles cambian los nombres de sus vicios" [III, 766]), all make clear his belief that a physical departure from Spain solves no problems, whether for the individual or for the country. In *Tormento* his remarks on the train to France, symbol of

---

[23] Reproduced in Fernando Díaz-Plaja, *La historia de España en sus documentos: el siglo XIX* (Madrid, 1954), p.334.

that emigration, reveal his awareness of this futility: "Un tren que parte
es la cosa del mundo más semejante a un libro que se acaba. Cuando los
trenes vuelvan, abríos, páginas nuevas" (IV, 1583). Rather than a
change of location, it is a change of attitudes that is required.

If Amparo is the ideal New Spain that was never possible, Refugio, her sister, must be the embodiment at this point of the Spain-of-
the-Revolution-that-will-be. She is a wild, impetuous girl who quickly
throws off the yoke of the Bringas family, seeing through their pompous pretensions. She ignores Amparo's advice that she earn a decent
living rather than rely on favours from male admirers or her earnings as
an artist's model. Significantly, her current pose is for the figure of a
"maja Calípije ayudando a enterrar a las víctimas del 2 de mayo" (IV,
1539). Surely Galdós is implying, through Refugio's way of living and
her attitudes towards others, the moral corruption of the coming revolutionary movement, which will be a debasement of the revolutionary
ideal as represented by the heroic sacrifice of the victims of the famous
May 2, 1808 slaughter in Madrid by Napoleon's troops. It is again not
without import that Galdós should choose a burial scene for Refugio's
latest picture and not a Goya-like skirmish, for the 1868 Revolution
"buried" the heroic sacrifice of its 1808 forerunner beneath its egotism
and materialism.

The fiction of *Tormento* is encased by two sets of dramatized
dialogues. We have already seen that the concluding piece links Amparo
and Agustín's behaviour with the coming revolution. This association
of history and fiction is present, albeit in a somewhat different form, in
the opening dialogue in which Ido describes the details of his current
literary concoction, an historical romance set in the times of Felipe II,
but inspired, it is to be noted, by the contemporary reality of 1867-
1868 and in particular by the daily lives of Amparo and her sister
Refugio. Despite the patent absurdities of characterization and plot, as
outlined by Ido, some of his remarks do have a special meaning if
applied to the subsequent story of the two girls as told by Galdós's
narrator:

> Todo es cosa de Felipe II, ya sabes: hombres embozados, algua-
> ciles, caballeros flamencos y unas damas, chico, más quebradizas
> que el vidrio y más combustibles que la yesca; el Escorial, el Al-
> cázar de Madrid, judíos, moriscos, renegados, el tal Antoñito
> Pérez, que para enredos se pinta solo, y la muy tunanta de la
> princesa de Eboli, que con un ojo solo ve más que cuatro; el
> cardenal Granvela, la Inquisición, el príncipe don Carlos; mucha
> falda, mucho hábito frailuno, mucho de arrojar bolsones de

dinero por cualquier servicio; subterráneos, monjas, levantadas de cascos, líos y trapisondas, chiquillos naturales a cada instante, y mi don Felipe, lleno de ungüentos.

(IV, 1472)

Ido's picture of the immoral times of Felipe II is not inaccurate on the whole, but it could also be suitably applied to the life and times of Isabel II's Court and anticipates the general outlines of Amparo's story: a romance that is really a cover for repressed sexual or materialistic urgings and clerical involvement (Polo and Nones). Ido's apparently absurd ramblings thus serve to place the fictional story in an historical context of the distant past which, to the observant reader of 1884, appears remarkably similar to that of a very recent historical period, 1867-1868 or the whole of Isabel II's reign, and if we believe the narrator, possibly to that of the period 1884.

The important scene that sets in motion the denouement of *Tormento* is Amparo's discovery, on reaching Agustín's house one day, that he has gone to see Marcelina Polo. She had come prepared to confess her secret, but now she concludes that her dream is destroyed, as Marcelina will undoubtedly tell Caballero the story of her affair. Commenting on this about-turn in events, the narrator calls it "esta lógica escondida [chance, coincidence], sobre cuyos términos descansa la máquina de los acontecimientos privados y públicos, así como éstos vienen a ser pedestal del organismo que llamamos Historia" (IV, 1569). The aside is a timely reminder to the reader of the historical referentiality of the fiction, a reminder that underneath the fiction runs the current of history which surfaces from time to time through authorial comments, plot structure, character symbolism and parallelism of episodes. These are the ingredients which combine to make *Tormento* a novel of the historical imagination in line with its predecessors in our Group I. Abandoning the figure of the potential pupil of history, Galdós now includes characters closer to the centre of national politics; but self-interest blinds them to the real meaning of events occurring around them.

CHAPTER 5

IN HISTORY'S ANTECHAMBER:
LA DE BRINGAS (1884)

If one work best exemplifies Galdós's novel of the historical imagination or historical allegory, and shows how it differs from the more traditional type of historical novel or even his own *episodios nacionales*, that work must be *La de Bringas*. For, although Galdós situates his story and characters in the most national setting of all that he has hitherto used or will use hereafter in the *serie contemporánea* — the Madrid Royal Palace —, he regularly and studiously avoids any substantial direct vision of figures or events of history, when it could almost legitimately be expected that they would appear on every other page of the novel. At this point we might be well advised to recall the words of George Eliot: "The exercise of a veracious imagination in historical picturing seems to be capable of a development that might help the judgement greatly with regard to present and future events."[1] Were we to adapt this counsel and apply it to the treatment of recent history in *La de Bringas*, we might perhaps perceive history etched in on every page.

Certainly our historical imagination is quickly kindled in this novel because of the historical setting provided for the first two thirds of the novel by the Madrid Royal Palace, the national epicentre from and to which all other movements and thoughts in the novel inevitably gravitate.[2] More specifically, it is the servants' quarters perched atop

---

[1] Reproduced by Deegan, p.25.
[2] See my "The use of distance in Galdós's *La de Bringas*", *Modern Language Review*, 69 (1974), 88-97; Andrés Amorós, "El ambiente de *La de Bringas*", *Reales Sitios*, 6 (1965), 61-68; Ricardo Gullón, *Técnicas de Galdós* (Madrid, 1970), pp. 103-34.

the Royal Palace and not the royal apartments on the ground level that are the novel's epicentre. And yet how could Galdós ignore the more sizeable component of this colossus which is the nation's symbolic core? The answer is, of course, that if he plays down or omits any mention of the royal apartments, it is not because he is not interested in them or in what is happening inside them, but because he is able to suggest through the location inhabited by his fictional characters that of the historical characters. In the meanderings of the narrator and Pez the Palace is described as a closely interconnected unit with no separation between upstairs and downstairs, or servants' quarters and royal apartments. In fact, the former are termed, in an oxymoronic phrase, "una real república" resembling a city "asentada sobre los espléndidos techos de la regia morada", or a crown studded with all sorts of diamonds or social classes which the Monarchs have placed on top of their head (IV, 1591). These images imply more than just the normal physical contiguity of two adjacent areas. What matters is the unusual nature of that contiguity. The image of the crown evokes dazzling superstructures, but in the Madrid Royal Palace the exact opposite is true: the servants' quarters are a ramshackle collection of absurd constructions which confuse and disorientate new visitors like the narrator.[3] The image of the quarters as a city placed above the roof of the royal apartments, immediately and confusingly reminding the reader of the real city of Madrid below,[4] suggests an overweight, ill-proportioned Royal Palace which might topple over. The final image of the servants' quarters as "una real república" extends the representativeness to a national level: one might conclude that the whole of Spain is quartered atop these royal apartments, as in one sense it is, because of the traditional and spiritual bond between the Monarch and her people symbolized by the crown. The image of the republic applied to the Monarch's servants is, of course, highly ironic; but it is also prophetic: the Bourbons will be overthrown, toppled over by the nation that they are supposed to serve. As a result of this revolutionary process, a republic will eventually be established.

Furthermore, the position of the Bringas apartment serves as a reminder of what is to be found below stairs. Whenever people enter, the reader knows that they have had to pass through the public area. The royal apartments and their owners are always felt to be off-stage;

[3] See Chad C. Wright, "Imagery of light and darkness in *La de Bringas*", *AG*, 13 (1978), 5-12.
[4] Cándida returns to her apartment after visiting her friends on other floors of the Palace "como si hubiera corrido medio Madrid" (IV, 1596).

indeed, this impression almost becomes a reality when, after a few weeks' occupation of their new quarters, the Bringas family rather pretentiously call the rooms in their crammed area by the names of some of the royal rooms below:

> ... llamaban a la sala Salón de Embajadores, por ser destinada a visitas de cumplido y ceremonia. Al gabinete de la derecha, donde estaba el despacho de Thiers y la alcoba conyugal, se le llamaba Gasparini, sin duda por ser lo más bonito de la casa. El otro gabinete fue bautizado con el nombre de la Saleta. El comedor-alcoba fue Salón de Columnas; la alcoba-guardarropa recibió por mote el Camón, de una estancia de Palacio que sirve de sala de guardias, y a la pieza interior donde se planchaba, se la llamó la Furriela.
>
> (IV, 1594)

Nor is the number of the Bringas apartment — 67 — inappropriate for the history-fiction parallel, for the beginning of the end of Isabel's reign occurred in 1867 with the death of her faithful supporter O'Donnell, as we saw in the previous chapter. The move to the Costanilla de los Angeles at that time signalled the start of the break-up of the Bringas family. Their move to the Palace in the Spring of 1868, which could coincide with the death of the Queen's other pillar of support, General Narváez (April 20), accelerates that process.

This indirect, allusive procedure is also applied to the historical figures. Although often mentioned by the palace servants, who are always interested in her whereabouts, Isabel II is never presented directly to the reader's attention. The closest view that Galdós permits — in the Salón de Columnas during the Maundy Thursday ceremony — is completely dehumanized by the elongated perspective selected (from the staircase opposite the chapel entrance, and from the higher skylights) and by additional layers of distortion. The Monarchs, like many of their servants on other occasions, are here presented only by their titles, except for a mildly individualizing reference to their "aire de benevolencia y cortesía, única nota simpática en la farsa de aquel cuadro teatral" (IV, 1599). This distant perspective, so essential for the effectiveness of the *esperpento*,[5] contrasts markedly with the close-ups of historical characters found in the *episodios nacionales*. In *La de Bringas* Galdós does not need to humanize such characters directly, for they are humanized indirectly by their fictional counterparts (in Isabel's case, by Rosalía).

The parallel between Monarch and subject, initiated in *Tormento*,

[5] See Ricardo Gullón, "Reality of the 'Esperpento' ", in *Valle-Inclán: Centennial Studies* (Austin, Texas, 1968), pp.135-36.

is renewed by Isabelita Bringas in a dream recalling the Maundy Thursday ceremony: "Despues oyó [Isabelita] tocar la marcha real. ¿Era que la reina subía a la terraza? No; aparecían por la puerta de la escalera de Damas su mamá, asida al brazo de Pez, y su papá, dando el suyo a la marquesa de Tellería" (IV, 1600). In *La de Bringas* the physical similarity between Rosalía and the Queen is now accompanied by a moral similarity which reaches its climax in the novel's denouement when Rosalía commits adultery with Pez and then resorts to high-class prostitution. There are other similarities of character which Galdós adds from time to time: the main reason Rosalía is able to overcome her husband's opposition to the incredible number of new dresses entering the house is her constant claim that they are gifts from the gracious and generous Sovereign. The excuse is a convenient device to forward the plot, but it also reveals that Rosalía's consuming passion for clothes is shared by her Monarch. In the closing pages of the novel the parallel becomes complete when Rosalía manages to seduce the narrator, who now occupies the important position of administrator of the Royal Palace for the Revolutionary Junta of Madrid.[6] For not only had Isabel previously maintained amorous relations with General Serrano, the leader of the new Provisional Government, but for a few moments Rosalía actually becomes the uncrowned Queen of the Royal Palace.

A warning that both fictional and historical character might share the same fate (of moral degradation and physical exile from the Palace) is sounded in the scene when Rosalía and Pez, emerging from the Retiro Park after a particularly intimate stroll, pass the Glorieta Gate where in 1865 the famous avenues of horse-chestnut trees were cut down and the land put up for sale by the Queen as a public gesture to help reduce the nation's debt. This so-called *rasgo* was bitterly attacked as an empty public relations exercise by the Republican, Emilio Castelar, whose subsequent dismissal from his post at Madrid University, along with that of the Rector, led to the bloody *Noche de San Daniel* riots, and ultimately to Isabel's overthrow in 1868. In case this is not well known to the readers, the narrator interjects at this point some direct commentary: "Esta palabra [rasgo] fue muy funesta para la Monarquía, árbol a quien no le valió ser más antiguo que los castaños, porque también me lo descuajaron e hicieron leña de él" (IV, 1614). The clear implication is that Rosalía will similarly suffer a downfall, especially as the word "rasgo" had been applied a short while earlier to her inventiveness in explaining away her sewing activities

6 See my "The use of distance . . .", pp.94-95.

when caught in the act by Francisco (IV, 1612).[7]

However, Rosalía is also a figure in revolt, a revolutionary determined to break out of the domestic straitjacket in which Francisco maintains her. Significantly, her rebellious urges are translated into forays in which she abandons the Palace and takes to the Madrid streets. Condemned to remain in the capital while her friends are holidaying in the north, she thinks of herself as an exile banished from Court society (IV, 1655, 1659), a pertinent reminder to the reader of those generals who had just been exiled for political reasons. She is thus associated with the September Revolution, which she welcomes in a passage which betrays her materialism and echoes Isidora Rufete's reaction in *La desheredada* to the news of King Amadeo's abdication:

> Vendrían seguramente tiempos distintos, otra manera de ser, otras costumbres; la riqueza se iría de una parte a otra; habría grandes trastornos, caídas y elevaciones repentinas, sorpresas, prodigios y ese movimiento desordenado e irreflexivo de toda sociedad que ha vivido mucho tiempo impaciente de una transformación.
> (IV, 1682)

Earlier, in a nightmare, Isabelita had imagined her mother outgrowing the Palace: "Su mamá era tan grande como todo el Palacio Real, más grande aún" (IV, 1641). In effect Rosalía outgrows her identification with the Queen and thus her monarchism and, as we have seen, eventually supplants her mistress, albeit briefly. A former representative of the fallen Monarch, Rosalía is now identified with the Revolutionary regime that has usurped her place. The clear implication is that the new order will be little different from its predecessor.

The parallelism between Francisco Bringas and his royal namesake is also deepened in *La de Bringas*. The ironic religious references applied to Bringas and which echo the Royal Consort's religiosity are now increased: a "santificador de las fiestas" (IV, 1598), "nuestro buen Thiers" has been promised by the Consort the award of the royal decoration of "caballero del Santo Sepulcro" along with the corresponding uniform and accessories (IV, 1600). Even the recriminatory Rosalía will later acknowledge her husband's saintliness (IV, 1670). Yet Francisco's outward meekness is deceptive, covering a selfish concern for his own material comforts, and the reality behind the religious comparisons is clearly exposed in the narrator's comments on his promotion to the

[7] See my *Benito Pérez Galdós: La de Bringas*, Critical Guides to Spanish Texts, 30 (London, 1981), pp.84-88, for a detailed study of other ironic verbal reprises.

Intendencia del Real Patrimonio, with its corresponding perk of a Palace apartment: "Tal canonjía realizaba las aspiraciones de toda su vida, y no cambiara Thiers aquel su puesto tan alto, seguro y respetuoso, por la silla del Primado de las Españas" (IV, 1591).[8] The parallel with Francisco de Asís is further developed when Bringas is cuckolded by his wife. No direct mention is made of the state of the royal marriage, but it was sufficiently well known for the contemporary reader to draw the parallel for himself. Here as elsewhere Galdós achieves greater effect by omitting the most damaging details.

Bringas's parasitism is more markedly exposed than in *Tormento*, his rapaciousness having been encouraged, it seems, by residence in the Royal Palace. His ready utilization of royal "left-overs" has developed into an obsessive exploitation of the Queen's famous munificence and he now thinks that she has a duty to keep him supplied with these extra rewards: she should reinstate his full pay or give the family free train tickets for their summer vacation. The Queen does oblige at times, as when she sends her own doctor to treat his blindness, but even then Bringas is not satisfied, for he expects such medical attention to be free. In all of these instances it is difficult to remember the proper social relationship: as Francisco lists his requests for the Queen he appears to be the imperious monarch, whilst Isabel II assumes the role of obliging servant. Thus, the social order of Spain seems dangerously inverted, in much the same way as the description of the servants' quarters as a city atop the Royal Palace had seemed a dangerous inversion of spatial dimensions. A similar inversion of values is evident in Bringas's plans to build a magnificent wardrobe out of materials scrounged from various parts of the Palace, for the finished product would be made of public property for individual possession. The Monarchs' personalization of State duties has fomented in their servants a reciprocal personalization which sees the State, the Queen and the Civil Service as their personal property. This inversion of values effectively exposes the driving egotism and materialism of the royal servants, but it reflects, too, on the Monarchs, who, by association, are tainted with the same faults.

La de Bringas also differs from preceding novels in its employment of a group of secondary female characters to reinforce the historical symbolism of the protagonist, Rosalía. Stressing the obvious may have been an artistic blunder by Galdós, but the method does have

---

[8] The irony of this promotion in February 1868 is that two months later Marfori, the Queen's current lover, was appointed head of the Real Intendencia by González Bravo. See Olivar Bertrand, p.197.

the advantage of extending the range of historical symbolism beyond the nexus of main characters, thus deepening the historical mould of the book. Appearing before Rosalía, Doña Cándida prefigures her in her spendthrift ways. The Queen has paid off Cándida's debts and given her living quarters in the Palace where she survives parasitically off bits and pieces she scrounges from other inmates or the Palace kitchens. The narrator's naïveté and ignorance of her identity when he first meets her cause him to believe that he is "*hablando con el más próximo pariente de su majestad. Aquel derribar de tabiques y aquel disponer obras y mudanzas, hicieron en mi candidez el efecto de un lenguaje regio hablado desde la penúltima grada de un trono.* El respeto me impedía desplegar los labios" (my italics; IV, 1594). In spite of the regal identification she will welcome and readily accommodate herself to the Revolution when it reaches the Palace, eagerly reporting the activities of the militia guards after the take-over of the Palace, just as she had earlier related the arrest of the Unión Liberal generals. The harbinger of political news, she is quick to identify with its sources and neither political principle nor personal gratitude can resist her overriding parasitism.

The aristocratic Milagros will likewise welcome the Revolution as a chance to reverse her financial bad luck. The cosmetics applied to her face recall the chaotic, gaudy refurbishing of the Palace quarters so minutely described in the opening chapters of the book. Above all, she shares with Rosalía and the Queen a passion for clothes and is, of course, responsible for leading the former along that particular road to perdition. The typical palace retainer, she and her dependants rely on the Queen's active connivance and support for their advancement. And because of this relationship Milagros, and the other females, are really "creations" of the Monarch, extensions and reflections of her inner weaknesses. For Ricardo Gullón, this process of transformation operates in the opposite direction: "Las figuras, figurones y figurillas de la historia, sin perder su carácter, se asimilan sustancialmente a los personajes novelescos, son como ellos, participan de su sustancia, y a la vez los incorporán de algún modo al plan histórico."[9]

Refugio Sánchez Emperador is the fourth and final figure in this series of fictional mirrors of Queen Isabel. Her appearance in the first three quarters of the novel is limited to the odd occasion, but her famous confrontation with Rosalía (Chapters 45 to 48 inclusive) establishes her significance for the main theme. In these climactic chapters, the reflective role that she, Rosalía and Milagros discharge is

9 Gullón, *Técnicas . . .*, p.122.

appropriately resumed. Refugio's buxom figure and her appearance in a night-gown and high-heeled shoes, perfect emblems of the *demi-monde* (IV, 1672), immediately remind us of Isabel II's habit of appearing in similar attire at Palace meetings with diplomats or politicians.[10] Her dress-covered rooms reflect the disorder of Rosalía's own dress-making room and the general chaos of the Palace upper structures. It is Refugio's remarks on the Queen's relationship with Rosalía and her imagined presence in this scene which in one flash combine and actualize all the levels of action in the novel (financial, sartorial, political and private) and which forge the clearest connecting-thread between all of these female characters:

> — Si estuviera aquí la *Señora*, no pasaría usted esos apurillos, porque con echarse a sus pies y llorarle un poco . . . Dicen que la *Señora* consuela a todas las amigas que le van con historias y que tienen maridos tacaños o perdularios. Ya se ve: si yo tuviera en mi mano, como ella, todo el dinero de la nación, también lo haría. Pero déjese usted estar, que ya le ajustarán las cuentas. Dice un caballero que viene a casa, que ahora sí que se arma de veras . . .
> — Sí, lo que es ahora — añadió Refugio con desparpajo — cambiaremos de aires . . . Vayan con Dios. Habrá libertad, libertades . . .
> Esta falta de respeto, esta manera de hablar de su majestad, enfadó tanto a la dama.
>
> (IV, 1676)

The final blow to Rosalía's pride — Refugio's disclosure of Milagros's pejorative description of her as "cursi" — is really an insult applicable to all of these female figures. The net effect of the scene is to confirm the interchangeability of these characters, historical and fictional (underlined by the common pejorative use of the female definite article before their surnames). They are reproductions, more or less, of the same character type: the immoral, pretentious, appearance-loving female who is blind to defects even when they are held up before her eyes. The word "cursi" sums up the type in a nutshell. Isabel and her subjects are alike: one and all contribute, because of their moral shortcomings, to the general pre-revolutionary chaos of 1868 which is vividly conveyed in the jumble of material in Refugio's dwelling.

All the main political developments of the novel's time period, April to October 1868, seem to be included: the rumours of revolution which had thickened the air since Narváez's death; the exile of the Unión Liberal generals, Montpensier and the Infante Enrique to distant

---

[10] See Gribble, p.175.

points; the movements of Prim; the wedding in May of the Infanta Isabel to an Italian prince. The course of the September Revolution is also faithfully recorded: the *pronunciamiento* in Cádiz by Topete, Prim and Serrano, followed by other risings across Andalucía and Prim's naval trek along the Eastern seaboard to secure important ports; Serrano's inland advance on Madrid from Seville, momentarily delayed by Novaliches's forces at the brief, bitter battle of Alcolea on September 29. The possibility of the Queen's return to Madrid to save her throne, as advised by Marfori, is included in Cándida's colourful talk: "Yo sostengo que si la reina tuviera ánimo para venirse acá y presentarse y echar una arenga diciendo: 'Todos sois mis hijos', se arreglaría esto fácilmente" (IV, 1680). It is Pez who indicates the step she was to take: exile in France. The events in Madrid, the establishment of the Junta and the Gobierno Provisional, are also mentioned, but it is the militia's occupation of the Royal Palace that is described in the greatest detail.[11]

The most surprising feature about all these historical references is their brevity, all the more surprising not only because of the national location from which most of the novel is narrated, but also because the narrator eventually reveals himself as an important political figure in the revolutionary movement. This reticence creates a certain distancing between the event and the reader which is increased by the contexts of these references – generally personal conversations between Francisco and the other characters. Other layers of distortion are usually added. Thus, the first mention of the exile of the Unión Liberal generals crops up as part of a conversation between Pez and Bringas, but the latter is more interested in his hair-picture (IV, 1607). Pez's empty triplicate sentences also distance the historical reality to which he is referring, as does the theatrical format in which the whole scene is presented. Fuller details about the generals' arrest and exile are presented in subsequent pages, but only very gradually, and always parcelled up by other matters. Francisco is again told of the event, this time by Cándida, but it is as one item in a long list of news topics and just before he has his traumatic seizure of blindness. Furthermore, the whole scene is recorded through the ears of Rosalía who is sitting in another room. The brief, staccato presentation, with the italicization by the author, amounts to a rapid succession of disconnected, almost incomprehensible words: "Rosalía la oía [a Cándida] desde su taller, sin distinguir más palabras que *administrador y papel del Estado ... Consolidado ...*

---

[11] For a more detailed description of the historical events and their recording in *La de Bringas*, see my "Galdós, the Madrid Royal Palace and the September 1868 Revolution", *Revista Canadiense de Estudios Hispánicos*, 5 (1980), 1-17.

*Revolución . . . Generales Canarias . . . Montpensier . . . Dios nos asista
. . .* Hablaban de negocios altos y de política baja. De repente la dama
oyó violentísimo estrépito, como de un mueble que viene a tierra y de
loza que se rompe" (IV, 1621).

More information about the generals' arrest and exile is advanced by the narrator's fragmented recollection of words pronounced
at Tula's soporific *tertulia*: the exiled generals have now reached the
Canary Islands; Prim is in Vichy; the Queen is about to go off to her
summer residences, first at La Granja, and then at Lequeitio; González
Bravo is ill and Cabrera, the famous Carlist general of the First Carlist
War (1833-1840), is conferring with the Pretender. Overlaying the distortion of the accompanying fashion talk are several other barriers
which further distance the historical reality: Pez's speech, which lulls
the narrator into a half-sleep; the filtered coloured light of the room in
which they are sitting, and other minor irritants (Cándida's yawning
and throat-clearing, the dazzling spots on Rosalía's dress, the prettiness
of one of Milagros's daughters and the noise of the rocking chairs and
fans). Political developments are thus an insignificant component of a
kaleidoscope of mundane activities and conversation topics. Milagros's
relation of the same political events to the Bringas couple shortly afterwards (IV, 1642) is more directly presented but for an ulterior purpose:
to curry favour with them so that they will lend her some desperately-
needed money. Their reaction, one of ecstatic delight, is absurdly
unrealistic, as any reader of 1884 would instantly appreciate. Pez's
more alarmist view of the generals' arrest and the rivers of blood which
will flow as a result, is suitably reproduced later that evening in Isabelita's nightmare amidst visions of her mother and parents arguing over
the arrival of more dresses (IV, 1651). His bitter analysis on another
occasion (IV, 1653-54) is similarly distanced because of his annoyance
at Francisco's interruption of his romantic overtures to Rosalía.

After such persistent, almost monotonous repetition of the
same historical event, it is clear that contemporary history is very much
part of the daily lives of these characters and talked about incessantly;
but it is subordinated to more dominant personal interests in an unrealistic way, when they should have shown a greater awareness of the
direct implications of events for servants of the Crown. This distanced
recording of the political events (which the narrator also maintains
when he eventually informs the reader of his own political appointment
as Palace administrator) appropriately reproduces the isolation of this
Palace society from the rest of the country. Cocooned in their labyrinthine structures, they can only perceive a distant echo of events, only

vaguely appreciate the direction of those events. This basically un-realistic vision is superbly and conclusively illustrated by the reaction of Francisco Bringas and his family to the take-over of the Palace by the revolutionaries. At last fiction and history will meet face to face, it seems. But Francisco still persists in refusing to face up to the reality of the situation: he barricades himself in the apartment firmly believing there will be a bloody repeat of the French Revolution. The ironic counterpoint to this hallucination is contained in Cándida's report that the militiamen are ambling through the royal apartments, gawping at the furniture, killing the odd pigeon and in need of a good meal: "En fin, es una risa. Baje usted y verá, verá. No hay miedo; son unos ange-lotes. ¿Robar? Ni una hebra" (IV, 1681). By refusing to take the reader downstairs and present history in the making, even at this climactic moment, Galdós shows that the narrator and his characters will always have an elongated perspective on the events of reality.

The important corollary of this argument, here and in the other novels of our Group I, is that the historical events which Galdós selects are inherently empty, devoid of great meaning, absurdly irrelevant in the final analysis. As Varey has summed it up, the outcome of *La Gloriosa* as presented in *La de Bringas* was a damp firework which only dislodged a few pigeons, another example of the dictum "plus ça change, plus c'est la même chose".[12]

As in *La desheredada*, the main fictional developments are made to coincide with the main occurrences leading up to the political event which closes the novel, the September Revolution. We have already noted that the second mention of the arrest of the Unión Liberal generals coincides with Francisco's first attack of blindness, the de-velopment which will enable Rosalía's revolution, her emancipation from her husband, to proceed apace. The Bringas couple's jubilation at the confirmation of the news of the generals' exile parallels their joy the previous evening on the premature recovery of Francisco's sight (IV, 1639). Pez's fateful letter to Rosalía, awaited with the same ex-pectancy with which Francisco had looked out for Golfín's bill, is suitably inserted after Paquito Bringas reads aloud to his father the threats against the Queen circulating in clandestine news-sheets and the prediction of her fall from the throne (IV, 1670). The use of the same word "papeles" in both cases reveals the intended parallel. For the twinning of other episodes, Galdós prefers more subtle suggestions, counting on the reader's awareness of the carefully structured chronological references and his ability to draw inferences.[13] Rosalía's growing infatuation with Pez in the Retiro walk occurs around the same time as the suspension of the Cortes by González Bravo (May 19, 1868) and the marriage of the Royal Infanta. The deadline for the repayment of Milagros's loan falls the same day that Montpensier is arrested. Galdós does not suggest these parallels openly in the text, but an awareness of their coincidence strengthens the chronological structure of the allegory.

La de Bringas follows *Tormento* in excluding from the gallery of characters the figure of the pupil of history whom Galdós had incorporated into the first three novels of our Group I. However, in the bureaucrat Pez it does contain a character who, like Nones in *Tormento*, has been and still is at the centre of the country's political life: "Había pasado toda su vida al retortero de los hombres políticos, *y tenía conocimientos prolijos de la historia contemporánea, que en sus labios componíase de un sinfín de anécdotas personales*. Poseía la erudición de los chascarrillos políticos, y manejaba el caudal de frases parlamentarias con pasmosa facilidad" (my italics; IV, 1606). Pez is ideally placed to be the man who possesses the inner secrets of Spain's recent history, the expert who, having seen governments at work from inside, can suggest remedies to the nation's problems. Indeed he likes to put himself forward as a deep thinker with regenerationist ideas and in matters political he is revered as a master. Yet he is the antithesis of the earlier guide figures who believed – erroneously – that they were teaching contemporary history to their pupils. For the result of his intimacy with politicians is cynicism and, assuming that his compatriots are incapable of instruction or improvement, he adopts a pose of moral and intellectual superiority:

> . . . El país no pensaba, el país no obraba, el país era idiota. Era preciso, pues, que el Estado pensase y obrase por él, porque sólo el Estado era inteligente. Como esto no podía realizarse, Pez se recogía en su espíritu, siempre triste, y *afectaba aquella soberana indiferencia de todas las cosas. Considerábase superior a sus contemporáneos, al menos veía más*, columbraba otra cosa mejor, y como no lograra llevarla a la realidad, de aquí su flemática calma.
>
> Se consolaba acariciando mentalmente sus principios, en medio del general desconcierto. *Para contemplar en su fantasía la regeneración de España*, apartaba los ojos de la corrupción de las

---

[13] See Roberto G. Sánchez, "The function of dates and deadlines in Galdós's *La de Bringas*", *Hispanic Review*, 46 (1978), 299-311, and Jennifer Lowe, "Galdós's use of time in *La de Bringas*", *AG*, 15 (1980), 83-88.

costumbres, de aquel desprecio de todas las leyes que iba cundiendo ... ¡Oh! Pez se conceptuaba dichoso con el depósito de principios que tenía en su cuerpo. Adoraba la moral pura, la rectitud inflexible, y su conciencia le indemnizaba de la infamias que veía por doquier ... Quisiera Dios que aquel ideal no se apartase de su alma ...

(my italics; IV, 1637)

Yet Pez's pompous rhetoric betrays an inner vacuity of intellectual substance and, like the palace footmen, he appears ultimately as an empty marionettish figure.

Moreover, Pez is presented as the embodiment of

esa España dormida, beatífica, que se goza en *ser juguete de los sucesos* y en nada se mete con tal que la dejen comer tranquila; que no anda, que nada espera y *vive de la ilusión del presente*, mirando al cielo, con una vara florecida en la mano; que se somete a todo el que la quiere mandar, venga de donde viniere, y profesa el socialismo manso; *que no entiende de ideas, ni de acción, ni de nada que no sea soñar y digerir.*

(my italics; IV, 1607)

His cynicism is far removed from that of the Marqués de Beramendi or *Confusio* in the later *episodios nacionales*, whose political amorality was a defensive response to a situation perceived as intolerable. For Pez is the epitome of the opportunistic civil servant and his cynicism is a convenient rationalization of his opportunism. Thus, when his contacts in revolutionary circles ensure his survival in the Civil Service, the narrator ironically defines his philosophy of history as knowing how to manipulate the system in one's own interest: "En el Gobierno provisional tampoco le faltaban amistades y parentescos, y dondequiera que volvía mi amigo [Pez] sus ojos, veía caras pisciformes. Y antes que casualidad, llamemos a esto Filosofía de la Historia" (IV, 1683). In Pez the anguish of the sensitive Relimpio has given way to indifference to the march of political events so long as personal interests are not threatened.

In the preceding novels of our Group I, Galdós had been concerned that the contemporary reader should draw moral edification from the fiction. In such an artificial novel as *La de Bringas* where he is narrating events at a time distance of sixteen years, there is, surprisingly, no such clear tying of the story to the year 1884. The narrator, previously the most important medium through which Galdós made this association, is paradoxically the largest obstacle to any such achievement, and his lack of candour inspires little confidence, even if he had expressed a didactic intention.[14] None the less, the confines of this 1868 period picture are not so hermetically sealed as they first appear, for they are broken down in a number of ways. The references to the subsequent social decline of Milagros and Cándida as they are recorded, for example in the latter's case, in *El amigo Manso*, advance the tentacles of the novel to the 1880s. From our reading of *Tormento* we know that in 1884 Bringas was in very bad health. *La de Bringas*, therefore, is not as isolated from the other novels of our Group I as it might seem. Moreover, the narrator's silence about the period in which he is writing his book is ominously deceptive. If we assume that the narrator, whose lack of political and moral principles is very similar to that of his friend Pez, is still a political figure in the year that he is narrating his story (there is no indication to the contrary), then the application of the novel's message to the Spain of 1884 is more than probable and appropriate. In a novel where the question of getting the perspective right is so crucial and the reliability of the narrator has to be qualified, such an interpretation is within reason.

This point is made in the emblematic pictorial image which Galdós masterfully constructs at the commencement of his narrative (to the confusion and dismay of many a reader of the novel!). The immobilising description of the hair-picture fulfils the same purpose as Ido del Sagrario's dramatized prolegomenon in *El doctor Centeno*, serving to establish the correct perspective in which the subsequent story has to be read. The first of many scenes of repugnant material chaos, the hair-picture is itself a work of physical perspective with its successive layers of attached hairs creating the illusion of a moonlit landscape. Secondly, the accessories are taken from a motley collection of models which, significantly, have some historical connections: the weeping-willow tree comes from a drawing of Napoleon's tomb at St. Helena; the puckering angel had originally appeared in a drawing of the tomb of one of Fernando VII's wives. Even this apparently innocuous description, then, has some relevance for recent Spanish history, the reader being reminded by these brief allusions of the antecedents of the contemporary political scene. Naturally, the "gallardo artificio sepulcral de atrevidísma arquitectura" with its "piramidal escalinata, zócalos grecorromanos, y luego machones y paramentos ojivales, con pináculos, gárgolas y doseletes" (IV, 1587) is, in retrospect, reminiscent of the mammoth structure of the Madrid Royal Palace described in a subsequent chapter as a colossus. Secondly, and more importantly, the

---

[14] See my "The use of distance . . .", pp.94-95.

hair-work is a personal token of gratitude from Francisco to Pez's wife in return for the political favour from Pez of a job in the Civil Service for Paquito Bringas. The picture is, thus, part of the traditional process of favour-buying by prospective bureaucrats which is still in operation after the Revolution when it is elevated, in the case of Pez, to the status of a philosophy of history. At a deeper level, the elegiac subject of the composition is a neat anticipation of the death knell sounded at the novel's close for the Isabelline regime and the Bringas family honour. But the hair-picture is never really finished; it never really exists as it is described in the opening chapter. The description that is given is an optical illusion, like so many others in this novel, and like the political changes which were supposedly to be ushered in by the 1868 Revolution. In the incompleteness of the hair-picture rest Galdós's words of warning for the readers of 1884: to dismiss *La de Bringas* as a period comedy with no relation to contemporary Spain would be to ignore the novel's subtlety.[15] This indirect, elusive reference to other epochs is, of course, very possible and likely in a novel of the historical imagination or an historical allegory, but not in the more traditional historical novels, the recognizable moulds of which *La de Bringas* — unique among the novels of our Group I of the *serie contemporánea* — seems to possess on a first reading.

[15] In this respect, it is interesting to note Galdós's comments (certainly ironic) on the glittering ball held at the Madrid mansion of the Duques de Fernán-Núñez on February 25, 1884, during the period in which he was writing *La de Bringas*. See Shoemaker, pp.63-71.

CHAPTER 6

HESITANT EMERGENCE
OF A REDEMPTIVE AHISTORICISM:
LO PROHIBIDO (1884-1885)

With the novelistic interest concentrated on social development and sexual immorality, *Lo prohibido* does not immediately appear to be a novel of the historical imagination like its predecessors in our Group I. The absence of any clearly outlined historical events, along with the abandonment of the symbolic representativeness of fictional characters, seems to mark this novel as an exception. However, the important role played by the narrator in his autobiography; his political status; the presence of a considerable number of faulty guide characters; allusions to English politics; verbal twinning of the public and private spheres; all point to a determination on the part of Galdós to surround his story with a pertinent political reference of some application for the contemporary reader. Indeed, in its tentative elaboration of a positive attitude towards the absurdity of contemporary history, *Lo prohibido* registers a new development in Galdós's novel of the historical imagination which supersedes the static cynicism of *Tormento* and *La de Bringas*, or the depressing failures of *La desheredada*, *El amigo Manso* and *El doctor Centeno*, and initiates the redemptive ahistoricism to be developed in our Group III novels.

After the intense political parallelism of *La de Bringas*, the apparent avoidance of sizeable references to political developments in the period under study (September 1880 to November 1884) is somewhat disconcerting, especially considering the narrator's position as a Sagasta deputy. The euphoria of the Liberal party on its accession to power in 1881; Alfonso XII's controversial visit to France and Germany in the same year, leading in 1883 to the fall of the governments of

Sagasta and Posada Herrera; the offensive behaviour of the Unión Católica leader, Alejandro Pidal y Mon, who criticized the Italian Government and then created a storm over the inaugural lecture of Professor Miguel Morayta at Madrid University in the autumn of 1884; all of these incidents go unrecorded in the diary-cum-memoir of our Liberal deputy, José María Bueno de Guzmán.[1] A few other events are recorded, but in such a vague and nonchalant manner that the narrator could not be credited with any intentions of documenting the political history of the period. The insurrection of the garrison at Badajoz in August 1883, provoked by agents of the exiled Radical leader, Ruiz Zorrilla, surfaces slightly in the anguished exclamations of the noble patriot Medina (IV, 1809). The inevitable return of Cánovas to power in January 1884, anticipated by Gustavito Tellería, conditions the financial climate of the period. The campaign of terror launched by the secret movement, La Mano Negra, in Andalucía in 1883, is adduced as a reason for José María's absence from his Jérez estates. The continued exploitation of a debilitated Cuba is visible in the career of Sánchez Botín and in the plans of the scheming Eloísa.[2] Among José María's friends are the Army Minister, Quesada, and the Finance Minister, Camacho, and the latter's character is lightly sketched in (IV, 1795). The revival of Republican plotting on the return of Cánovas in 1884 and the subsequent hard line adopted by the Conservatives are the motives behind Torres's alarmist tactics on the Stock Exchange (IV, 1831). This is the sum of identifiable allusions to concrete political developments or characters of the period. It is certainly not a comprehensive account, but probably enough to add an authentic touch to the narration.

But is there a deeper reason for these brief, imprecise, almost reluctantly-given details? The fragmented, oblique style conforms with that of the preceding novels, for sure; but it is even more appropriate in José María's case, for he is a politician who unabashedly confesses that he is uninterested in politics. He contemptuously dismisses his profession as a sham: "Francamente, el Congreso me parecía una comedia, y no tenía ganas de mezclarme en ella" (IV, 1733).[3] The anonymous

---

[1] Galdós did comment on some of these events in articles for *La Prensa* written during the composition of *Lo prohibido*.

[2] See Shoemaker, pp.126-28, for Galdós's view of the depressed Cuban economy at this time.

[3] Very similar sentiments were expressed by Galdós in his *La Prensa* columns at the same time. In an article published on July 15, 1884, he wrote: "La política, tal como aquí se practica, me es soberanamente antipática. Todo se reduce en ella a un juego de personalidades y a un discutir eterno y mareante capaz de acabarle la paciencia al lucero del alba" (Shoemaker, p.104).

narrator of *La de Bringas* was coy about his political appointment, but he was not uninterested in his job. José María, on the other hand, has been press-ganged into representing an Andalusian constituency notorious for its exploitation by previous deputies, and he continues the tradition of indifference to his electors:

> Yo era diputado cunero, y no me cuidaba ni poco ni mucho de cumplir los deberes de mi cargo. Jamás hablaba en las Cortes, asistía poco a las sesiones, no formaba parte de ninguna Comisión de importancia, no servía más que para sumarme con la mayoría en las ocasiones de apuro.
>
> (IV, 1733)

All requests from his constituents are regularly thrown into the wastepaper basket. When he is called to account for this political apathy by the Minister of Development, he follows the advice of Villalonga and takes up a career as a stockbroker. This so-called "patriotic service" is still nothing more than a means for personal advancement commonly practised by his acquaintances – Villalonga, Torres, Barragán and Medina –, all of whom profit from Government activities. Torres's fortune, for instance, begins to mount with Amadeo's abdication in 1873 and increases phenomenally with the second Carlist War of 1873-76. Consequently, financial detail looms larger than political fact in *Lo prohibido*. Politics do not pay, stockbroking does, as the career of José María's uncle, Rafael, has also proved, and only when political storms threaten the cash supply from his investments and, therefore, his amorous adventures, does Bueno de Guzmán manifest any interest in politics. And as was the case with Pez in *La de Bringas*, belief in their own importance encourages his financier friends to consider themselves more suitable than the professional politicians for governing the country, a claim ridiculed in the narrator's description of an encounter between Barragán and the Republican leader Castelar:

> . . . Barragán manoteaba y alzaba la voz delante del rey de los oradores, escupiendo a la faz del Cielo los mayores disparates que de humana boca pueden salir. El otro se reía, y le hacía el honor increíble de contestar a sus gansadas. Cuando se separaron, don Isidro dijo a Villalonga:
> – Se va porque no puede conmigo. Le he apabullado. Estos señores de las palabras bonitas se vuelven tarumba en cuanto se les ataca con razones.
>
> (IV, 1825)

Contemporary public life, as depicted by José María, is indeed an egotistical farce.

Yet through this narrator who is indifferent to politics, Galdós directs his lesson to the contemporary reader. The period he is now covering is no longer pre-1868 but rigorously contemporaneous. This change of temporal focus is pointedly established in the opening lines: José María leaves his Jérez estates in September 1880 to travel to Madrid, and in the capital, which he has not visited since 1868, "los tiempos de González Bravo" (IV, 1687), he is shocked to see the multitude of changes that have taken place in the intervening years. A sense of contemporaneity is also encouraged by José María's stipulation that his memoirs are to be published only after his death, and by the revelation that names, including his own, have been changed to protect the identity and reputation of real people who are still alive. He also presents himself as the Political Everyman of 1884 Spain:

... yo no soy *héroe*: yo, producto de mi edad y de mi raza, y hallándome en fatal armonía con el medio en que vivo, tengo en mí los componentes que corresponden al origen y al espacio.

(IV, 1787-8)

Moreover, José María claims that he started writing his memoirs partly for his own moral instruction, with the aim of reforming his way of life, and although in practice he tends to forget his avowed intention, it serves to establish an interpretative frame for the novel, inviting the reader to draw the conclusion that a reformation of political and moral behaviour is essential for the improvement of corrupt contemporary Spain.

As Arthur Terry has pointed out, José María is not a totally reliable narrator whose words can be taken at face value.[4] However, when describing other people he tends to be more trustworthy than he is when talking about himself, and his evaluation of them can be sharply perceptive. In his account of the other characters there emerges a coherent pattern of contrasting attitudes towards national affairs and through this, for the first time in the *serie contemporánea*, Galdós is able to advance a solution to the problem of the relation of the individual to the flow of surrounding historical events.

José María's two older cousins and their respective husbands (María Juana and Cristóbal Medina, and Eloísa and Pepe Carrillo) represent in varying degrees the basic bankruptcy of the Restoration system in which personal desires (sexual, monetary or social) are always satisfied through the socio-political system. Cristóbal rejects a position

[4] Arthur Terry, "*Lo prohibido*: unreliable narrator and untruthful narrative", *Galdós Studies*, ed. J.E. Varey (London, 1970), pp.62-89.

of public responsibility in order to concentrate on the accumulation of his private fortune. Eloísa, who often dreams that she is Rothschild's wife, yearns for another civil war to renew her fortunes, and reckons that Cuba should be sold for a good price to the United States, presumably to the benefit of individual speculators like herself.

If Cristóbal and Eloísa exploit, or would like to exploit, politics for personal gain, their respective partners, María Juana and Pepe Carrillo, use politics as a mask for inner vanities or disorders. María Juana's vehement calls for a revolution to rid the country of parasites conveniently conceal her lust for José María. Pepe is a more difficult case. At first he appears to be Galdós's answer (practical, modest) to the corrupt political system which the others typify. An assiduous attender at the sessions of the Senate, he takes his duties very conscientiously: he speaks out in the debates for all sorts of worthy causes, and canvasses the high and mighty, from the King down, for donations to these projects. His burning ambition is to regenerate Spanish aristocracy on the lines of the British model, about which he has read much in Macaulay and Erskine May. He naïvely believes that traditionalist and revolutionary political principles can be combined harmoniously, a notion that Galdós had effectively pooh-poohed in Don Florencio Morales in *El doctor Centeno*. Apart from the dubious merit of all this political do-goodism, Pepe spends less and less time with his wife, giving her grounds for adultery with cousin José María. The direct relation of Pepe's public life to his private life is unwittingly suggested by Eloísa in an appropriately striking political image: "No sé cómo Pepe, que tiene talento, emplea su dinero en hacer de Galeoto entre la Democracia y el Trono, sabiendo que esa señora y ese caballero no se han de casar, y *lo más, lo más, harán lo que hacemos nosotros, quererse a espaldas de la ley*" (my italics; IV, 1731). Private morality takes its cue from the trends in national politics. Pepe's deathbed exclamation ("No he hecho mal a nadie" [IV, 1770]) evinces a smug self-satisfaction with his public role as a national senator. While he seems to press for all the correct reforms, admire all the right models of English parliamentary theory and practice, he fails to see that any true reforms for the good of the country will have to be of a moral/spiritual nature which will affect the individual.[5] Parliamentary committees may be good for Pepe's public image, but they hardly effect any change, indeed none at all, in the

---

[5] Galdós makes fun of Carrillo's anglomania when, on a visit to Eguía's shop, he is prepared to purchase any British *objet d'art*. The detailed passages on British political life in *Lo prohibido* are more a collection of names and dates than an elaboration of political ideas.

country's moral climate. This acute criticism of the moral ineffective-
ness of the parliamentary system, even in one of its most altruistic
servants, marks the nadir of Galdós's disillusionment with the supreme
arbiter of the country's public life. To all appearances, Pepe is the
perfect deputy; but his motivation and style exert a negative effect.

As in *La de Bringas*, the Guzmán family circle is well populated
with kindred spirits, actors of equal competence in the socio-political
farce. The Marqués de Cicero with his handsome historical mien is in
reality a Civil Service nonentity; the Carlist General Chapa is more of a
handsome social fixture than a military leader. Characters we have seen
in earlier novels are still on their winning ways: Sánchez Botín is exploiting Cuba as he had done in *La desheredada*; Peña is well up the
social and political ladder he had started to climb in *El amigo Manso*.
However, not all the characters in *Lo prohibido* are uncritical of the
masquerade. Like Refugio in *La de Bringas*, some make accurate assess-
ments of the surrounding reality (the Marqués de Fúcar, Raimundo,
Sacamantecas, General Morla, Don Serafín and Rafael). Certainly there
are more such figures than in any of the preceding novels, yet the
acceptability of their criticism is weakened by countervailing defects.
This is especially true of *Sacamantecas* who, for all his perceptive comments, is as much an exploiter of the State as the cynical Villalonga.
Raimundo is more complex. Basically, he is a rather frivolous State
employee who delights in making eccentric imitations of, or telling
anecdotes about, politicians. Yet Galdós entrusts to him the presentation of an accurate historical analysis of the country's decadence,
with words that "escondían algo de verdad" (IV, 1762) and are intended to be taken seriously. His famous moral map of Spain, perhaps
the logical sequel to the map in Canencia's office that had appeared at
the beginning of *La desheredada*, is a bitter condemnation of the vices
of the whole country, the provinces as well as the capital, from the
moral, political, financial, physical and religious standpoints. His remarks on the country's political corruption are revealing:

> ... hasta en política lleva ventaja Madrid a las provincias, y las
> capitales de éstas, a las cabezas de partido. En la Memoria pruebo
> que los políticos de aquí, tan calumniados, son corderos en pa-
> rangón de los caciques de pueblo, y que el ministerio más concusio-
> nario es un ángel comparado con el secretario de Ayuntamiento
> de cualquiera de esas arcadias infernales que llamamos aldeas.
>
> (IV, 1811)

Since *Lo prohibido* shows us only the corruption of Madrid politicians,
the national implications of his remarks are staggering. Yet, needless to

say, Raimundo's own behaviour falls short of his perceptiveness about others' weaknesses.

Don Serafín, another member of the Guzmán family affected by the hereditary disease, seems to be a most positive guide figure. An old soldier who loves to see the changing of the Palace guard, and who has "ideas tan puras y hermosas sobre la justicia, sobre el derecho, y *que había sabido darlas a conocer con algo más que con palabras*" (my italics; IV, 1705), he also has a head like that of Christopher Columbus; but all of this potential is wasted by his incorrigible kleptomania.

General Morla has been more at the centre of national events than most characters over the decades; indeed, he is a walking encyclo-paedia of historical anecdotes, having been associated with most of the country's leading figures since 1834. He served as aide to the Liberal general, Luis de Córdova, during the First Carlist War; he was an in-timate friend of Narváez and an inseparable companion of the famous financier and urban developer, Don José Salamanca. More significantly,

> Los motivos secretos de los cambios políticos en el anterior reinado los sabía al dedillo, y las paredes de Palacio eran para él de una transparencia absoluta ... Le incitamos a escribir sus memorias, que serían el más sabroso y *quizá el más instructivo libro de la época presente.*
>
> (my italics; IV, 1739-40)

As guide to the inner secrets of Spain's nineteenth-century history, he could have been an excellent source of instruction for contemporary youth. However, it is clear that his knowledge, while extensive, is only anecdotal; like Morales in *El doctor Centeno*, he shows more interest in name-dropping than in deducing principles of political action or ana-lysing patterns of events. His inclusion of Pepe Carrillo's death in the long list of those of historical figures he has witnessed illustrates the purely superficial character of his historical concern. In *La desheredada*, despite obvious extravagance and some touches of absurd patriotism, Relimpio had made an attempt to see the continuum of Spanish history, linking its recent varied manifestations. Morla's pattern con-struction, on the other hand, is purely circumstantial: by coincidence he happens to be dining at the Carrillos' the evening that Pepe dies and therefore has another opportunity to display his historical knowledge. In the novels following *La desheredada* no historically-minded character has been able to match Relimpio's patriotic anguish.

In *Lo prohibido*, Galdós veers in the opposite direction, seemingly making a virtue out of a lack of historical consciousness. The important ahistoricist role now given to Camila and Constantino, the third couple of José María's cousins, foreshadows a development which will occur in our Group III of the *serie contemporánea*.[6] In many respects, the Constantino of the beginning of the novel is the continuation of such absurd army types as Pedro Minio in *La de Bringas*: he is solely interested in career advancement despite an alarming lack of field experience. None the less, he undergoes a character change during the course of the novel and is transformed from a brutish simpleton into a somewhat sensitive individual with an inkling of moral values. This change is tested by the series of events at the novel's close when José María falls downstairs and is taken ill. To the latter's surprise, the husband of his latest prospective seduction victim displays heroic Christian charity by tending the moribund narrator. This transformation is inspired and nurtured by his wife's example. Selling her valuables to help pay off José María's debts, taking charge of his house and looking after his needs even during the most difficult part of her pregnancy, Camila, whom the narrator had initially characterized as an "escandalosa, una mal educada, llena de mimos y resabios" (IV, 1695), is really the first example of a new and limited breed of Galdosian heroes and heroines. Overcoming the pull of pride and egotism, these will devote their energies to the welfare of others in complete oblivion of the historical moment in which they are living and of the historical society of which they form part. National politics, which claim the interested attention and subsequent profit of others, fail to disturb the matrimonial happiness of Camila and Constantino. Galdós is tentatively inaugurating in this couple, especially in Camila, the idea of rejection of the public world in favour of individual sentiments and acts of generosity between individuals. The key to such joint efforts by couples is love, equally shared and based on a healthy physical fulfilment, not upon a perverted lust, and a pointed contrast is drawn between the athletic love-play of the two and José María's scheming, obsessive adultery.

Paradoxically, the role played by history in Constantino's transformation is important. However, it is not the narrow, sterile history of Spain, but a wider, more balanced absorption of European history. When he is browsing over José María's collection of books, Camila urges him to read history and novels, "prosas claras que enseñen lo que se debe saber" (IV, 1854). This support of historical reading by

---

[6] Walter T. Pattison, *Benito Pérez Galdós* (Boston, 1975), p.85, and Robert Ricard, *Galdós et ses romans* (Paris, 1961), p.86, both note the exceptional role played by this couple in the novel, but only from the viewpoint of social rebelliousness, not from that of any lack of historical attitude or a redemptive ahistoricism.

Camila is not to be confused with the superficial name-dropping of General Morla. She urges her husband to read French history as well, seemingly for the pure instructional delight, and without any of the cultural snobbery in which Pepe Carrillo indulges. Galdós indicates the difference between this broad intuitive historical vision of Camila and Constantino and the narrowly Spanish identification of Morla and others by choosing markedly different names for the couple. Their progeny will also have the names of figures from universal history: Alexander, Constantine and Napoleon. This is fitting, for their own final example of abnegation is of universal application. Constantino's earlier humorous allusion to his wife's regal status is not inappropriate either: "su majestad está en sus habitaciones ... con la camarera mayor, que es ella misma" (IV, 1723). Likewise, José María recounts that he once kissed Camila with a respect "como el homenaje que a los reyes haría el monárquico más sincero y leal" (IV, 1888). Christian love should be society's new ruler, it is implied. Not until our Group III novels (1895-1897) will Galdós once more be able to introduce a similar character with Camila's sense of Christian charity and personal abnegation which is at peace with the antithetical dictates of a traditional historically-framed society.

One final word of caution is necessary, though. The reborn Camila and Constantino are the literary creations of a narrator who was never fully aware of his statements or reliable in his judgements. Now, on his death-bed, he adores the divine Camila. This state of affairs could be interpreted in two different ways. On the one hand, this picture of the couple might be distorted by the peculiar condition of the narrator and, therefore, be exaggerated. On the other, José María's fall may represent the necessary prerequisite for the rebirth of any individual, if he is to put reality in the proper perspective.[7] If the latter interpretation is accepted, José María's fall and subsequent change of heart is a dramatic lesson for the contemporary reader, who must also undergo some kind of readjustment of his historical frame if he is to perceive the inner reality of life. No longer, it seems, must one think in terms of getting in tune with the historical note of the times, but of replacing it with a stronger note of universal Christian charity. That indeed is a new lesson for the regular reader of our Group I of novels of the *serie contemporánea* ... if he can ever come to accept the reliability of the narrator of *Lo prohibido*.

[7] In *Misericordia* Frasquito Ponte suffers a similar fall (from his horse), which is a prelude to his public recognition of Benina's angelic nature.

CHAPTER 7

OLD AND NEW TRENDS RESUMED:
FORTUNATA Y JACINTA (1886-1887)

In view of Galdós's sustained interest in the treatment of contemporary historical material in the *serie contemporánea*, it is not
surprising that *Fortunata y Jacinta*, the longest and most celebrated of
all his novels, should contain his most comprehensive treatment of the
topic. The 1970 study by Geoffrey Ribbans, one of the few monographs hitherto published on the subject and the inspiration behind this
study, suggested that this was one of several important themes in the
novel.[1] If Ribbans hesitated to call the novel an historical allegory, the
anonymous *TLS* reviewer of the Penguin translation was more assertive,
but explored only a few aspects of the treatment.[2] For a Marxist critic
like Carlos Blanco Aguinaga, the political references do not constitute
so much an historical allegory as a series of fundamental reminders of
the concrete historical reality from which they are taken.[3] History,
then, is basic to the texture of Galdós's masterpiece, which not only
resumes and expands his previous experiments in the allegorical painting
of history, but also continues and advances the debate on the advantages or disadvantages of an interest in national affairs.

Galdós still directs his study to the contemporary reader.
Though the major events fall in the period 1869-1876 – he is once
more jumping back a few years, a decade and a half, for his story –, he
ensures that the novel is not just a period piece, by relating it in various
ways to the period in which he is writing. The behaviour of the Madrid
students in the *Noche de San Daniel* riot, the opening scene of Part I, is

---

[1] Ribbans, "Contemporary history . . .".
[2] "Five years . . .".
[3] Blanco Aguinaga, "Entrar por el aro . . .".

put into perspective by the observation that modern youth do not behave so indecorously. Changes in customs such as alms-giving or contraband-running are also recorded. Moreover, some of the characters who appear in the novel and are personal friends or acquaintances of the narrator (especially those in the Santa Cruz circle) are still alive. In the political context Galdós is fairly explicit about the similarity of politics then (1876) and now (1886) in his long description in Part III of the various *tertulias* arranged in a café. The effect of the slip from the imperfect to the present tense is to suggest that the immoral collusion of the different political parties exemplified by the inter-connecting *tertulias* is still a reality in 1886 Spain, as Galdós would have known from his position as a Sagasta deputy:

> Allí brillaba espléndidamente esa fraternidad española en cuyo seno se dan mano de amigo el carlista y el republicano, el progresista de cabeza dura y el moderado implacable . . . Esto de que todo el mundo sea amigo particular de todo el mundo es síntoma de que las ideas van siendo tan sólo un pretexto para conquistar o defender el pan. Existe una confabulación tácita (no tan escondida que no se encuentre a poco que se rasque en los políticos), por la cual se establece el turno en el dominio. En esto consiste que no hay aspiración, por extraviada que sea, que no se tenga por probable; en esto consiste la inseguridad, única cosa que es constante entre nosotros; la ayuda masónica que se prestan todos los partidos, desde el clerical al anarquista, lo mismo dándose una credencial vergonzante en tiempo de paces que otorgándose perdones e indultos en las guerras y revoluciones . . . La moral política es como una capa con tantos remiendos, que no se sabe ya cuál es el paño primitivo.
>
> (V, 294-5)

This passage indicates not only the continuation of these practices (the *turno pacífico* to which the narrator refers was still operating), but also their disastrous effects. The net result is the loss of all political ideas behind government measures: only expediency and opportunism prevail. There can be no doubt that Galdós was vitally interested in the principles behind political events, not just the superficial succession of names and dates. He was a thinker who wanted to probe beyond the pomp and circumstance or the political crises which attracted the whole attention of so many of his contemporaries. External evidence to support the view that this 1876 café scene is relevant to the political situation of 1886 is provided by an article he published in *La Prensa* on December 19, 1885 (while he was writing Part I of *Fortunata y Jacinta*): "Es que hemos aprendido mucho en los últimos quince años; conocemos prácticamente cuán infecundos son los cambios en la forma de gobierno; hemos escarmentado en cabeza propia y desconfiamos de las panaceas, lo mismo en medicina que en política" (*OI*, VI, 302).

Moreover, if we accept the narrator's famous words that the oscillations in Juanito's affections for Fortunata, or for any female, are a representation of the constant lurches in Spanish politics during the period 1872-1876, there is justification in our suggestion that this symbolism extends beyond the novel's chronological limits into the later years of the Restoration period in which Galdós is writing: the political changes in the Spain of 1886 are still governed by caprice. This is the reference point that the reader must not forget in reading the novel.

For the first time in the *serie contemporánea* Galdós goes back over ground covered earlier, the period 1872-1878 which he had already treated in *La desheredada*. Moreover, through the involved histories of the Santa Cruz and Arnáiz businesses, the encyclopaedic historical knowledge of Estupiñá and the historical events coinciding with Isabel Cordero's child-bearing, he is able to refer back to Spanish history of the middle and early years of the nineteenth century. *Fortunata y Jacinta* is as much a history book of nineteenth-century Spain as *War and Peace* is of an earlier period in Russian history.[4] Connecting the very recent and the intermediate past, Galdós's masterpiece emphasizes the continuum of these periods which were treated separately in the *episodios nacionales* or the preceding novels of the *serie contemporánea*.

The space allotted to historical occurrences can vary conssiderably. Most of the references to the early nineteenth century, for example, are made through Estupiñá's conversations with his prospective customers and take the form of one-word or one-line allusions with no accompanying comment. This sketchy method is also applied to events of the recent past: Prim's death, for example, crops up indirectly in a lament by Baldomero Santa Cruz II, and the various manoeuvres between the leaders of the major monarchical parties in 1874 (Cánovas, Sagasta and Romero Ortiz) are mentioned in Caña's café gossip. Sometimes, Galdós treats the same event in two different ways: in the café *tertulias* (V, 298) major episodes of the Second Carlist War such as the siege of Bilbao, the death of General Concha and the Sagunto *pronunciamiento* are treated very summarily; the same conflict receives more extensive coverage in Juan Pablo's colourful account of his Carlist

---

[4] Pattison, pp.90-93, relates that Galdós had read the 1884 French translation of *War and Peace* before he started writing *Fortunata y Jacinta*.

camp experiences (Part II, Chapters I, IV). At other times, an adjective with political overtones is sufficient to suggest the historical period or event without further comment from the narrator: Jacinta's simple allusion to the *cantonales* in December 1873 when thinking primarily of her husband's renewed relationship with Fortunata ("¡Si yo pudiera ganarle de una vez para siempre y derrotar en toda la línea a las *cantonales!*" [V, 88]) is enough, with Galdós's italicizing of the word, to remind the reader of the rebellious cantons in Cartagena and Murcia who were resisting the attacks of the Government forces at this time. Clearly, the amount of space occupied by an historical incident is not necessarily proportional to its purpose. Economy of expression may conceal a deeper function.

As always, Galdós avoids direct description of political events even when he is close to them. The principal example in this novel is the entry of Alfonso XII into Madrid on January 14, 1875. Jacinta's convenient fainting-fit at this moment, after learning of her husband's renewed liaison with Fortunata, effectively prevents any attention being focussed on the procession passing below in the street:

> Desde aquel aciago instante ya no se enteró de lo que en la calle ocurría. El rey pasó, y Jacinta le vió confusa y vagamente, entre la agitación de la multitud y el *tururú* de tantas cornetas y músicas. Vió que se agitaban pañuelos, y bien pudo suceder que ella agitara el suyo sin saber lo que hacía ... Todo el resto del día estuvo como una sonámbula.
>
> (V, 310)

A precise photographic reproduction of the procession is not called for, not because Galdós is uninterested in the great occasion, but because the fictional developments are much more effective in providing the correct emotional gloss on the historical event. The historical imagination of the reader can make the necessary tie-up without further direction from the narrator. Granted that the triumphant entry is synchronized with Juanito's resumption of his relationship with Fortunata, Jacinta's fainting-fit could be regarded as the sign of an intuitive reaction to the Restoration, a premonition of the disillusionment that it will bring in the future. In the reciprocal transfer of meaning encouraged by this sophisticated correlation of fiction and history, the change in political regimes underlines the change in Juanito's affections, and in turn Jacinta's reaction has a bearing on the simultaneous historical event.

The historical imagination of the reader is activated even during the heavy accounts of the Santa Cruz family history, for it is significant that Galdós structures the stages in the development of their clothing business according to important political watersheds of nineteenth-century Spain, not just for historical convenience, but because the coincidence of events is mutually illuminating. The business is given a firm foundation by Baldomero I during the First Carlist War when it is contracted to supply uniforms to the Government army. After 1848, that cataclysmic year of Liberal revolt throughout Europe (including Spain), the firm, now under Baldomero II, takes off, expanding into the manufacture of foreign clothes, thanks to the tariff reform of 1849. By 1868, another cataclysmic year in Spanish history, Baldomero II is ready to retire and pass over the family business to relatives, humorously named Los Chicos. Galdós underlines the essential role that political developments have played in the increase in the wealth of the Santa Cruz family:

> ... Fué preciso que todo Madrid se transformase; que la desa-mortización edificara una ciudad nueva sobre los escombros de los conventos; ... que las reformas arancelarias del 49 y del 68 pusieran patas arriba todo el comercio madrileño; ... y, *por fin, que hubiera muchas guerras y revoluciones y grandes trastornos en la riqueza individual*.

> (my italics; V, 28)

Personal family fortunes are thus amassed at the expense of the nation's suffering, the corollary being that the more wars and internal disorders there are, the better it is for the Santa Cruz business.

The historical parallel is also suggested by the way in which Galdós converts the Santa Cruz into a kind of royal dynasty. Juanito, the heir to the family wealth, is often called "el delfín", while Jacinta is occasionally "la delfina" and Juan Evaristo "el delfinito". The style by which Juanito's father is occasionally described, Baldomero II, reminds the reader of his historical homonym, Baldomero Espartero (1793-1879), the famous *progresista* general and leader in the 1840s and 1850s, who in 1870 was put forward as a candidate for the vacant Spanish throne with the title of Baldomero I. Appropriately, Baldomero Santa Cruz II was a supporter of the more moderate faction of the *progresista* party in the 1860s: "... figuraba *con timidez* [my italics] en el antiguo partido progresista; mas no era socio de la re-voltosa *tertulia*, porque las inclinaciones antidinásticas de Olózaga y Prim le hacían muy poca gracia" (V, 13); and in 1875 he prides himself on retaining those same political views, despite the innumerable political battles, *pronunciamientos* and wars that have occurred since and which, according to the narrator, have been responsible for the spectacular growth of his wealth. In practice, though, it is the profit motive rather than ideology which is behind his reactions to political events. Thus, the emergence of the First Republic inspires gloom, while Pavía's coup d'état in January 1874 arouses delight and the return of the Bourbons in 1875 unbridled elation. The correct slant on this last reaction is provided by the introspective Jacinta: "Pero a este buen señor, ¿que le va ni le viene con el rey?" (V, 309).

Baldomero's self-centredness is expressed in a phrase which neatly suggests the parallel with political events. After his marriage he constantly repeats that "no se cambiaría por un rey, ni por su tocayo Espartero, pues no había felicidad semejante a la suya" (V, 25). Is Galdós evoking here Espartero's reluctance to accept the candidacy in 1870, and, indeed, his failure in earlier decades to capitalize on the good will of the country and fulfil the promise of a firm Liberal or *progresista* administration?[5] Maybe it is only a whiff of a suggestion, but there is something strange about Santa Cruz's abandonment of the headship of the family firm in 1868 on the pretext that the times called for somebody else to take it over and he wanted to enjoy retirement; for he is still in good health and his youthful appearance is often commented upon by the narrator. This tacit criticism of his early retirement could also be levelled at Espartero for preferring isolation in Logroño in the 1860s and 1870s.

Certainly Santa Cruz's concept of progress, which is behind his decision to retire in 1868, is called into question by Galdós. His naïve belief in the differences between generations is responsible for his tolerance of Juanito's wayward spirit and juvenile excesses: "Cada cual en su época. Juanito, en la suya, no puede ser mejor de lo que es" (V, 17). This moral attitude is firmly linked to his political credo: "¿En qué consistía que habiendo sido él educado tan rígidamente por don Baldomero I, era todo blanduras con su hijo? *¡Efectos de la evolución educativa, paralela de la evolución política!* ... Esto no era una falta de lógica, sino la consagración práctica de la idea madre de aquellos tiempos, el progreso" (my italics; V, 27). His mistake is to equate moral and political progress when he can hardly be said to understand or practise the latter. His determined character, apparent in the treatment of the Pitusín question, when he unnecessarily wounds Jacinta's feelings, is also evident in the opening page of the novel when he immediately resorts to his contacts in the Isabelline administration (no less a functionary than González Bravo) to secure Juanito's release from prison after

[5] See Carr, p.183.

the *Noche de San Daniel* revolt. The *progresismo* of Baldomero II is really a political and social slogan which masks an authoritarian, egotistical materialism. His progressive ideas seem to apply only to the misguided encouragement of his son's wayward behaviour. Could Galdós also be suggesting that in the same way the inner contradictions of the Liberals, separated from 1833 to 1868 into *moderado* and *progresista* wings or parties, at a time when the charismatic figure of Baldomero Espartero could have exercised firmer control and influence, were the root cause of the lurches in the Spanish political scene after 1868, so well symbolized by Juanito's continuous alternations in affections and opinions?[6]

The obviousness of these parallels is increased by explicit glosses: "El *Delfín* había entrado, desde los últimos días del 74, en aquel período sedante que seguía infaliblemente a sus desvaríos. En realidad, no era aquello virtud, sino cansancio del pecado; no era el sentimiento puro y regular del orden, sino el hastío de la revolución. Verificábase en él lo que don Baldomero había dicho del país: que padecía fiebres alternativas de libertad y de paz" (V, 311). Not all the stages of Juanito and Fortunata's relationship are plotted against important historical developments, but there are sufficient correspondences to suggest the allegorical frame. Juanito's first action in the novel, it should be noted, is as a political activist in the *Noche de San Daniel* protest, as "el revolucionario, el anarquista, el descamisado Juanito" (V, 13). He is an actor of history first, before he ever becomes a character of fiction. Through this notorious incident we are given our first glimpses of his inner personality: on the one hand, he engages in illegal anti-government activity, yet, on the other, he is prepared to accept the order and authority of others and in the following years at university he devotes himself to regular studies with great enthusiasm. The alternation in his character between the two opposite poles of order and disorder has thus been suggested in the novel's opening chapter and, significantly, in an incident which had important repercussions in nineteenth-century Spanish history. The bases of the historical allegory which forms the structure of the novel have been laid.[7]

Furthermore, doubts are raised about Juanito's real interest in

[6] See Ribbans, "Contemporary history . . .".

[7] Various historical allusions bolster Juanito's representativeness. He bears the same name as a famous Carlist guerrilla leader (see Fernández Almagro, I, p.144), who, by chance, is the cause of a heated argument between Juan Pablo and Nicolás Rubín. The Santa Cruz family also live close to the church of the same name, the destruction of whose tower in the post-Revolution year of the new Constitution, 1869, so upsets Estupiñá.

the event of national importance in which he has engaged. The jocular tone adopted to describe his participation, so different from the grave condemnation of the same event in Galdós's memoirs (VI, 1671), tends to equate the political episode with pranks like egg-frying in university classes. The implication is that Juanito is not a seriously committed political activist, just as he does not appear to be a serious history student of Salmerón. Later he may have enormous influence with the Republican leaders (according to Doña Guillermina), but he refuses to enter politics. He does profess some political ideas, but they are always dictated more by the need to impress a listening public than by any firmly or deeply held convictions. He is forever changing sides: in 1870 he is in favour of a monarchy, yet when the throne of Spain is given to Amadeo, he begins to call for a republican system. As the representative of a period of Spanish history filled with chaotic alternations in political structures, it is fitting, then, that he should hold fickle political opinions and participate only sporadically in the political network.[8] Lamentably, Juanito fails to draw the obvious conclusions from the historical parallels so carefully marshalled by the author and made explicit for him by his father's comments. A potential student of contemporary history and a part-time actor in its ebb and flow, Juanito cannot absorb the full lesson offered by history even as regards his own emotional predicament. He conveniently blames the inconsistency of political ideas or regimes on the weakness of the human condition. In many respects he resembles Isidora Rufete in *La desheredada* in this obtuse or cynical disregard of the history lessons that Galdós thrusts at him.

    In comparison with her husband, Jacinta has no interest in politics, obsessed as she is with having a baby and monitoring her husband's errant ways: "Los pensamientos políticos nacidos de las conversaciones de aquella noche huyeron pronto de la mente de Jacinta. ¿Qué le importaba a ella que hubiese República o Monarquía, ni que don Amadeo se fuera o se quedase? Más le importaba la conducta de aquel ingrato que a su lado dormía tan tranquilo" (IV, 83). It is rather ironic that she should take umbrage at Alfonso during his processional entry into Madrid, for her only previous political act was to express support for the young Bourbon monarch (albeit because of her dominant maternal instincts). Is Jacinta perhaps a symbol of the impassive, tolerant Spanish public who, because of greater absorption in personal matters and benign tolerance of a wayward political system,

---

[8] Stephen Gilman, "The birth of Fortunata", *AG*, 1 (1966), p.75, notes that Juanito bears an ironic surname for a *señorito* without any political mission.

contribute to their own future suffering and disillusionment?

Those members of the Santa Cruz circle who do take an interest in politics (and there are many: Villalonga, Aparisi, the Marqués de Casa-Muñoz, Ruiz, Guillermina, Estupiñá and Isabel Cordero) do so in a way which brings further ridicule on the political attitudes of that circle and its principal actors through a process of inner reverberations, as it were. It is the deputy Villalonga who recalls the take-over of the Cortes by Pavía's troops in January 1874, another pivotal episode linking fiction and history. Juanito's renewed interest in Fortunata (above all, in a clothes-conscious Fortunata) parallels the desire of the country for another change of political form, a return to more stable political ways after the chaos of the First Republic. The twinning of these two strands is aided by the fact that Fortunata's latest lover, with whom she has returned to Madrid, is an arms-dealer who has been supplying the Republican government with weapons. However, Villalonga's account of the seizure of the Cortes is more important for the attitudes shown towards it by both the narrator and the listener, especially as Villalonga is a confidant of the rebels Serrano and Pavía. No less than Juanito, he prefers to enthuse over Fortunata's appearance instead of emphasizing the national importance of the event. His description of the leaders' ignorance of the coup's progress, of the comic antics of the deputies in the Chamber and the final absurd touch (the cannons outside the Parliament building are unloaded), all contribute to create a sense of farce. The narrator makes the explicit comment:

> ¡El 3 de enero de 1874! . . . ¡El golpe de Estado de Pavía! No se hablaba de otra cosa, ni había nada mejor de que hablar. Era grato al temperamento español un cambio teatral de instituciones, y volcar una situación como se vuelca un puchero electoral . . . Deseaban todos que fuese Villalonga a la casa para que les contara la memorable sesión de la noche del 2 al 3.
>
> (V, 151)

In reality the episode was not totally farcical and Galdós's description of it in *De Cartago a Sagunto* (1911), an *episodio nacional* of the fifth series, is considerably more bitter. Only a small part of this feeling comes across in *Fortunata y Jacinta*, and, significantly, this is not in Villalonga's account, but in the narrator's comments on reports of the defiant resistance of one Republican deputy, Díaz Quintero, and of Castelar's heart-attack later at home: "Estas referencias o noticias sueltas eran *en aquella triste historia* como las uvas desgranadas que quedan en el fondo del cesto después de sacar los racimos. Eran las más maduras, y quizá por esto las más sabrosas" (my italics; V, 155). Because of his chosen economical style Galdós cannot analyse or enlarge upon the ramifications of the incident, but the depth of his interest and his desire to comment can be gauged from the insertion of these clipped, emotive phrases.

Villalonga is only one of several of the Santa Cruz circle who help to incorporate history into fiction and at the same time unconsciously downplay and ridicule it in much the same way as the leaders of the circle. The Marqués de Casa-Muñoz and Aparisi are always engaging in absurdly rhetorical arguments over politics, but the most instructive example of this verbal pugilism occurs between Aparisi and Ruiz, the pedantic archaeological researcher, at the 1873 Christmas Eve party in the Santa Cruz house. Juanito plies the two with drink to make their behaviour appear even more ridiculous:

> [Aparisi] brindó por *los héroes de Trafalgar*, por *los héroes del Callao* y por otros muchos héroes marítimos; pero tan conmovido el hombre y con los músculos olfatorios tan respingados, que se creería que Churruca y Méndez Núñez eran sus papás y que olían muy mal. A Ruiz también le daba por el patriotismo y por los héroes, pero inclinándose a lo terrestre y empleando un cierto tono de fiereza. Allí sacó a Tetuán y a Zaragoza, poniendo al extranjero como chupa de dómine, diciendo, en fin, que *nuestro porvenir está en Africa*, y que el Estrecho es un arroyo español.
>
> (V, 138)

However, when Estupiñá suddenly stands up to toast the future (impossible) birth of grandchildren in the Santa Cruz household, the author has neatly turned the laughter back towards Juanito. At the same time, this non-event that is the cause of Jacinta's constant anxiety is integrated into the rest of the series of historical allusions: in its improbability, this longed-for "episodio nacional" is as comical as the exaggerated versions of the other (real) ones.

If Ruiz is the professional historian of the distant past whom the Santa Cruz household retains on its staff, as it were, then Estupiñá is the professional contemporary historian who honours the tables of the Madrid bourgeoisie with his after-dinner anecdotes. His expertise is not based on a minute examination of texts and old artefacts (indeed he is no lover of books!) but upon his personal witnessing of historical events in nineteenth-century Spain. At last Galdós may be presenting a character with an intimate knowledge of and an ability to analyse recent Spanish history, a combination of Relimpio of *La desheredada* and General Morla of *Lo prohibido*, as it were, who could also be an admirable guide figure for Spain's youth (he is guardian-tutor of Juanito

Santa Cruz). But we have already noted that Galdós's interest in these types gradually disappeared after *La desheredada* because their experience of historical events had become little more than an excuse for vain name-dropping. The words which introduce Estupiñá sound the same note of authorial criticism: "En 1871 conocí a este hombre, que fundaba su vanidad en *haber visto toda la historia de España* en el presente siglo" (V, 34). In other words, he has seen all the great names of Spanish nineteenth-century history (Joseph Bonaparte, María Cristina, Fernando VII, the Duc d'Angoulême, Wellington, Canterac, O'Donnell, Merino, Chico, Espartero, Rodil and Sergeant García) as they passed in street processions, embraced on balconies, ascended the gallows or appeared in other public fora. The only time he stands really close to the historical action is when he appears on the platform on which the priest Merino is executed for his assassination attempt on Queen Isabel in 1852. Otherwise "la historia que Estupiñá sabía estaba escrita en los balcones" (V, 35). Ribbans is right to say that this listing of names and dates represents a compact synthesis of nineteenth-century history, but surely he is at fault when he criticizes the compilation for not being explained or analysed for the benefit of the reader.[9] The listing is an important reminder of the drift of events since the beginning of the century, events which have affected the lives of all Spaniards, and in this chronological sweep Estupiñá unwittingly reminds us of the historical forces which explain the present social condition of the fictional characters.

Furthermore, Estupiñá's history lessons to shop customers or bourgeois dinner hosts reveal the uselessness of such nostalgic reminiscing. He is quite content to spend all day talking about the moves the generals should have made in the First Carlist War, for example, instead of trying to sell material to prospective customers in his shop. The result is that his business is a failure and he is reduced to running errands for the Santa Cruz family. One could say that if nineteenth-century Spanish history is responsible for the prosperity of some businesses, an obsessive nostalgic interest in it can contribute to the bankruptcy of others! Nor does Estupiñá instruct his pupil in the meaning of all this history which he has witnessed with eager eyes. The instruction he gives Juanito is limited to the finer points of tauromachy! Estupiñá's interest in history is, above all, an excuse for personal vanity, which will not tolerate any impudent questioning of his presence at the events which he narrates. He may possess Mesonero Romanos's ability

[9] See Ribbans, "*Historia novelada . . .*", p.134.

to bring the past alive for his listeners but he lacks the moral insight of the great *costumbrista*. Indeed how seriously can one take a person who resolutely claims that he has seen absolutely everybody of public importance in the previous fifty years "como le estoy viendo a usted ahora" (V, 34)? In short, Galdós makes it clear that this "vicio hereditario y crónico" (V, 35) is another mania akin to those of the Santa Cruz whom he serves, an obsession that is really directed to inner self-satisfaction and little else.

One could also say that Estupiñá binds the whole novel – its action, characters and themes – into this panoramic survey of nineteenth-century Spanish history which he has had the privilege of witnessing. As the narrator observes (V, 40), the novel could not have been written, the story of Fortunata and Juanito would not have been possible, without Estupiñá. The latter's exceptional illness (he had been described earlier as the healthiest man in the world) prompts the visit of Juanito to No. 11, Cava de San Miguel, a visit that leads to the cataclysmic staircase encounter with Fortunata. Estupiñá's role in the same setting at the end of the novel is no less important, for he is responsible for delivering the Santa Cruz heir to Doña Bárbara and Jacinta in another room of the same building.[10] The guardian angel of the Santa Cruz family, he has presided over the initiation and termination of the process by which the all-important question of the family's succession is finally and satisfactorily resolved. Although it is not a traditional story of royal romance and succession to be added to his list of after-dinner conversation topics, this particular "episodio nacional" could well be of more real relevance for the future of the country than any of those which he does relate.

On another level, Estupiñá's smuggling activities mirror the Santa Cruz family's commercial exploitation of the country. He relishes every chance to challenge the authority of the police and the power of the Treasury to levy taxes, and although his activity slackens in the more liberal times of 1871-1872, he would still like to have an encounter with the police "para probar al mundo entero que era hombre *capaz de arruinar la Renta si se lo proponía*" (my italics; V, 75). Here Estupiñá represents an attitude which had an effect on national finances, and in turn on national politics, for that attitude could well have contributed to the depressed economic condition of the country in 1865-1868, which was one of the causes of the 1868 Revolution.

[10] See my "Fortunata and no. 11, Cava de San Miguel", *Hispanófila*, 20, No. 59 (1976-1977), 31-48.

Galdós may not go so far as to make this point openly, but the reader is encouraged to use his historical imagination to correlate the attitudes of the fictional characters with historical phenomena. Estupiñá's "theft" of Juan Evaristo from Fortunata at the end of the novel is a manifestation of the same vice, and joins fiction and history once more: "¡Van a decir que le he robado! Anda, los ladrones serán ellos. Que digan lo que quieran. A mí, ¿qué? Les presento el papelito firmado por ella, y en paz" (V, 538). Whereas before he had robbed the Spanish State of money, he is now robbing it (if we see Fortunata as the embodiment of the Spanish nation) of a more precious asset, its human vitality and energy, which will now be marshalled and brought under control for empty bourgeois purposes. Paradoxically, at the same time the narrator has been presenting Estupiñá as the inflexible, tyrannical agent of the landlady Doña Guillermina (V, 480-1). Authority and delinquency are strangely mixed in Estupiñá's character and actions, as they are in those of his pupil, Juanito, and his master, Baldomero II.

A very similar role as contemporary historian, likewise only partially considered by Ribbans,[11] is played by Isabel Cordero. It is perhaps important to remember that though her relationship with history extends only to a parallelism between the births of some of her children and important political events, she is also the daughter of Benigno Cordero, the hero of Boteros, probably the most positive embodiment in the first two series of *episodios nacionales* of Galdós's briefly-held ideal of the ordinary citizen who combines industry, reason, tolerance and patriotism. The characterization of Isabel as a symbol, in name and fecundity of offspring, of Queen Isabel II shows how far the Galdosian ideal represented by the earlier, historically-attuned Cordero has given way to a type whose interest in contemporary politics consists only in making name comparisons and whose over-riding motivation is her family's business success (not just its economic survival). She thus becomes a positivist, materialist caricature of her father, her heroism confined to bringing up her children and marrying them off. Carlos Blanco Aguinaga correctly points out that Isabel's business acumen is stressed before her fertility.[12] There is great irony in the fact that this woman, who uses historical comparisons to re-member the identity of her children and appears the embodiment of patriotism, is responsible, with her colleagues in the clothes trade, for ruining the trade in the colourful Spanish *mantones de Manila* and for

---

[11] See Ribbans, "Contemporary history . . .", p.93.
[12] Carlos Blanco Aguinaga, "On 'The birth of Fortunata' ", *AG*, 3 (1968), p.23.

encouraging the spread of *novedades*. As in the Santa Cruz family, materialism dominates any political thinking. Since she finds her flock of children such an imposition, the association that she (not the narrator, let it be noted) makes between the children's births and historical events does not bespeak an interest in the wider national sphere. In this respect it is hard to accept Gilman's view that Isabel's children "are by their own right 'episodios nacionales' with Isabel representing the daily heroism of Spanish womanhood",[13] for the historical incidents, mostly relating to civil strife or violence, constitute an ill omen for the lives of the Cordero children:

> Mi primer hijo ... nació cuando vino la tropa carlista hasta las tapias de Madrid. Mi Jacinta nació cuando se casó la reina, con pocos días de diferencia. Mi Isabelita vino al mundo el día mismo en que el cura Merino le pegó la puñalada a su majestad, y tuve a Rupertito el día de San Juan del cincuenta y ocho, el mismo día que se inauguró la traída de aguas.
>
> (V, 31)

Lacking an insight into contemporary history, Isabel does not realize that the parallel between Jacinta's birth and the Queen's wedding is an ominous one, for, like the royal marriage, her daughter's will be wrecked by infidelity. She herself does not live to see Jacinta marry, dying of excessive delight at the forthcoming alliance which marks the fulfilment of all her dreams: "Aquella gran mujer, heroína y mártir del deber, autora de diecisiete españoles, *se embriagó de felicidad sólo con el olor de ella, y sucumbió a su primera embriaguez*" (my italics; V, 47). Her demise coincides with that of the historical figure of Don Juan Prim and the language used ("heroína y mártir del deber") might seem to identify the two, but the parallel is incongruous, for Prim's sacrifice was for the nation, while her "inebriation", similar to that of Estupiñá, Juanito, Izquierdo, Ido, Ruiz or Aparisi, demonstrates the self-absorption of the Spanish society she represents. By the same token, however, the analogy has belittling repercussions on the historical occurrence. Is Galdós suggesting that the *progresista* leader's death could have been avoided had he shown greater prudence?[14] Granted that Juanito's marriage to Jacinta could represent the six years of Spanish political history from 1870-1876, Isabel Cordero's decease, which casts a cloud over the wedding preparations, could well correspond to Prim's

---

[13] Gilman, "The birth . . .", pp.71-72.
[14] In *España trágica* (1909), an *episodio nacional* of the fifth series, Galdós hints as much when Halconero's list of suspects ready to assassinate Prim is rejected by the *progresista* leader (III, 999).

inopportune death which was to prefigure the failure of Spain to accept the fruits of the 1868 victory. The low-keyed wedding of Juanito and Jacinta parallels the sombre installation of Amadeo I soon after Prim's assassination.

Doña Guillermina Pacheco, another prominent member of the Santa Cruz *tertulia*, reflects the attitudes to politics and the State held by the Santa Cruz and Estupiñá. In her mania to establish an asylum for orphans she tackles all and sundry for contributions: beggars, whores and even King Amadeo and Queen María Victoria (renowned for their generosity, as Galdós was to point out in *Amadeo I* (1910) in the fifth series of *episodios nacionales*). This resourceful canvassing for her own egotistical glory is put into relief when news is received of Amadeo's abdication, for Guillermina merely gives a sigh and utters a "Todo sea por Dios" before resuming her sewing. Her desire for the return of the Bourbons is motivated by the same driving ambition to secure funds for her orphanage: ". . . porque le hemos traído con esa condición: que favorezca la beneficencia y la religión" (V, 310). In keeping with this imperious attitude, Galdós likens her to a despot, a captain-general or a parade marshal, who is not averse to using the law for her own purposes: either to threaten Fortunata about her relationship with Juanito, or to force prostitutes like Felisita to go to Las Micaelas against their wishes, or to abduct Mauricia *la Dura* from the clutches of the Protestant couple, Don Horacio and Doña Malvina. In this way Guillermina underscores the contradictory attitudes of others in the Santa Cruz family, where public respect for order very often conceals severe abuses of that order for personal reasons.

Within their own circle the Santa Cruz are criticized by what one might call an *extranjerizante* element: the quasi-expatriate Moreno Isla, who takes a perverse delight in disparaging all aspects of Spanish life. The latter abandons the country after the stock-market crash which followed the abdication of Amadeo I, and when he returns on a brief visit soon after the Bourbon Restoration he again launches into criticism of his fellow countrymen. This anti-patriotism, Galdós indicates, is as misfounded as his relations' chauvinism: "Moreno Isla no cedía una pulgada del terreno antipatriótico en que su terquedad se encerraba" (V, 319). His picture of an undernourished Spain in need of foreign blood to invigorate it is unbalanced, for while the family of Ido del Sagrario is evidence enough that there is plenty of poverty and illness in the country, Moreno's view is somewhat contradicted by the numerous references in the novel to the good health of Fortunata, the Santa Cruz and Estupiñá and to the fecundity of Isabel Cordero. In an inversion of the eighteenth-century literary tradition represented by Swift, Montesquieu and Cadalso, the foreign residence of Moreno Isla does not produce in him an accurate assessment of the native land that he revisits. He may back the import business of Aurora and allow Guillermina to steal his money for the construction of her asylum but he does so without realizing or even considering the merit of such actions.[15] The cheap presents he gets for his English friends perpetuate a distorted view of Spain as much as his own sardonic remarks. His comments to King Alfonso XII, both uttered and unuttered, when the new Monarch sets sail from Dover, are typically ungenerous to his fellow-countrymen:

> ¡Lástima de rey! Yo le dije: "Vuestra majestad va a gobernar el país de la ingratitud; pero vuestra majestad vencerá a la hidra." Esto le dije por cortesía; pero yo no creo que pueda barajar a esta gente. El querrá hacerlo bien; pero falta que le dejen.
>
> (V, 319)

As Jacinta does with her prophetic faint when the King enters Madrid some time later, Moreno Isla may be sounding a note of warning amidst the general euphoria of the bourgeois Santa Cruz circle over the return of the Bourbons. However, by the time he dies Moreno's anti-patriotism has undergone some hesitant reappraisal as he comes, under the influence of his love for Jacinta, to feel pity for the outcasts of Spanish society, such as the blind female singer or the crippled boy whom he had previously ignored in the streets. For the first time he realizes that he might possibly be able to do something to help them, whereas before he had dismissed them as regrettable and objectionable examples of Spanish poverty or barbarity. Moreno thus comes to discover that there is more in life than repeating anti-patriotic sentiments in the Santa Cruz *tertulia*.

Like the Santa Cruz circle, families lower down the social ladder are cast in a representative historical mould. Such is the case of the Rubín family:

> La venerable tienda de tirador de oro que desde inmemorial tiempo estuvo en los soportales de Platerías, entre las calles de la Caza y San Felipe Neri, desapareció, si no estoy equivocado, en los primeros días de la revolución del 68. *En una misma fecha cayeron, pues, dos cosas seculares: el trono aquel y la tienda aquella, que si no era tan antigua como la Monarquía española,*

---

[15] Ironically, as absentee landlord of No. 11, Cava de San Miguel, Moreno provides the setting for the liaison of Fortunata and Juanito that will make Jacinta, his eventual obsession, an unhappy woman.

éralo más que los Borbones, pues su fundación databa de 1640,
como lo decía un letrero muy mal pintado en la anaquelería.
(my italics; V, 157)[16]

Here Galdós chooses the strategic point of the beginning of Part II to display again his continuing interest in the facts of history and their relation to the lives of his fictional characters. The death of Nicolás Rubín the same year, that of his wife a year earlier and the subsequent dispersion of the three sons, rumoured to be of different parents, clearly represent the collapse of the Bourbons in 1868 and the factious disputes of the 1868 Revolutionaries which surfaced after their victory.

Like Baldomero Santa Cruz, the anti-clerical Doña Lupe, the Rubíns' aunt, could be said to represent mid-nineteenth-century Liberalism, but her political beliefs are soon exposed as a superficial attitude inherited from her husband Jáuregui (also the name of a Liberal general in the First Carlist War), more for sentimental reasons than anything else. She really does not understand a word of politics, and her principles are as unattractive and inappropriate as the gaudy portrait in militia uniform of her husband, whose sole intervention in political history consisted in supporting the rising in favour of Isabel II — not quite an inspiring example of Liberalism. The legacy of this militia hero to his wife, like that of Benigno Cordero to his daughter Isabel, is a certain residue of political awareness limited to the nominal externals, and a successful business acumen which becomes the vehicle for the satisfaction of egotistical desires. The successful balance between political self-sacrifice and material prosperity realized by Cordero, and to a far lesser extent by Jáuregui, has been disrupted in the Spain of the 1870s by individual materialism, as the example of Lupe's business colleague, Torquemada, sufficiently demonstrates. Once again Galdós is illustrating the degeneration of the Liberal ideal of the earlier years of the century.

Behind her veneer of professed liberalism Lupe is a despotic character who wants to control other people's lives, particularly that of Fortunata. Indeed she feels capable of governing Spain: "... ¡qué tiempos y qué Gobiernos! ¡Ah!, si yo gobernara, si yo fuera ministra, ¡qué derechitos andarían todos! Si esta gente no sabe ..., si salta a la vista que no sabe" (V, 358). This illusion almost becomes a reality in

---

[16] John H. Sinnigen, "Individual, class and society in *Fortunata y Jacinta*", in *Galdós Studies II*, ed. Robert J. Weber (London, 1974), pp.49-68, notes the parallel with the Santa Cruz family, but attacks Galdós on spurious ideological grounds. Ribbans, "Contemporary history ...", p.102, is mistaken in his view of the Rubíns' role. Nimetz, p.200, perhaps, gets their function into the proper perspective.

the narrator's style: "Estas ideas ... fermentaron en el cerebro de aquella gran diplomática y ministra durante todo el mes de marzo" (V, 498). In view of the fact that Mauricia *la Dura* likens her to Cánovas, it is significant that the *pronunciamiento* of Sagunto, which brought back the Bourbons in December 1874, coincides with her move to a new house.[17] Through her loans to the country's soldiers, politicians and bureaucrats, Lupe exerts some real control in the sources of national political action. Her authoritarianism, which prompts her to use threats of police retaliation and, on the other hand, to show disregard of the laws when it suits her purpose, links her with Guillermina, who, not surprisingly, holds a special fascination for her. The domestic crisis posed by Maxi's relationship with Fortunata again solders the two spheres of fiction and history:

> Sentía desvanecida su autoridad sobre el enamorado joven; veía una fuerza efectiva y revolucionaria delante de su fuerza histórica, y si no le tenía miedo, era innegable que aquel repentino tesón le infundía algún respeto ... Pensó entonces con admirable tino que *cuando en el orden privado, lo mismo que en el público*, se inicia un poderoso impulso revolucionario, lógico, motivado, que arranca de la naturaleza misma de las cosas y se fortifica en las circunstancias, es locura plantársele delante; lo práctico es sortearlo y con él dejarse ir, aspirando a dirigirlo y encauzarlo. *Pues a sortear y dirigir aquella revolución doméstica*; que atajarla era imposible, y el que se le pusiera delante, arrollado sería sin remedio.
>
> (my italics; V, 202)

Cánovas-like, Lupe has a Republican revolutionary on her hands. The political parallel may or may not be appropriate to describe this change in relationship between aunt and nephew, but its employment by Galdós serves to remind the reader of the political events occurring at the same time: it is the period after Pavía's coup d'état when Spain was still a nominal Republic under the leadership of Serrano, and Cánovas was actively campaigning for the return of the Bourbons.

The eventful political life of Lupe's nephew, Juan Pablo, provides another opportunity for Galdós to relate factual details of recent history and at the same time to incorporate this lower-middle-class character into his pattern of mutually illuminating figures. Juan Pablo's affiliation to the *alfonsistas* after a mysterious expulsion from the Carlist

---

[17] In retrospect, Juanito's rhetorical outburst when he and Jacinta reach Sagunto on their honeymoon in May 1871 is ironically significant (V, 56-57). Spanish history shows a tendency to repeat itself, but clearly the 1874 Sagunto episode is a pale reflection, if not a comic distortion, of the heroic struggle of the Celtiberians against the Romans.

camp (because of financial irregularities, it is rumoured), reflects the political opportunism, at a higher level, of the Republican-then-Monarchist deputy, Villalonga (significantly the provider at the end of the novel of Juan Pablo's provincial governorship), and, since he is always singing the praises of the side he is currently supporting, the empty rhetorical speeches of Juanito Santa Cruz. The vacuity of his political ideas can be appraised from his rote-learning and regurgitation of left-wing political theorists. Like Juanito Santa Cruz, Juan Pablo is imprisoned for taking part in political disturbances, those of 1874. Lupe's contacts in high places secure his release just as Baldomero Santa Cruz had called upon political friends to release Juanito after the *Noche de San Daniel* disturbances almost a decade earlier. A long thread of interdependent scenes and associations thus links this incident in Juan Pablo's life to the concrete historical example at the beginning of the novel. By association, if nothing else, Juan Pablo's incarceration casts an ironic note, not on that historical event itself, but on Juanito's participation in it. Just as Juanito returns to the fold of social respectability, Juan Pablo subsequently becomes a secret policeman, a jailor and, finally, a provincial governor responsible for law and order. All of these Restoration characters evince an alarming mixture of disregard and respect for the law, according to whichever suits their overriding personal interest.

Nicolás Rubín, identified with the Carlist cause, assumes the responsibility of re-educating Fortunata along religious lines, but the true motivation for this proselytizing is an ambition for glory in ecclesiastical circles. In terms of the political allegory we are trying to trace, if we see Fortunata as the incarnation of the Spanish nation during the period 1868-1876, then Nicolás's efforts to subject her to a religious regime are as erroneous as the Carlists' attempts to impose an *absolutista* State on Spain.

Maxi may not participate at all in politics but, nevertheless, his life's development is sewn into the historical fabric of the novel. Before his momentous meeting with Fortunata, he is a dull, weak lad who obeys his aunt in everything. After that meeting, he undergoes a profound character transformation that is described in political language, as we noted above. Lupe even believes that he is participating in political conspiracies because he returns home late at night. A more precise historical parallel is made when, under Feijoo's persuasion, she tries to convince Maxi that he should take back his errant wife:

— Francamenta, tía, eso de que pase hambre ... Yo no la perdono, no puede ser ... Le aseguro a usted que eso ... *Jamás,*

jamás, jamás.
— Ya te he dicho que no es prudente soltar *jamases* tan a boca llena sobre ningún punto que se refiera a las cosas humanas. Ya ves el bueno de don Juan Prim qué lucido ha quedado con sus *jamases*.
— Pues a mí no me pasará lo que a don Juan Prim, porque sé lo que digo ... *Y como la restauración depende de mí* [my italics] y yo no he de hacerla ... Pero de esto no se trata ahora. Aunque no ha de haber las paces, me duele que pase hambre. Es preciso socorrerla.

(V, 361)

The allusion is to Prim's famous assurance in the *Cortes Constituyentes* of 20 February of 1869 that the Bourbons would never return to Spain. Galdós is not comparing the personal characters of Maxi and Prim, but rather the situations in which they find themselves. Both try to guarantee the impossibility of the future event whose realization, in retrospect, appears inevitable: the Bourbons did return to Spain just as Maxi takes back Fortunata. If Fortunata is a symbol of Spain, is there any reason for not seeing Maxi as a symbol of Prim's service to the country? The analogy is risky because of the lack of other examples of parallelism between the two figures; but this fact should not deter the interpretation encouraged by these occasional cryptic allusions. Of all Fortunata's lovers and educators, Maxi is the most sincere and the most sympathetically presented by the author. Prim, as we have seen in our chapter on *La desheredada*, elicited Galdós's deepest praise and sympathy during his brief period of power: he had been the one ray of hope in post-1868 Spain for the realization of a truly Liberal government before his tragic death destroyed that cherished dream. Maxi is not guiltless or fault-free, but he genuinely tries to provide a better life for Fortunata at a time when she wants to become a respectable member of society. His failure is in part his own making and in part that of others, as was Prim's assassination. Not all details in the parallel correspond exactly, but enough indicators are given to the reader for his imagination to explore and expand the similarities. Ribbans is right to note the frequency with which Prim is mentioned in the *serie contemporánea*,[18] but more could have been read into its use in this instance. It is not just an isolated reference but part of an intricate mosaic of allusions which can be put together to form a coherent and meaningful historical allegory.

Towards the end of the book Maxi takes on the appearance of a philosopher of history. However, he is no Máximo Manso and is

---

[18] Ribbans, *"Historia novelada ..."*, p.137.

reduced to the role of nodding enthusiastic approval in a Madrid café *tertulia* for Ido del Sagrario's wise words on the dangers of too much political control or freedom. Yet in their respective ways the two men are expressing in terms of abstract theory the whole political theme of the novel: the incessant alternation between the extremes of order and disorder. This is the general theme on which Baldomero Santa Cruz II and the narrator have expatiated at earlier points and which the private lives of Juanito, other characters in his circle and the Rubín family have exemplified:

> . . ."Porque, mire usted, cuando el pueblo se desmanda, los ciudadanos se ven indefensos, y, francamente, naturalmente, buena es la libertad; pero primero es vivir. ¿Qué sucede? Que todos piden orden. Por consiguiente, salta el dictador, un hombre que trae una macana muy grande, y cuando empieza a funcionar la macana, todos la bendicen. O hay lógica o no hay lógica. Vino, pues, Napoleón Bonaparte, y empezó a meter en cintura a aquella gente. Y que lo hizo muy bien, y yo le aplaudo, sí, señor, yo le aplaudo."
> — Y yo también — dijo Maxi *con la mayor buena fe, observando que aquel hombre razonaba discretamente.*
>
> (my italics; V, 488)

What Ido is really advocating is a happy medium between the extremes of dictatorship and anarchy, a political ideal that had eluded Spain in the decade of 1868-1878:

> Me gusta la libertad; pero respetando . . ., respetando a Juan, Pedro y Diego . . ., y que cada uno piense como quiera; pero sin desmandarse, sin desmandarse, mirando siempre para la ley . . . cuando hay libertad mal entendida y muchas aboliciones, los ricos se asustan, se van al extranjero, y no se ve una peseta por ninguna parte . . . y el bracero que tanto chillaba dando vivas a la Constitución, no tiene qué comer. Total, que yo digo siempre: "Lógica. liberales", y de aquí no me saca nadie.
>
> (V, 488)

But this is precisely what the Restoration *turno pacífico* had achieved: prosperity, stability, freedom from anarchy and tyranny. Ido and, through his enraptured admiration, Maxi, thus appear to be the somewhat Quixotic apologists of Restoration order. However, as the narrator had made abundantly clear in his description of the *compadrazgo* of the current political parties as mirrored in the café *tertulias*, the cost of such stability in the political machine is a complete loss of ideals of any kind.

The political cynicism of Moreno Isla in the Santa Cruz circle is duplicated in the Rubín circle by Feijoo, especially towards the end of his liaison with Fortunata. Like Moreno Isla, Feijoo is portrayed largely with sympathy: he is very generous to needy acquaintances, and above all, discreet with that charity. Foreign service has left him with a jaundiced view of domestic Spanish politics too: "Yo . . . soy progresista desengañado, y usted, [Juan Pablo] tradicionalista arrepentido. Tenemos algo de común: el creer que todo esto es una comedia y que sólo se trata de saber a quién le toca mamar y a quién no" (V, 295). Spanish politics do not hold his interest; of far greater concern to him are his sexual relationships with women, and it is noteworthy that, recounting to the enthralled Fortunata his service with the Spanish army in Cuba and Italy, he slides into a catalogue of his amorous conquests abroad. In his philosophy of life, lovers must be prepared to rebel against society's laws in order to satisfy their physical desires: ". . . soy tan indulgente con los y las que se pronuncian" (V, 339). In all other respects, how-ever, he insists that the laws of society must be strictly obeyed. This code of moral hypocrisy, which he tries to impose upon Fortunata, and which he carries into practice by engineering her return to Maxi, is also the system which Juanito follows in his behaviour with Fortunata and which the country follows in its political life. In love and politics it is really the law of whim that holds sway in Spain. Besides ridiculing the method which Feijoo employs to inculcate this code into his pupil, with his schoolmasterish phrase-by-phrase reproduction of the salient points ("Guardando . . . las . . . apariencias, observando . . . las reglas . . . del respeto" [V, 342]), Galdós emphasizes that it becomes a mania which does not take into account Fortunata's real need and aspiration, the permanent love of Juanito. Is Galdós suggesting, on a political level, that the Restoration of the Bourbons was not the wisest move for Spain, that it did not take into account the real needs of the country, whatever they were? After a decade of the *turno pacífico* this message had ample justification, and this interpretation of Fortunata's return to Maxi is more than encouraged by the political language Galdós has deliberately used to describe the fictional occurrence and by the political methods Feijoo adopts to effect her "Restoration" to the Rubín family: the gift of a government job for Juan Pablo through the good services of Villalonga.

The Fourth Estate also provides a number of characters, in-cluding the protagonist, Fortunata, who are intimately connected with the historical framework so far established for the novel; but because they are at the other end of the social spectrum they have a correspondingly less conscious association with history than the Santa Cruz circle. Their distance from the centre of political activity leads to an even greater distortion than that afforded by the lower-middle-class characters. José Izquierdo's description of his participation in earlier historical events is a grotesque parody of the actions of Juan Pablo and Villalonga. His stories of service with both Carlists and Republicans during the 1870s, related to Ido in a café, are pure fantasy, a farcical distortion of the historical reality made even more comical by the colloquial syntax and pronunciation and the fact that his listener shows greater interest in his meal:

> ¡Republicanos de chanfaina . . ., pillos, buleros, piores que serviles, moderaos, piores que moderaos! . . . No colocarme a mí, a mí, que soy el individuo que más bregó por la República en esta judía tierra . . . Es la que se dice: *Cría cuervos* . . . ¡Ah señor de Martos, señor de Figueras, señor de Pi!
>
> (V, 109)

The account cannot be considered in any way an objective view of the First Republic and the kaleidoscope of violent events of that novel political experiment. That is not the author's purpose; but in Izquierdo's resentment, greed and delusions of grandeur, he is showing that behind the patriotic service of individuals lurk some distasteful emotions. Even before Izquierdo starts his absurd speech, Galdós pulls the carpet from under him by informing the reader that now, "en plena Restauración" (V, 109), he is a great success as an artist's model for paintings on ancient and medieval history.[19]

His recollections of earlier national events offer further grotesque shafts of light on the accounts of Estupiñá and Isabel Cordero, those other oral historians introduced in earlier chapters:

> . . . toda mi vida no he hecho más que derramar mi sangre por la judía libertad. El cincuenta y cuatro, ¿qué hice? Batirme en las barricadas como una presona decente. Que se lo pregunten al difunto don Pascual Muñoz . . . que era el hombre de más afloencias en estos arrabales, y me dijo mesmamente aquel día: "Amigo *Platón*, vengan esos cinco." Y aluego juí con el propio don Pascual a Palacio y don Pascual subió a platicar con la reina.
>
> (V, 109)[20]

---

[19] Galdós had attacked the absurd escapism of contemporary historical painters (see Shoemaker, pp.97-104), suggesting that they should choose their subjects from contemporary history. James Whiston, "Language and situation in Part I of *Fortunata y Jacinta*", *AG*, 7 (1972), p.89, notes Galdós's parody of heroic language to describe Izquierdo's success as a model for historical paintings.

[20] Izquierdo is referring to the Revolution of 1854, which was headed by O'Donnell and led to the *Bienio progresista* of 1854-1856.

Galdós does credit Izquierdo's account with some particles of truth, but by and large we are to accept it as pure fantasy. His inclusion of his encounter with Fortunata in Barcelona amongst his "historical" adventures again integrates fiction and history with reciprocal exchanges of meaning. This interrelation is underlined by the parallel preoccupation of Ido del Sagrario with the previous day's conversation with Jacinta about Pitusín. There is a definite correlation between the two men's interests at this point: Izquierdo's largely untruthful account of his exploits is paralleled by Ido's fabricated story about the spurious son of Juanito and Fortunata. Yet if Izquierdo downgrades national history with his absurd inventions, his insistence that Guillermina secure him a position with the Republican government of 1873 as a condition for surrendering Pitusín to the Santa Cruz raises the fictional element to the domain of national history: "– La señora se aboca con Castelar . . ., que me tiene tanta tirria . . ., o con el señor de Pi. – Déjame usted a mí de *pi* y de *pa* . . . Yo no le puedo dar a usted ningún destino. – Pues si no me dan la ministración de El Pardo, el hijo se queda aquí" (V, 117). The Pitusín affair is an "episodio nacional", but unfortunately it is as fantastic as Izquierdo's exploits.

In Mauricia *la Dura* the *pueblo* also has its own *extranjerizante* element corresponding to Feijoo and Moreno Isla in the lower- and upper-middle classes. However, with her the pattern is varied slightly by Galdós: she is a female and her "foreignness" is limited to the Napoleonic comparisons made by the narrator. With her violent protest against the rigid order of Las Micaelas, Mauricia could be a symbolic figure of the growing anarchist movement of the period. Certainly her advice to Fortunata at critical junctures could be thought to be representative of wider attitudes as it is couched in terms which suggest an anarchist viewpoint: ". . . a la que nace pobre no se la respeta, y así anda este mundo pastelero. Siempre y cuando puedas darle un disgusto, dáselo, por vida del santísimo peine" (V, 247). The anonymous *TLS* reviewer of the Penguin translation noted this aspect of her characterization but failed to observe that it is intimately combined with a disconcerting respect for firm control and order, whether it be exerted by Doña Guillermina or the cripple Sor Marcela in Las Micaelas.[21] As much as any other character in the novel, Mauricia is a perplexing mixture of opposing moods of order and disorder, or in Galdós's own words, a "naturaleza desordenada, con alternativas misteriosas de depravación y de afabilidad" (V, 235). In this sense, then, the Napoleonic comparisons

[21] See "Five years . . .", p.1227.

are entirely apposite and link her with the revolutionary-monarchist
Santa Cruz dynasty, for Napoleon was the epitome of the revolutionary-
turned-autocrat.

On her first appearance in the novel Mauricia is likened to Bonaparte before he became First Consul. Continued confinement in Las
Micaelas emphasizes the likeness, especially when she comes into conflict with the other inmates. Her ignominious exit from the convent is
amid the derision of the municipal roadsweepers, who accompany her
"como una escolta de burlesca artillería, haciendo un ruido de mil
demonios y disparándole bala rasa de groserías e injurias" (V, 260). On
her death-bed, she again receives the imperial designation, but now,
significantly, the comparison is with the Napolean of the great European
victories recalled in the old etchings hung up around the room:

> Eran excelentes grabados, *ya pasados de moda* [my italics], el
> papel viejo y con manchas de humedad, los marcos de caoba, y
> *representaban asuntos que nada tenían de español, por cierto*
> [my italics]: las batallas de Napoleón I, reproducidas de los *un
> tiempo* [my italics] célebres cuadros de Horacio Vernet y el baron
> Gros. ¿Quién no ha visto el *Napoleón en Eyleau*, y *en Jena*, el
> *Bonaparte en Arcola*, la *Apoteosis de Austerlitz* y la *Despedida
> de Fontainebleau*?
>
> (V, 367)

The moribund Mauricia is the final picture in the series: "En fin, que la
Dura completaba la historia aquella expuesta en las paredes: era el
Napoleón en Santa Elena" (V, 367). History, now foreign, and fiction
are once more intimately fused. Mauricia is an oddity of Dionysiac
proportions within the corrupt Spanish family. The point is reinforced
emblematically by the other gaudy pictures adorning the walls of
the room where she will die: "el cuadrito de los *dos corazones amantes*,
el de la *Numancia*, en mar de musgo; los retratos de militares cuñados
de Severiana, la estera de esparto, flamante y sin ningún agujero, de
pleitas *rojas y amarillas* [my italics]" (V, 367); "una lámina del Cristo
del Gran Poder, ... un cuadrote que representaba a Pío IX echando la
bendición a las tropas españolas en Gaeta" (V, 371).[22] Enveloping them
all, a Spanish flag, made from some old curtains, offers conclusive
evidence of Galdós's contrastive intentions in this scene. In a moribund
Spanish society the Napoleonic vitality of Mauricia *la Dura* represents

[22] In 1849 Narváez, in league with Austria, France and other Catholic powers,
sent an expeditionary force of about 5,000 men to defend the Papal States against
the incursions of Garibaldi. The grateful Pius IX blessed the Spanish troops in his
palace-refuge of Gaeta.

a dangerous foreign body that must be exterminated. Her death thus symbolizes the impossibility of her code of values as a viable alternative in Spanish society.

Napoleon had of course been Spain's scourge during the War of Independence chronicled by Galdós in the first series of *episodios nacionales*. In combining to expel this common enemy Liberal and Conservative Spaniards had temporarily buried their own antagonisms, which were destined to reappear after 1815 and continue right through the decades of the nineteenth century in one form or another. In *Juan Martín el Empecinado* (1874), an *episodio nacional* of the second series, Galdós had commented on this fact in an authorial aside:

> Vino Napoleón, y despertó todo el mundo. La frase castellana *echarse a la calle* es admirable por su exactitud y expresión. España entera se echó a la calle o al campo; su corazón guerrero latió con fuerza, y se ciñó laureles sin fin en la gloriosa frente; pero lo extraño es que Napoleón, aburrido al fin, se marchó con las manos en la cabeza, *y los españoles, movidos de la pícara afición, continuaron haciendo de las suyas en diversas formas, y todavía no han vuelto a casa* [my italics].
>
> (I, 976)

The characterization of Mauricia *la Dura* as an image of the different faces of Napoleon is thus a reminder of the origins of this violent civil discord that was still continuing in the Spain of the 1870s. Galdós had written this commentary in the *episodio nacional* with the events of 1874 in mind: the civil wars in the north and south-east against the central Republican Government. This turbulent year − 1874 − falls straight in the middle of the period covered by *Fortunata y Jacinta*, so that Mauricia *la Dura* could well be the embodiment of that violent discord. She is presented for the most part as an unruly, wild element in this Madrid society. Her countenancing of social rebellion in the realm of matrimonial relationships determines the continuation of Fortunata's liaison with Juanito. Yet on her death-bed and in earlier relapses of peaceful calm with Guillermina and Marcela, she can be the obedient and humble citizen. As she dies she enjoins Fortunata to mend her ways and repent of everything except her love for Juanito (V, 370). Earlier Fortunata had received the same contradictory advice from Feijoo, for all of these *extranjerizante* characters are alternately attracted and repelled by the fluctuating moral condition of Spanish life.

Aurora is another female character who exerts a strong influence on Fortunata in the final part of the novel. Her French connections are also pertinently stressed; she lived in France for many

years because of her marriage to the French businessman, Fenelón. Her
seduction and that now awaiting Jacinta, both at the hands of Moreno
Isla, are likened by her to famous battles of the Franco-Prussian War of
1870: "Yo fuí Metz, que cayó demasiado pronto: y ella [Jacinta] es
Bellfort, que se defiende; pero al fin cae también" (V, 444). Aurora has
an important role to play in the novel's denouement in that her de-
ception of Fortunata leads to the latter's death; but with her French
connections she also has some relevance for the allegorical framework.
Prim's energetic search in 1870 for a suitable candidate amongst Europe's royal houses to occupy the vacant Spanish throne had been one
of the root causes of the Franco-Prussian conflict, because the French
had opposed the candidacy of Prince Leopold of Hohenzollern-
Sigmaringen.[23] In Aurora's betrayal of Fortunata we may like to see
France's betrayal of Spain in 1870, for had Prim been allowed to bring
back the German prince, the course of Spanish history thereafter would
certainly have been different and Prim's tragic death, like that of
Fortunata, would probably have been avoided. It might be objected
that earlier we noted that at one point Galdós makes an explicit comparison between Maxi's situation and that of Prim. If he can now
suggest through Fortunata's betrayal and death those of Prim and the
Spanish Liberal ideal, it is not because he is confusing his images of
historical characters but because he is comparing political and fictional
situations in the broadest of outlines.

Having referred a number of times already to Fortunata's political symbolism, we must now explain what we mean by this. As the
central character of the novel, Fortunata holds the key to any solution
that Galdós may be proposing for the chaotic oscillation in the public
and private behaviour of Spaniards, represented by the other characters.
As if expanding the argument that he had briefly advanced in the
figures of Camila and Constantino in *Lo prohibido*, Galdós puts forward the possibility of a redemptive love capable of withstanding the
forces of history. However, this possibility materializes for only one
brief, tragic moment when Juanito meets Fortunata for the first time
on the steps of No. 11, Cava de San Miguel and during his subsequent
visits to the same house whilst Estupiñá is ill. The deep and rich layers
of meaning attached to this scene have received full and excellent
analyses from Gilman and others.[24] The dramatic, unheralded entry of
Fortunata into the public setting of the stairway without any fore-

[23] See H. Butler Clarke, *Modern Spain 1815-1898* (Cambridge, 1906), p.317.
[24] See Gilman, "The birth . . ." and Blanco Aguinaga, "On 'The birth . . .' ".

warnings from the narrator, in stark contrast to his overpowering verbosity when presenting the history of the Santa Cruz circle, points to her characterization, in this very first instance only, as a person not in any way connected with the historical society of Madrid and Spain which thereafter engulfs her. By the novel's end she has undergone a process of "historicization" well represented by the narrator's change in his description of No. 11, Cava de San Miguel, her residence at the beginning and ending of her fictional existence.[25] Her status as representative of the Spanish nation for the period covered by the plot of the novel is first apparent in Juanito's slip of the tongue when speaking of his relationship with her: "Hay momentos en la vida de los pueblos, quiero decir, en la vida del hombre" (V, 59, 60). Fortunata is indeed subject to the caprices of a string of lovers, just as the Spain of 1868-1876 was subject to the whims of its political masters, and in that sense her name is not inappropriate. In this context it is also interesting to note that, referring to a more explicit allegorical symbol of Spain in *El caballero encantado* (1909), Galdós specifies that her constantly changing facial expression is the result of the constant stream of conflicting actions by her sons, the people of Spain:

> Me verás rozagante y alegre cuando la muchedumbre de mis criaturas se muestra enmendada de sus delirios y con inclinaciones al bien y a la paz. Me verás triste y caduca cuando la grey que lleva mi nombre se desmanda y quiere precipitarme por senderos abruptos.
>
> (VI, 293)

A common desire held by both Fortunata and her more serious would-be educators (Juanito, Maxi, Feijoo, Nicolás and Lupe) is that this naïve, golden-hearted girl who has plied the trade of prostitute become an honourable woman acceptable within their respective social circles (V, 180, 186). Could Galdós be here making an ironic allusion to the famous slogan of the 1868 Revolutionaries, "la España con honra", the recovery of Spain's honour after the humiliation of Isabel's immoral reign? If so, he is implying that the aim of the 1868 Revolutionaries was certainly not achieved, just as Fortunata's acceptance into respectable society is never really completed, despite the final sacrifice of her child to that society. She dies the outcast, unconfessed. The various characters in the novel have different ideas as to how this state of honour is to be achieved and they all try to impress upon her their own conception of respectability, so that she becomes their own creation,

---

[25] See my "Fortunata and No. 11 ...".

subject to differing emphases, much as Spanish history between 1868-1876 and earlier was shaped by interminably conflicting currents. Only continued cohabitation with a faithful, stable Juanito would fulfil her inner wishes and desires, just as the solution for Spain is marriage to a truly stable Liberal government faithful to its ideals. But neither Juanito nor the post-1868 Liberal party ever live up to these high expectations.

However, manipulated though she is by a stream of domineering people, it cannot be said that Fortunata bears none of the blame for her fate. Her abiding weakness is her total love for Juanito, a love which dominates her whole being and blinds her to his basic character defects. "Hooked" on Juanito, she never really condemns him in the way that Jacinta does at the end. This attitude emerges very clearly in the description of her surrender to him just after her wedding to Maxi:

> Fortunata *estaba como embriagada*, con cierto desvarío en el alma, perdida la memoria de los hechos recientes. Toda idea moral había desaparecido, como un sueño borrado del cerebro al despertar ... Y ni podía dejar de hacerlo, ni discutía lo inevitable, ni intentaba atenuar su responsabilidad.   (my italics; V, 276-7)

Fortunata's "inebriated" conduct in the sole area of life that absorbs her interest reflects that of other characters bent on the satisfaction of personal needs less natural and forgivable. Love may have replaced egotistical and perverted lust as an antidote to an absorption with the political processes of the time, but its success as a motivating force of disinterested behaviour, as exemplified by Camila and Constantino in *Lo prohibido*, is now questioned in the life of Fortunata, for when a breakdown of the relationship threatens her individual happiness, the egotism of love reacts in a natural, impulsive outburst and her other qualities are eclipsed. Moreover, in hankering after an ideal relationship with Juanito, Fortunata is behaving unrealistically, although Galdós controls her choice to a great extent by never presenting to her attention a male who combines the physical attraction of a Juanito with the inner love of a Maxi. In the same way, Spain is always hankering after the love of a Liberal party that does not know how to treat the country properly.

As character and symbol, Fortunata must die at the end.[26] The

---

[26] The significance of Fortunata's death for a true interpretation of the novel is still the subject of considerable disagreement. Most critics have tended to take the view that she achieves a degree of nobility with her sacrifice of Juan Evaristo to Jacinta and that she is the effective catalyst in the new social mix in Spanish society between bourgeoisie and proletariat; see Stephen Gilman, "The consciousness of Fortunata", *AG*, 5 (1970), p.59. The other tendency stresses the tragedy of Fortunata's end; see Anthony N. Zahareas, "El sentido de la tragedia en *Fortunata y Jacinta*", *AG*, 3 (1968), pp.32ff.

Spain of 1868-1876 has traversed many an up-and-down before pro-
ducing its offspring, the Restoration political settlement. Juan Evaristo,
Fortunata's sole surviving child, is portrayed, through comparisons with
the statue of Felipe III located in the Plaza Mayor below the Cava de
San Miguel apartment, and the baby-talk of his mother and great-aunt,
as the ruler of a new order. Fortunata's gift of him to the Santa Cruz
family is accepted by Doña Guillermina as a "rasgo feliz y cristiano"
(V, 539), a phrase that, in the context of our sustained historical
allegory, inevitably reminds the reader of Isabel II's famous *rasgo* to
the nation in 1865, the significance of which we have already noted in
our chapter on *La de Bringas*. Isabel II's *rasgo* had led directly to the
bloody *Noche de San Daniel* riots, the historical episode which
launched the fiction of *Fortunata y Jacinta*. Our novel has indeed come
full circle, with little substantial change between beginning and end, for
Fortunata's gift of a son to the Santa Cruz is likewise doomed to be a
token gesture, although she intends it to be more than that. Certainly
the boy's upbringing in the Santa Cruz circle does not bode well for
the future synthesis of Spanish classes. If Spain is to change, more
fundamental reforms of a moral kind are called for, not just furtive
class intermarriage or public relations gestures by the Monarch.

Like the Spain of 1868-1876, Fortunata's life-story may appear
to be a succession of whimsical changes, but it is really the inevitable
result of earlier happenings, and this determinism underlying the
chaotic swirl of events is explicitly stated as a fundamental principle of
public and private lives when Galdós discusses her return to Maxi:

> Y de este modo se verificó aquella restauración, aquel restableci-
> miento de la vida legal. Fué de esas cosas que pasan, sin que se
> pueda determinar cómo pasaron, *hechos fatales en la historia de
> una familia como lo son sus similares en la historia de los pueblos.*
> (my italics; V, 362)

Even that initial seed of the novel's plot — Juanito's chance meeting
with Fortunata on the staircase of No. 11, Cava de San Miguel — is not
so fortuitous, given the circumstances of Estupiñá's unusual illness, the
bond of affection between master and pupil and Fortunata's residence
in the same building. Fortunata cannot escape the web of her relationships once established, any more than Spain can avoid the pull of her
history. A code of individual moral values which can be practised
within society, during the historical moment, and yet transcend that
historical moment, is still not possible in Galdós's novel of the historical
imagination.

There is, however, one glimmer of light in this gloomy conclusion. Through the discussion between Ponce and Segismundo as they
return from Fortunata's burial, Galdós posits the relevance of the novel
for the contemporary reader. More than the headstone that Segismundo
is devotedly going to erect, the novel itself is Fortunata's monument, or
rather a monument to the memory of an imperfect Fortunata and the
failed Liberal Spain of 1868-1876. The irony of the two admirers'
remarks is that Fortunata and her age will be perpetuated in a novel
which will disprove Segismundo's theory of oblivion, precisely on the
level that Galdós intended: the moral and spiritual. The sacrifice of
Fortunata and the Spain of 1868-1876 has been for the benefit of the
Spain of the future, that is, the present Spain of the contemporary
reader of 1886. In the hope that the reader will not follow the faults
of his fictional and historical forbears lies the one note of optimism in
Galdós's tragi-comic picture both in *Fortunata y Jacinta* and in the
other novels of our Group I of the *serie contemporánea*.

CHAPTER 8

THE END OF AN ATTEMPT:
MIAU (1888)

In the intense reassessment that the eighth novel of the *serie contemporánea* has undergone in the last ten years, surprisingly little attention has been given to Villaamil's participation in the public sphere, his political affiliations or opinions, all of which contribute to a better understanding of the character and his actions. In this final novel of our Group I political details, general and particular, are given, but scenes and episodes in the manner of those found in *La desheredada* or *Fortunata y Jacinta* are not. The existence of an allegory is perhaps now contentious, for the political data is included not so much to paint an historical period as to highlight the inner weaknesses of individual characters, and this would seem to indicate that Galdós is developing a different attitude towards the representation of contemporary historical material, an attitude that will become more apparent in the novels of our Group II.

Galdós does continue in *Miau* the debate, initiated with *La desheredada*, on the relation of the individual to the contemporary political reality. However, his conclusions are still as bleak as those of *Fortunata y Jacinta*: the well-intentioned individual who has so much to offer the country is again defeated by the march of contemporary history and by his own inner weaknesses. Ramón Villaamil is a character aware of the possibilities of his contribution to the national good, and it is in this awareness and its potential positiveness that he differs from Fortunata and Camila. However, although he appears to incorporate positive features of earlier idealistic characters in the series, Villaamil is as much a failure as they were. The ultimate impracticability of his financial plans reflects the nature of similarly idealistic theories on education advanced in *El doctor Centeno* by Jesús Delgado, whilst his suicide recalls that of José de Relimpio in *La desheredada* and of Máximo Manso in *El amigo Manso*.

Weber has accurately pointed out the care with which Galdós, as usual, frames the plot with chronological references.[1] However, in comparison with the preceding novels, *Miau* offers very few allusions to the precise year of the events. The only noticeable reference is a parenthetical allusion which associates the pawning of the Villaamil possessions with the marriage of Alfonso XII and María de las Mercedes: 23 January 1878. From the presence of Alfonso XII and Mercedes at the Opera when the Queen is described as being very pale, we deduce that the action of the novel is completed before her death in May 1878, since otherwise that event would surely have been mentioned. Indeed the action of the novel covers a short period in 1878: from the winter of February to early spring. Abelarda's wedding to Ponce, which we do not see, is fixed for the third of May, and Villaamil's final excursion to the city limits takes place on one "de estos días precozmente veraniegos en que el calor importuna más por hallarse aún los árboles despojados de hoja" (V, 675).[2] The comparative brevity of this period will contrast with the retrospective look at Villaamil's career and the forward glance to the period of the reader, for although he is still narrating events at a decade's distance, Galdós is once more anxious to link immediate past and actual present in a meaningful manner. Direct comparisons between the two periods are made: the open space between the Paseo de Areneros and the Guardias' barracks is still occupied by rubble, rocks and washing-lines in 1888 as it was in 1878 (V, 576). At other times, it is the disappearance of objects and people between those years that focusses attention on their contrast: "De este tipo de funcionario [Pantoja], que *la política vertiginosa de los últimos tiempos se ha encargado de extinguir*, quedan aún, aunque escasos, algunos ejemplares" (my italics; V, 614). If the implication is that the Civil Service has now passed into the hands of adventurers like Víctor, then the novel does indeed have relevance for the contemporary reader of 1888. Galdós felt compelled to express the prevalent corruption of the Restoration system in 1888, but it had to be done indirectly.

Furthermore, Pantoja's retrospective picture of the political

[1] See Robert J. Weber, *The Miau Manuscript of Benito Pérez Galdós: a Critical Study*, University of California Publications in Modern Philology, 72 (Berkeley, 1964), pp.24-25.

[2] According to Weber, pp.62-63, Galdós reinforced the chronological frame of the novel in the Beta version with the purpose of creating ironic religious connotations.

favours that Pez has been forced to incur from before the fall of Isabel
II up to the Restoration and, by implication, up to the present time of
the novel's composition, binds the whole period 1865-1885 into a
connected whole and serves to remind the regular Galdós reader of the
author's treatment of that period in the previous seven novels. By
means of the flow of political events past and future are inextricably
linked in a chain of cause and effect:

> Esa gente, que sirvió a la Gloriosa primero y después a la Restau-
> ración, está con el agua al cuello, porque tiene que atender a los
> de ahora, sin desamparar a los de antes que andan ladrando de
> hambre. Pez ha metido aquí a alguien que estuvo en la facción y
> a otros que retozaron con la cantonal. ¿Cómo puede olvidar Pez
> que los del gorro colorado le sostuvieron en la Dirección de
> Rentas, y que los amadeístas casi casi le hacen ministro, y que los
> moderados del tiempo de sor Patrocinio le dieron la gran cruz?
>
> (V, 616)

The bureaucratic world examined in *Miau* is another important
component in the gallery of official circles portrayed in this group of
novels. And because Villaamil's problem is intimately connected with
his former job and employers, his visits to the Ministry of Finance
afford excellent opportunities for Galdós to delineate in detail an important part of the 1878 political scene. But as in *La de Bringas* he
refrains from exploiting this government forum to full effect. There is
another dense picture of an internal labyrinthine structure, but little
reference to contemporary politico-financial realities. The difficulties
of the Cánovas government during this period, brought about by the
growing militancy of Sagasta's Liberals inside the Congreso, Ruiz
Zorrilla's continued plotting from Paris for a Republic, and Vizcaya's
refusal to sign an economic agreement with the Madrid Government,
are only briefly mentioned and without further elaboration (V, 587,
629).[3] The Finance Minister responsible for much of Villaamil's woe,
Fernando Cos-Gayón (1825-1898), is never presented directly to the
reader, except on one occasion through the comments of Pura on his
presence at the Opera with Cánovas: "Ahí tienes a don Antonio, en el
palco de los ministros, y a ese Cos-Gayón . . ., así le fusilaran" (V,
632).[4] This reluctance to provide concrete, identifiable examples of

---

[3] Manuel Ferrandis and Caetano Beirao, *Historia contemporánea de España y
Portugal* (Barcelona, 1966), p.318.

[4] Weber, p.57, maintains that the Finance Minister's name was also included
in God's letter in the Beta manuscript but omitted in the printed text. The purpose, he reckons, was to heighten the light note of the vision and the funda-
mentally ironic tone of Beta. There is a similar lack of precision about the identity

historical names from the contemporary period (as opposed to the detailed historical pictures of the intermediate past provided by Villaamil's nostalgia) represents an important departure for Galdós: it is almost as if he is slowly turning his back on the world of contemporary history which has obsessed him hitherto. The novels of our three remaining groups will see this development confirmed.

If the Finance Ministry seems vaguely located in a Madrid street without any given external features, and somehow suspended in Madrid air space at a vague historical moment, then its servants like to consider themselves as holders of a permanent position, unaffected by time or outside pressures. Hence general universal principles and comparisons have a purpose in this bureaucratic circle: they are a subconscious confirmation of the characters' desire for a permanent position. Víctor, Ruiz, Ponce, Argüelles, Cucúrbitas, Cañizares are, or will soon be, civil servants. Villaamil and Mendizábal are the only male adult characters shut out of this bureaucratic world, and it is their lot to make most of the precise historical references in the novel, for they are figures of the past who for basically similar reasons have recourse to their experiences to justify their present complaints. Víctor may refer to the "ley de Cánovas" to justify his claim for promotion; Argüelles may recall his halcyon days during the era of Julián Romea;[5] other former colleagues may spread absurd rumours of national crises to scare Villaamil (V, 629); but the principal voice of the precise past is Villaamil, because he is forced to live in that past to substantiate his case for a future entitlement to his pension. This, though, is not the way the current Civil Service functions, for, oblivious of the past, it occupies a present which it seeks to perpetuate into the future. Galdós as narrator makes the explicit comment that civil servants are "una honrada plebe *anodina, curada del espanto de las revoluciones, sectaria del orden y la estabilidad, pueblo con gabán y sin otra idea política que asegurar y defender la pícara olla; proletariado burocrático, lastre de la famosa nave"* (my italics; V, 660).

Fittingly, it is the chief bureaucrat, Pantoja, who best expresses this basic apoliticism or anti-politicism of the civil servants: "¿Hablábase de Hacienda? Pues en el acto tremolaba Pantoja su banderín con este sencillo y convincente lema: 'Mucha administración y poca o ninguna política' . . . Al propio tiempo sostenía que . . . la política [era] el arte de cohonestar las defraudaciones y el turno pacífico o violento en el

---

of the aristocratic lady who favours Víctor and of the deputy who might speak to the Government on Villaamil's behalf.

[5] A famous Spanish actor (1816-1868).

saqueo de la Hacienda" (V, 614). None the less, Pantoja's concluding advice to Villaamil is that he should be friends with all politicians and enemy of none, for the Civil Service ultimately depends on politicians for its survival. Other means are to be used too: help from influential women can be bought with sexual favours, as Víctor demonstrates in a grotesque way with his old, ugly mistress, and it is even hinted that Pantoja owed his first position to his wife's influence with a politician. Pantoja has surpassed the petty favour-buying and corresponding indebtedness of figures like Pez, because he has cultivated the highest friendship possible in the political parties without identifying with the respective political principles or ideology. He has climbed above the political hurly-burly to an Olympian summit of loyal and noble service to the faceless entity of the State, and by so doing he believes that he has put himself in an untouchable position where he is accountable to none but the State. In fact this belief is erroneous, for Galdós's forward glance to 1888 (V, 614) has shown that politics do still drastically intervene in the appointment system of the Civil Service. Thus Villaamil's litany of service under various political masters is still very relevant for the Spain of 1888.

In a brilliant anticipation of twentieth-century bureaucratic mentalities, Galdós shows in Pantoja how such loyalty to the invisible entity of the State is really a mask for the maintenance of one's own ideas and interests, no different in results from the traditional political patronage that Pez tries all the time to cultivate. It comes as no surprise, then, to learn that any attempt like that of Villaamil to introduce administrative reforms or to implement economic expansion is regarded by Pantoja as a direct threat to his own position.[6] Other civil servants lack Pantoja's dedication to this impersonal deity of the State but not his hidden concern for his own job security. In a crucial argument between Víctor and Villaamil in Chapter XI, the former tells his father-in-law: "Mil veces le he dicho a usted que el mismo Estado es quien nos enseña el derecho a la vida. Si el Estado no muere nunca, el funcionario no debe perecer tampoco administrativamente" (V, 582). Víctor, who has appropriated the taxes in Valencia considering them his due reward from the State for services rendered, concludes his speech with a confusing theoretical argument that justifies his concern for his own position as being in the national interest: ". . . mediador entre el

---

[6] In his 14 March, 1887 *La Prensa* article on the awarding of a contract to the Transatlántico Company, Galdós sharply criticized the politicians who professed an attitude similar to Pantoja's (*OI*, III, 302).

contribuyente y el Estado, debo impedir que ambos se devoren, y . . . tengo que asegurar mi vida para seguir impidiendo el choque mortal entre el contribuyente y el Estado" (V, 582). Spokesman, as it were, for the whole mass of civil servants swarming through the labyrinth of the Finance Ministry, Víctor is the reverse of the coin of which Pantoja is the face; the common denominator is their defence of their own interest.

Given the prevalence of this attitude, it is not surprising that Villaamil should tend to exaggerate his predicament and to see himself as the victim of a gross injustice: "En este mundo no hay más que egoísmo, ingratitud, y mientras más infamias se ven, más quedan por ver" (V, 555). Eventually, he comes to long for a political revolution as the sole answer to his problem: "Así saltara esta noche el cantón de Madrid y la *Commune* inclusive, y tocasen a pegar fuego" (V, 629). Yet his only physical act of rebellion – his final, futile mutilation of the municipal saplings – is a pathetic gesture that adequately sums up his identification with the State. Striking out against a minor symbol of the entity which is the cause of his personal ills, Villaamil reveals a love-hate relationship with the State which is the traditional frame of mind of the civil servant and which, ultimately, he cannot escape.

However, Villaamil is no longer a member of the Civil Service. Now on the outside and terribly anxious to be reinstated, he has to recall his past record in order to convince himself, former colleagues and superiors of the justness of his cause. It is because of this need to justify a problematic future pension by the record of past years that a number of precise historical references are documented in a tedious manner by Don Ramón for his listeners, and by the narrator for his readers. In the first substantial passage of exact references, Villaamil is reminiscing to himself about his career and his periods of unemployment:

> . . . carrera lenta y honrosa en la Península y ultramar, desde que entró a servir, allá por el año 41, y cuando tenía veinticuatro de edad (siendo ministro de Hacienda el señor Surrá). *Poco tiempo había estado cesante antes de la terrible crujía en que le encontramos*; cuatro meses en tiempo de Bertrán de Lis, once durante el bienio y tres y medio en tiempo de Salaverría. Después de la revolución pasó a Cuba y luego a Filipinas, de donde le echó la disentería. En fin, que había cumplido sesenta años, y los de servicio, bien sumados, eran treinta y cuatro y diez meses. Le faltaban dos para jubilarse con los cuatro quintos del sueldo regulador, que era el de su destino más alto, jefe de Administración de tercera. "¡Qué mundo éste! ¡cuánta injusticia! ¡Y luego no

quieren que haya revoluciones . . .!"

(my italics; V, 562-3)[7]

Later, when he harasses his former colleagues, the details of his *curriculum vitae* are related to the memory of the individual ministers whom he has served:

> Yo entré a servir en tiempo de la Regencia de Espartero, siendo ministro el señor Surrá y Rull, excelente persona, hombre muy mirado . . . Mi primer ascenso me lo dió don Alejandro Mon . . ., buena persona . . ., y de mucho carácter . . . Como madrugador, no ha habido otro don Juan Bravo Murillo, y el número uno de los trasnochadores era don José Salamanca, que nos tenía aquí a los de Secretaría hasta las dos o las tres de la madrugada. Pues digo, ¿hay alguno entre ustedes que se acuerde de don Juan Bruil, que, por más señas, me hizo a mí oficial tercero? ¡Ah, qué hombre! Era una pólvora. Pues también el amigo Madoz las gastaba buenas. ¡Qué cascarrabias! Yo tuve el cincuenta y siete un director que no hacía un servicio al lucero del alba ni despachaba cosa alguna, como no viniera una mujer a pedírsela.

(V, 651)[8]

From the foregoing data, the political allegiance of Villaamil, probably broadly *progresista*, although it is never openly stated, does not appear to have played any significant role in his appointments or periods of *cesantía*. Weber believes that Villaamil was a *moderado* and that "the pattern of his periods of unemployment and release reveals that his political beliefs have influenced his appointments and that he has not altered his views since his youth".[9] The truth of this statement is hard to reconcile with the facts quoted above which show that Villaamil was employed by both *progresista* and *moderado* administrations. If most of the politicians he mentions are *moderados* this is simply due to the fact that *moderado* governments were in power more than *progresista* administrations during the 1843-1868 period. Moreover, Ramón's employment during the *Bienio* of 1854-1856 was during a period of

[7] An *exaltado* (Radical) in the Cádiz Cortes of 1823, Surrá was Finance Minister during the premiership of González y González (1841-1842). Bertrán de Lis, a *moderado*, was Finance Minister in December 1846. Salaverría was Minister during the Unión Liberal in 1858 and held the same portfolio again in 1864 and 1875.

[8] Finance Minister in 1837, 1844, 1846 and 1848, Alejandro Mon was famous for his *Reforma tributaria*. Bravo Murillo, a *moderado*, was Minister in 1849 and was responsible for the important *Ley de Contabilidad* of the same year. Salamanca, a member of the splinter *moderado* faction, the *puritanos*, was Minister in 1847. Bruil was Minister in 1855 during the *Bienio*, and Madoz, a *progresista*, was Minister in 1843 and 1855.

[9] Weber, p.70.

moderado and *progresista* coalition government under the dual leadership of O'Donnell and Espartero.

Villaamil's lack of political commitment and even concern for politics becomes more evident from the narrator's supplementary information. His highest position ever in the Civil Service as "jefe económico en una capital de provincia de tercera clase" is a political gift from a friend of González Bravo which – understandably – he has to forfeit with the 1868 Revolution. By March 1869, however, he has been given another job, with promotion too, presumably by the same Revolutionary government that had removed him from his provincial post.[10] He then spends two years in Cuba in a government position; after a period in Spain, he returns to the turbulent colony in another capacity, until finally forced to relinquish his position

> en los aciagos dias de los cantonales. El Gobierno, presidido por Serrano después del 3 de enero del 74, le mandó a Filipinas, donde se las prometía muy felices; pero una cruel disentería le obligó a embarcarse para España sin ahorros y con el propósito firme de desempeñar la portería de un Ministerio antes que pasar otra vez el charco. *No le fué difícil volver a Hacienda*, y vivió tres años tranquilo, con poco sueldo, siendo respetado por la Restauración, hasta que en hora fatídica le atizaron un *cese* como una casa.
>
> (my italics; V, 591)

The most obvious conclusion from the details of Villaamil's post-1868 career is that appointments to and dismissals from the government bureaucracy follow no political lines, that the political affiliations of the civil servants, even if they have any, are not considered, and that all government jobs depend upon the inscrutable whims of the unidentified people in power who make these appointments, in all probability the Minister or the head of a branch or department.[11] In Villaamil's case Galdós deliberately leaves this source a mysterious secret.

If politics play no overt part in these decisions, Villaamil would seem to have little justification for criticizing political developments, the Government or the State as he does at the end:

> ¡Ay, Dios mío, qué desgraciado soy y cómo me voy quedando fuera de juego! ... Con esta Restauración maldita, epílogo de una condenada revolución, ha salido tanta gente nueva, que ya se

[10] There had of course been some cabinet changes, but Prim, Serrano, Topete and Sagasta still held the major posts. See Fernández Almagro, I, p.52.

[11] Nimetz, p.49, quotes Mesonero Romanos's statement to the effect that the *cesante* loses his job through "un capricho de la fortuna, o más bien de los que mandan a la fortuna".

vuelve uno a todos lados sin ver una cara conocida. Cuando un don Claudio Moyano, un don Antonio Benavides o un marqués de Novaliches le dicen a uno: "Amigo Villaamil, ya estamos mandados recoger", es que el mundo se acaba.

(V, 610)[12]

In a later argument with Pura, he condemns the examples of the Pez clan who have served so many different political masters, but in his resentment he fails to see that he too had served the same regimes with the exception of the First Republic. His plea for a *turno* to operate again in the Civil Service is pointless and absurd, as it already exists and he is its current victim. The emphasis Ramón places on the poor personal quality of the new crop of politicians reveals the values that he holds. As in his praise of former Finance Ministers, quoted above, Villaamil looks to the Minister, not to the party or its programme. *Personalismo* is the name of his game, governing his recollection of the past and his attempt to use those recollections to press his claims for the future.

For the reader, if not for Ramón, the precision of historical detail underlines one important truth that must have some bearing on any interpretation of his character and the meaning of the novel as a whole: Villaamil has played the Civil Service system all his life, has endured periods of inexplicable *cesantía* (mercifully these periods have been very short) and at the same time has enjoyed some good fortune in his career. Has he the right to complain of rough treatment, now, with two months remaining before he retires?[13] Moreover, he did not hesitate to use the *cacique* system, first in an attempt to remove Víctor from the family circle and then, when that proved impossible, to push him up the Civil Service ladder. There is no gainsaying the plight of Ramón and his family during the period covered by the plot, but its pathos can be exaggerated if the case is taken out of context. Galdós does not allow this to happen precisely through the insertion of this background information about his career. There is still sympathy for the old man — dismissal from a job only two months before retirement is a cruel blow of misfortune —, but how can he expect better treatment from a system notorious for its insecurity and instability, defects which are well known to him from lifelong experience? His situation is inhumanly preposterous by any account, but he has failed to absorb the lessons of earlier years, and he now refuses to believe that the rules of

[12] All three men were *moderado* ministers in the middle of the century, but they held portfolios other than Finance.

[13] See A.F. Lambert, "Galdós and the anti-bureaucratic tradition", *BHS*, 53 (1976), 35-49.

the game still apply to him and that he is not in a special category. He could have campaigned more actively for a job, as he had done four years earlier in *Fortunata y Jacinta*; the final arrangements he makes before his suicide (sending Luisito to his aunts, and assuring the family's survival by allowing Abelarda to marry Ponce) were options open to him at the beginning of the novel; and if Víctor's arrival changes and complicates his position, it also offers him a further lifeline which he could have grasped had his pride and honour permitted him. In reality the Villaamils' situation is not beyond the point of despair, nor utterly irremediable, as Ramón likes to think, fettered as he is to a misconception about the way the Civil Service has unjustly treated him. In a novel where again the instruction offered by life, especially its political ups-and-downs, is ironically paralleled by the formal education of young children, the old veteran fails to learn from his own and other people's examples.

In possible mitigation of this harsh portrayal of Villaamil's self-concern, one might argue that his detailed plan, worked out over the years, for the reform of the tax system is the panacea that would solve Spain's problems. However, although forming an important part of Ramón's catalogue of service to the country and manifesting his concern for the desperate economic situation, the scheme is presented by Galdós as partly unrealistic in detail and completely incapable of implementation in the Spain in which Villaamil lives. The last point is vividly brought out by the hilarious reaction of his former colleagues, climaxing in Guillén's attachment of the anagram MIAU to the plan. Given their lazy, self-seeking attitudes, how realistic is it to expect that these civil servants will be even willing to flesh out the details of a plan in any government bill of measures? Nor is it any more realistic, given the examples of egotistical ambition and greed to be found in the novel (such as the moonlighting of Ildefonso with his secret import-export business in religious *objets d'art*), that Villaamil's plans for a sincere declaration of income by taxpayers or for high tariffs to protect national industries will remove this private blackmarket profiteering. One aspect of his plan, the unification of the National Debt, is a reasonably practical measure, as we already know from *Lo prohibido*. Yet José María Bueno de Guzmán's experience on the Stock Exchange in that novel shows that such rationalization of investment portfolios will only encourage greater stock-market profiteering.

The sketching-in of historical detail, whilst helping significantly to join public and private worlds, is also a useful indicator of the probable failure of Ramón's plan. In 1852 the famous tax-reformer Bravo

Murillo signalled out Villaamil's scheme for special mention, and the first version of the document was made in 1855 in the form of "un plan de presupuestos" (V, 563) which was highly praised by Pascual Madoz and Juan Bruil. The inference to be drawn is that Ramón's plan forms part of Spain's economic history over the last thirty years. Yet, from the list of Finance Ministers under whom he has served, it is clear that he has been a member of a losing team, for the record of these eminent, well-meaning financial reformers is depressing, their sensible reforms only being implemented for short periods, if at all. Placed in that context, Villaamil's plan appears as but one of a number of plans for economic reform which never see the light of day or are rendered unfeasible by the attitudes prevalent in Spanish society. Interestingly, in one visit to his old office, Villaamil and his former colleagues indulge in a game of fantasy in which they pretend to form a government from their own ranks and "elect" him Prime Minister and Minister of Finance (V, 629). This game of fantasy highlights the unreality of Villaamil's thinking and links him to the madman Tomás Rufete who, in the opening sequence of *La desheredada*, the first novel of the series, had envisaged himself in similar flights of fancy as the country's Prime Minister.

The reappearance of Don Basilio Andrés de la Caña, who had propounded a similar set of financial reforms in *El doctor Centeno*, also serves as a timely reminder that the enunciation of fine-sounding economic plans can conceal a greater personal concern for self-advancement. As the regular reader of Galdós knows from *Fortunata y Jacinta*, these economic theories on reform were quickly jettisoned when Caña found prosperity in the Restoration administration of Cánovas in 1875. Likewise the promotion of Villaamil's plan in *Miau* is dictated more by the old man's predicament and his attempts to remedy it than by the perceived current economic situation of the country, and in his excitement at at last finding an influential politician to put his case to the Government, he fails to see the deputy's obvious opportunism, which casts a pejorative light on his own plan and motives. This is not to say that Villaamil is not concerned about the country. He is, but like Pantoja and the others he believes, somewhat dangerously, that his own plans and concerns are identifiable with those of the country as a whole: ". . . es que miro las cosas *de la casa* [i.e. the Finance Ministry] como mías propias, y quisiera ver a este país entrar de lleno por la senda del orden" (V, 617). Behind what appears a noble patriotic spirit lurks an unhealthy intimacy with the State that will not tolerate criticism from outsiders nor encourage self-criticism. Thus he rejects all criticism of his plan, convinced that the country is sick and that he alone can cure it. His status as a concerned national reformer is further undermined by the manner in which he promotes his scheme. There is some point to Guillén's mischievous suggestion that he should have published his plan, but the old man is too set in his bureaucratic ways and has been content to submit proposals to his political bosses and to bask in their fine words of approval. And, incredibly, when he does find a deputy to support his scheme, he does not go himself to the Parliament building to press his case but, allowing his personal animosity towards his son-in-law to keep him away, spoils his chances by sending young Luisito instead.

In the closing stages of the novel, Villaamil undergoes a certain spiritual change as he finally casts aside all concern for his personal situation and the pension he so desperately wanted. However, this phase of total altruism and patriotic concern is soon replaced by uncontrolled hatred directed against the State he supposedly loved so much, and he strenuously counsels the three army recruits he meets in the tavern on the Madrid outskirts to rebel against their officers at the first opportunity because the "gran pindongo del Estado" is their enemy. Yet, despite the sincerity and intensity of the emotions, Villaamil's tirade to these army recruits and later to the four prostitutes in another tavern scene is out of place and ignores the reality before his eyes. Individual resentment has finally destroyed the last vestiges of common sense and realism. With an alarming profession of anarchism, as Lambert has noticed, Ramón is prepared to bring all society crashing down with him.[14] Appropriately, he now curses the distant figure of the Carlist sympathiser Mendizábal in political language: "Me futro en tu absolutismo y en tu inquisición. Jeríngate, animal, carca y liberticida, que yo soy libre y liberal y demócrata, y anarquista y petrolero, y hago mi santísima voluntad" (V, 681). In many ways Villaamil is the most tragic of the victims of historical conscience whose irremediable failures have been chronicled in successive novels of our Group I of the *serie contemporánea*. Closer to the centre of political activity than Relimpio, Máximo Manso or Florencio Morales, he has a sharp awareness of the historical needs of the country unlike other bureaucrats or politicians such as Pez, José María Bueno or Villalonga. Galdós's conclusions are still pessimistic because he has not discovered a character with a spirit of public regeneration who can overcome the pull of his individual ego when contemporary political processes offer great possibilities for the exploitation of that ego. Villaamil's failure to affect and be affected by

[14] Lambert, p.45.

the national situation is as complete as those of less nationally conscious characters.

In all of the preceding novels Galdós's determination to construct an historical allegory was more or less self-evident. In *Miau*, this intention is not so immediately obvious. However, certain details, when assembled together, would suggest that he still had some intention of chronicling a period. From the historical data so far presented in this chapter it is clear that Villaamil's career reflects the topsy-turvy development of Spanish politics in the nineteenth century. But Galdós carries over this identification of public events and private lives into his description of the Villaamil family as a whole. Their most recent pawning of possessions, we are informed in Chapter V, coincides with the wedding day of King Alfonso and his cousin, María de la Mercedes, in January, 1878. Despite the serious implications of the loss of these possessions, the three Villaamil women do not miss any of the public festivities of that day and even shoulder their way brazenly through to the best viewing positions in the street. There are two levels of irony to be appreciated here by the reader. Firstly, on the day they lose practically all their personal possessions the Miaus still find time, energy and interest to participate in the public event. On a second, less obvious level, the day is an inauspicious one, both for the Monarch and for these three particular subjects. From this day forward the Villaamil household will go even more downhill until its eventual tragic break-up and the death of its *paterfamilias*. Alfonso's marriage was to be short-lived too, ending with the universally lamented death of Mercedes (May 1878), roughly simultaneous with Villaamil's suicide (undated, but probably occurring in late spring or early summer). This means that the story is plotted against the very brief duration of the Monarch's first marriage, and that it is another "episodio nacional" in the life of the country, equal in importance to the more official events.

This association between the Royal Family and the Villaamils is reinforced later when the Miaus attend the theatre where Alfonso and the now sick Mercedes are also spectators: the familiar tone of the three women's comments on the Queen's pale appearance and on other political figures gives the impression that they are talking about members of their own family who hold the same empty values, symbolized by the locale of the theatre. Moreover, recent developments in the Villaamil family history correspond to those in Spanish history. The year 1868 is cataclysmic for both nation and family: "Vámonos, pues, al 68, que marca el mayor trastorno político de España en el siglo presente, y señaló, además, graves sucesos en los azarosos anales de la familia Villaamil" (V, 588).[15] Ramón loses his job with the September Revolution, as we have noted above, but once back in Madrid he secures another position. In 1869 the family starts to break up, just as the Revolutionary coalition was becoming a motley collection of warring factions: Luisa, the elder daughter, dies and Doña Pura commences her extravagant life-style. The sickly, almost orphaned Luisito, product of the unstable marriage between Luisa and Víctor and presumably conceived in mid-1868, could well symbolize the result of the *Septembrina*: isolated and lonely, he displays the same disorientation and bewilderment evident in Spanish society since 1868.[16]

In this broad political-historical representativeness of the Villaamil family, their relationship to the Mendizábals, the *porteros* of the tenement house, is not unworthy of attention. Socially, of course, the couple are inferior to the Villaamils, though the respective names of the two families constitute an ironic inversion of their social status: "Mendizábal", the name of the economic wizard of Spain in the 1830s, would have been a more suitable name for Ramón, whilst the pedestrian, commonplace "Villaamil" would have suited the *portero* better. Additional irony derives from the latter's extreme animal ugliness, for his historical counterpart was renowned for his fashionable, somewhat effeminate appearance.[17] The *portero* is undoubtedly a generous character, overlooking the inability of the Villaamils to meet some of their rent payments, feeding Luisito and being generally charitable in his opinion of Villaamil. However, at the same time Galdós intends us to note the man's weaknesses of character, especially his inability to perceive the complete truth about Villaamil or the current political situation. He thunders against the injustice of the age in much the same way as Villaamil and the other civil servants: "Ya no hay modestia, ya no hay sencillez de costumbres . . . Ya no hay honradez, ya no hay cristiandad, ya no hay justicia. ¿Qué es lo que hay? Ladronicio, irreligiosidad, desvergüenza" (V, 556). Yet, his accusations do not ring true, for they are not the fruit of his own experience but of his

[15] See my "Galdós, the Madrid Royal Palace . . ." for a discussion of Galdós's obsession with *La Septembrina*.

[16] Weber, p.47, is particularly insistent on this symbolism of Luisito.

[17] Juan Alvarez Mendizábal (1790-1853) was Spain's greatest Finance Minister of the century, responsible for the important sale of ecclesiastical property in 1836-1837, the so-called policy of *desamortización*. It is noteworthy that he is not included in Villaamil's list of famous and important Finance Ministers. Villaamil was not in Hacienda during Mendizábal's greatest and most controversial term of office, 1836-1837, but he must surely have been employed there when Mendizábal returned in 1843, for there is no indication that Ramón was a *cesante* at that time.

newspaper readings. Moreover, whereas that other avid newspaper reader, José de Relimpio in *La desheredada*, pawed endlessly over the inner meaning of the political events he read about, Mendizábal can only repeat the generalized rhetoric he reads and memorizes, and then only imperfectly: "¿Qué se hizo de aquella pobreza honrada de nuestros padres, de aquella – no recordaba lo demás – de aquella, pues ... como quien dice ...?" (V, 556). Mendizábal is an ironic echo of Villaamil, pointing to the notes of unreality in their respective yearnings, in the latter's case, for "moralidad", in the former's for "religión" (V, 577). The mistake of both men is to demand unrealistically such absolute virtues from a society and country that is manifestly incapable of ever developing them.

Mendizábal's first-hand experience of historical events is also employed as an ironic counterpoint to Villaamil's catalogue of public service in the Finance Ministry. His participation in these events has only hardened his *absolutista* convictions, instead of opening his eyes to the reality of the contemporary political process. He proudly re-counts his military exploits, even venturing to claim that they are an integral part of Spanish history, a chapter which has not yet been published. There is some truth in this claim but not in the way that he means. Like that other rent-collector, Estupiñá, Mendizábal is a potential historical guide whose value should not rest in the exaltation but in the deflation of the historical episode. Here Galdós is still pro-gressing from the emotional commitment to history of a José de Relimpio towards the cynical disillusionment of a Beramendi or *Confusio* in the later *episodios nacionales*:

> –Pero ¡cuánto ha visto usted en este mundo, amigo Mendi-zábal, y qué de cosas habrá presenciado tan trágicas, tan intere-santes, tan ...!
> Y el *gorila*, abarquillando los recibos, contestaba:
> –La Historia de España no se ha escrito todavía, amigo don Ramón. Si yo plumeara mis memorias, vería usted ...
> (V, 587-8)

The Villaamils laud Mendizábal's right-wing views when they cannot pay the rent, but in more prosperous times they ridicule him. But what Villaamil fails to realize is that Mendizábal is a silent reminder that had Spanish politics after 1833 taken a different course and the Carlists, not Queen Cristina's Liberals, triumphed in the First Carlist War, he and the other functionaries in Pantoja's office, whether of *progresista* or *mode-rado* persuasion, would never have enjoyed their comfortable positions.

Whether or not Luisito is intended as a precise symbol of the post-1868 political period, he and his school chums must represent at least in general terms the current youth of Spain or the future of the country, just as the gangs of lads in *La desheredada* had been cast explicitly in that role. Besides playing an important role in the development and final denouement of the plot, Luisito is an expression of Galdós's pessimistic vision of the Spain of the 1880s, of Restoration stability and material prosperity. Luisito is a human battleground for warring factions in and outside the family, and his developing personality is strongly influenced by these conflicting pulls. The epilepsy which he has inherited is not reduced by his experience in the Villaamil household, nor, one presumes, will it disappear with his move to Quintina's house, for Pura and Abelarda will still exert some influence. Pupil of life's lesson, Luisito cannot benefit positively from the example of his elders, his natural tendency to violence being allowed to go unchecked, as the after-school brawl with *Posturitas* brings out. On this occasion Luisito feels the satisfaction of an adult at his physical superiority over weaker brethren: "... sentía en su alma *los primeros rebullicios de la vanidad heroica*, la conciencia de su capacidad para la vida, *o sea, de su aptitud para ofender al prójimo*, ya probada en la tienta de aquel día" (my italics; V, 575). The operative phrase in this description of Luisito's reactions is "vanidad heroica". The school scene which opened the novel had already shown a world very similar to that of adults in which physical violence is prominent, as if the national revolution advocated by Villaamil as a solution to his individual problems were already in the author's mind:

> A las cuatro de la tarde, la chiquillería de la escuela pública de la plazuela del Limón salió atropelladamente de clase, con algazara de mil demonios. Ningún himno a la libertad, entre los muchos que se han compuesto en las diferentes naciones, es tan hermoso como el que entonan los oprimidos de la enseñanza elemental al soltar el grillete de la disciplina escolar y *echarse a la calle* piando y saltando. La furia insana con que se lanzan a los más arriesgados ejercicios de volatinería, los estropicios que suelen causar a algún pacífico transeúnte, el delirio de la autonomía individual, que a veces acaba en porrazos, lágrimas y cardenales, *parecen bosquejo de los triunfos revolucionarios que en edad menos dichosa han de celebrar los hombres*.
>
> (my italics; V, 551)[18]

[18] Eamonn Rodgers, *Pérez Galdós: Miau*, Critical Guides to Spanish Texts, 23 (London, 1978), p.22, is mistaken when he considers this scene solely in terms of comic irony. I would argue that the last line of the quotation sounds a completely different, more serious note in Galdós's picture of youth's tragic future, already anticipated in Mariano's gang fight in *La desheredada*.

Luisito, caught amidst the conflicts of an adult world that he cannot understand and which nobody will explain properly to him, is destined to become another part of the unthinking society of Restoration Spain. The point is firmly made in his visit to the Parliament building to deliver his grandfather's note to the deputy: "Total, que Luisín no podía formar juicio exacto, y su mente era toda confusión . . . 'Quien debía venir aquí a explicarse es Mendizábal, que sabe tanto, y dice unas cosas tan buenas' " (V, 637). The helpfulness of Mendizábal in this situation is probably debatable, but the undeniable truth that this scene rams home is that in this last novel of our Group I of the *serie contemporánea* the youth of Spain still have no reliable guide to help them understand the political events around them. Nor are there ahistoricist alternatives such as Camila and Fortunata had briefly offered in the two preceding novels, for Abelarda is neurotic and her charitable virtues and love are too heavily enmeshed in her sexual attraction for Víctor to allow her to offer an alternative mode of living to the Restoration system.

   Miau marks the end of Galdós's allegorical representation of historical periods through characters and their actions in the *serie contemporánea*.[19] He will still continue to avail himself of precise historical facts in order to give his novels a certain national representativeness or flavour, but the degree of that allegorical significance will be strongly diminished as he comes all the more frequently to present characters who deliberately set themselves against the trends of contemporary history in a more conscious manner than that effected intermittently hitherto. But though Galdós's interest in contemporary history may diminish, it will never disappear completely. After all, he was to continue writing political commentaries for *La Prensa* of Buenos Aires right into the twentieth century.

---

[19] Stephen Gilman, "Novel and society . . .", p.21, comes to roughly similar conclusions: ". . . the cast of each and every one of his novels prior to 1887 was a microcosm explicitly designed to communicate a developing understanding of the macrocosm, Spain's nineteenth-century experience." Gilman would omit *Miau* from the Group; I prefer to include it, although it is looking towards the novels of our Group II.

PART TWO
HISTORY'S ROLE
REDUCED

CHAPTER I

PRECISION ALMOST ABANDONED: *LA INCOGNITA* (1889) and *REALIDAD* (1889)

In the novels of our Group II of the *serie contemporánea* Galdós makes important changes in his technique of incorporating contemporary historical material into the so-called social novels. Precisely factual material is now reduced almost to a minimum with a growing emphasis being placed on abstract general reference to political structures and theories. Neither brand of historical reference is inserted with the purpose of creating an allegory of the historical period in question; we are no longer conscious of retrospective history lessons from the narrator's present. Nevertheless, history is still there and in such a meaningful way that we can still talk in Deegan's terms of a novel of the historical imagination: the historical material is now integrated into the bewildering character of the fictional protagonist in order to present the particular nature or mood of the politics of the time (not a diachronic outline) against which a deeper character analysis can be undertaken. At the same time Galdós continues his argument about the attitude of politically conscious characters to the question of national regeneration, not necessarily advancing beyond the position that he had reached with Villaamil in *Miau* and yet not retreating either from the presentation of characters who, while seeing through the political sham, cannot see ways of changing the system. The tragic isolation of the sensitive individual is still his pessimistic conclusion.

Employing a narrative technique considerably more complex than provided hitherto by a quasi-unreliable, albeit supposedly omniscient narrator, Galdós shows in *La incógnita* and *Realidad*, (discussion of which novels is obligatorily joint) that a definitive assessment of life's events must be limited. This hesitancy in proposing definitive explanations must then apply to the political material which at first reading appears quite straightforward. Because of Galdós's use of an ambiguous narrative voice, the two characters around whom the major political material is situated in *La incógnita*, Manolo Infante, the narrator, and Carlos Cisneros, his uncle, represent a strange mixture of political idealism and cynicism. Unaware of this inner contradiction, they are, none the less, advanced developments of a type – the unabashed political cynic – that we have already met in Pez in *La de Bringas*, José María Bueno de Guzmán in *Lo prohibido*, and Villalonga in *Fortunata y Jacinta*.

The political question is given an important position in the structure of the two novels. For a good part of the first half of *La incógnita* Manolo shows concern for the political views of his uncle and his own activity as a deputy in the Congreso. Only when he comes to know Augusta and her circle of friends does he dwell with increasing preponderance on the personal, amorous aspects of these relations. But at this point politics also assume an equally important alternative role in his life, so that the political theme is dominant to a great extent throughout the novel. This importance must then be carried over to *Realidad*, despite the apparent silence with which the dramatized sequel of *La incógnita* appears to gloss over the political dimensions of the latter. It is important to remember that *Realidad* is a gift from Infante's correspondent, Don Equis, who resides in Orbajosa, the district that Manolo represents in the national Congreso. Moreover, the manuscript of *Realidad* is delivered to Infante in Madrid by Juan Tafetán who has come from Orbajosa to solicit his deputy's help in getting his job back. Clearly, then, the whole question of *Realidad*'s relation to *La incógnita* is structurally soldered by the question of political roles and actions. If there is no mention of political history in the sequel this omission does not mean that Galdós has not sewn it into a political frame. Furthermore, if the characters do not show any interest in politics, then the main conclusion of *La incógnita* is substantiated: individuals are too engrossed in their own personal interests to bother about the destiny of the country. And yet public affairs are a dimension of Spanish life that cannot be ignored: national politics are as much a part of 1888 Spanish reality, so Infante reveals in the letters of *La incógnita*, as Viera's suicide which grasps the attention of all in *Realidad*. For the contemporary reader, at least, Galdós ensures that this important theme is not swamped by the others by placing the political material as a preface to the two novels, as it were.

As in *Miau* the barest of details are provided to fix the chronology of the political scene. If we do know the exact day and month of the letters of *La incógnita*, the year of their appearance is only corroborated by the notice on the title page of *Realidad*: "La acción es contemporánea" (V, 791).[1] Although there are direct shots of parliamentary debates in *La incógnita*, again little precise detail is provided beyond passing references to the political leaders, Cánovas, Castelar and Sagasta, or to the enactment of certain laws. This will be the tenor of the style in our remaining groups of the *serie contemporánea*, the bare details being just sufficient to ensure the contemporary historical status of these novels. The instructiveness of *La incógnita* for the contemporary reader is once more programmed by Galdós through the contradictory habits of the undiscerning narrator. Manolo pontificates on one occasion: "La invención realmente práctica consiste en abrir mucho los ojos y en acostumbrarse a ver bien lo que entre nosotros anda" (V, 766); earlier he had remarked: ". . . todo es aprender, observar y cursar la difícil carrera de la vida" (V, 748). Manolo applies himself to his task with much seriousness, trying to observe the visible reality around him, but failing to decipher its true meaning, which forever must remain an enigma, an "incógnita". At least the contemporary reader is in a privileged position to make a better attempt at deciphering the total reality than these actors, enmeshed in the web of fiction.

Manolo Infante impresses more positively as a public political representative than the blatantly cynical José María Bueno de Guzmán of *Lo prohibido*; but despite his conscientious discharging of his duties in Orbajosa, his election to the national Congreso had been rigged in a way sufficiently offensive to arouse local opposition. When participating in the work of the Congreso he introduces a bill to lower the taxes of the region in a move designed to curry favour with discontents at home and clearly not in the national interest. Politics in the Cortes become more important for him when he discovers that his position as a deputy can act as a spur or antidote to love. When Augusta and her friends visit the Cortes hoping to hear a political debate between great orators, they have to endure the turgid speech of an unidentified deputy who drones on and on, and for Manolo and the other equally bored deputies the great regret is that they cannot "dar a los debates un carácter divertido y sainetesco para aliviar la tristísima situación de aquellas desgraciadas"

---

[1] Gonzalo Sobejano, "Forma literaria y sensibilidad social en *La incógnita* y *Realidad* de Galdós", *Revista Hispánica Moderna*, 30 (1964), p.93, comments: "Las cartas de Manuel Infante comprenden un lapso de tiempo idéntico al de la redacción del libro por Galdós: de noviembre a febrero de 1889. La sincronización de ambos procesos (fingido y efectivo) quiere decir que la materia de la obra es rigurosamente actual."

(V, 699). The parliamentary debates become a great opportunity for Manolo to win Augusta's attention, for she will only return to the Congreso when he delivers a speech. Paradoxically, when she rebuffs him, he finds consolation in the heated debates which act as "un mareo reparador, una embriaguez" (V, 709).[2] The benefits of this rhetorical oratory achieve a physical effect positively unique in the *serie contemporánea*: ". . . la *res pública* es cosa muy buena, un emoliente, un antiflogístico eficacísimo para ciertos ardores morbosos de la vida . . . Si la política es un vicio, con este daño inocente se pueden matar otras diátesis viciosas que nos trastornan el seso" (V, 703-4).[3] Yet if at last we have a politician who actually expresses interest in national politics, his motives are obviously far from praiseworthy. Nor are his political affiliations all that stable, for he suffers from bouts of conflicting identification, feeling himself a democrat one day and the next an authoritarian.

As elsewhere in the *serie contemporánea*, politics are a farce: the hilarious style of Manolo's maiden speech, the exaggerated praise it receives from the few somnolent deputies in the Congreso, the prearranged reply from the Opposition benches, and the later redrafting of the speech for the parliamentary record, convey the utter absurdity of the political process and Infante's part in it. This picture of the emptiness of the political process is integrated into the main fictional interest: Viera's suicide; for, at the same time as this event occurs, the Congreso is debating an important proposed law which could have affected the outcome of his case. Yet the politicians who will chatter about the suicide at the Orozco *tertulia* are not interested in participating in the debate:

> . . . voy al Congreso. Animación en los pasillos, runrún de crisis, chismorreo largo, mucho secretico, mucho racimo de curiosos en torno a este y el otro personaje, pechugones aquí y allí por si tú debías votar y no votaste. Oyense las frases iracundas de siempre, y aquello de *ni esto es partido, ni esto es Gobierno, ni esto es nada.* En el salón reina la paz de los sepulcros. Discútese el proyecto de ley de Enjuiciamiento criminal; soledad en los escaños; el orador, rodeado de tres o cuatro amigos, trata de convencer a los bancos vacíos.
>
> (V, 739)

---

[2] Galdós may be alluding here to the crisis that Sagasta had to weather in the summer of 1888 when all parties combined to attack his policies, especially his free-trade and universal suffrage proposals.

[3] Pattison, p.115, predictably, makes the suggestion that Galdós is reflecting here his own behaviour as a Sagasta deputy.

Thus, even in a matter of direct relevance to a notorious murder case which absorbs the prurient interest of Madrid society, Restoration politicians are still blindly and pathetically uninterested, preferring to gossip, chatter or utter empty rhetoric. Galdós's picture has not changed since *La desheredada*, but now he is avoiding precise historical details.

Previous first person narrators had omitted such detail for a variety of reasons: philosophical choice (Máximo Manso), devious slyness (the anonymous narrator of *La de Bringas*), plain lack of interest (José María Bueno de Guzmán). In the case of Manolo Infante his basic attitude is that politics are a means to a comfortable end, as he explains to Viera, or to gain a love. At times he refrains from giving more detail of Congreso events out of a delicate sense of what might not interest his correspondent in Orbajosa. Above all, Manolo Infante has to contend with the enigmatic and confusing political guidance of his mentor, Don Carlos María de Cisneros, whose political affiliations he cannot classify at all during his first few days in Madrid, believing him one minute to be a Carlist, and then the next, the complete opposite. As a former politician himself, Don Carlos appears to speak words of eminent wisdom when criticizing the corrupt Restoration system:

> La política, tal como aquí se practica, le inspira despiadadas burlas. Atiende a ella, según dice, como quien asiste a un sainetón extravagante. Para él no hay ministro honrado, ni personaje que no merezca la horca.
>
> (V, 694)

Don Carlos has thought out an alternative system:

> En el fondo de este sueño late la revolución, no esa revolución pueril por que trabajan los que no tienen el presupuesto entre los dientes, sino la verdadera ... para que de la materia descompuesta salga una vida nueva, otra cosa, otro mundo, querido Manolo; otra sociedad, modelada en los principios de justicia.
>
> (V, 694-5)

These are only two extracts from a lengthy passage devoted to the exposition of Don Carlos's political ideas. Manolo, the political apprentice, soon notices that these splendidly idealistic attitudes are contradicted by Carlos's subsequent actions such as welcoming vain, egocentric politicians to his *tertulia*, his avid reading of the political press, his establishment of schools on his estates. Above all, his anarchistic ideals clash violently with his continued exploitation of the capitalist system: "... no pude menos de mostrarme asombrado de que tales ideas profesase un hombre que vive tranquilamente de las rentas extraídas de la propiedad inmueble y de la riqueza mobiliaria, es decir, un fortísimo sillar del edificio del Estado, tal como hoy existe" (V, 695). The visit of the ex-minister a short time later, with a request that he pull strings for him, sums up the contradiction in Carlos's thinking. In the same way his later intervention with the enquiry judge in order to have Augusta's involvement in the Viera case covered up, jars incongruously with his earlier indignant condemnation of the decadence of Spanish institutions (V, 764). This intervention not only relates the political material to the fictional interest in the same manner that more precisely detailed episodes were twinned in the novels of our Group I, but also points to the selfish interest behind his political beliefs.[4] From the ex-minister, this tax-paying pillar of society is able to secure promises of action to remove opponents from a town council and from local government offices. He may urge Manolo to join him in the revolutionary process by attacking the Government in the Congreso, but he will make sure that his own family is protected in any future social conflagration. Carlos could well be the eternal egotist who uses the political system and idealistic rhetoric for his own personal advantage. On the other hand, unconsciously or even consciously, in his own way, he could be contributing to a betterment of Spanish society which will be achieved by a preceding conflict. The question cannot be resolved because Galdós now presents life as full of contradictions and enigmas. In no sphere is this more evident than in the relation of individual politicians to the national political structure.

Given this type of political guide figure, it is no wonder that Manolo becomes guilty of the same shortcomings: able to criticize Don Carlos's failure to visit his country estates, he cannot see that he shows the same dereliction of duty to his own political estates, the constituency of Orbajosa. It is only the news of the dissatisfaction of his constituents at the loss of their local perks to neighbouring towns which causes him to hasten back to the country to repair his "*altarito*, o sea, mi poder político en el pedazo de España que tuvo la honra de elegirme su esclavo y opresor" (V, 786).

Galdós also appears to attach some nationally representative stature to Don Carlos, "esta figura eminentemente nacional", with the

---

[4] Politicians were also rumoured to have intervened in the Calle del Baño murder. The same was certainly true in the famous historical murder case of the time which is the source for this fictional episode: the murder in the Calle de Fuencarral about which Galdós wrote at great length in a number of articles for *La Prensa* during 1888-1889. See Denah Lida, "El crimen de la calle de Fuencarral", in *Homenaje a Casalduero*, ed. Rizel Pincus Sizèle and Gonzalo Sobejano (Madrid, 1972), pp.275-83, and "Galdós, entre crónica y novela", *AG*, 8 (1973), 63-77.

profile of his Renaissance namesake and possible relative, the Spanish Cardinal Cisneros. Manolo suggests to his correspondent that in order to visualize Carlos he should recall the images of those

> guerreros afeitados *que parecían* curas, aquellos señores *que seme-*
> *jaban* labriegos vestidos de seda, los comuneros de rostro recurtido
> por el sol y los hielos de Castilla; . . . *reconstruye el cuño de la raza*
> *y tipo de la madre Castilla*, y podrás decir: "Vamos, ya le tengo".
>
> (my italics; V, 690)

For Manolo, Don Carlos is Spanish society's historian, though not in the mould of Estupiñá, Relimpio, Morales or General Morla. As if to demonstrate that Galdós is now turning his back finally on that type of amateur historian, we have in Don Carlos the historian of the private lives of individuals, and in his accounts of those lives precise historical detail is pertinently omitted, as it never was in the accounts of those other walking historical encyclopaedias. Galdós is now deliberately playing down official political-military history, whereas in the novels of Group I, in authorial passages commenting on the juxtaposition of public and fictional lives, there had been an assumed equality of the two. In Infante's remarks the apology for the private history of individuals is made on the defensive, as it were, as if Cisneros, and hence Infante himself, really rate it higher than traditional public history:

> Era aquello la historia, *compuesta y adornada a lo Tito Livio,*
> *como arte verdadero; historia no inferior por su trascendencia y*
> *ejemplaridad a la que nos cuenta en fastidiosas páginas las bodas*
> *de los reyes y las batallas que se ganaron o se perdieron por un*
> *quítame allá esas pajas*. Mi tío me ilustró también con algunas
> particularidades de su vida, en las cuales no pude menos de ver
> esa mano de gato con que algunos cronistas desfiguran y en-
> galanan lo que les conviene.
>
> (my italics; V, 708)

Moreover, no longer is our voice of history prepared to defend his account of public history with the authority of his visual experience, as was Estupiñá's wont. Don Carlos deliberately distorts the truth of his history lessons, and Galdós is perhaps already tending towards what will be his final and probably most preferred type of historian, *Confusio*, the character in the later *episodios nacionales* who spends his time rewriting nineteenth-century Spanish history as he thinks that it should have happened. Don Carlos may be a symbol of Spain's historical past, but he is a disconcerting historian with dangerous nineteenth-century anarchist tendencies; after all, Galdós does make him reside in Madrid's Plaza del Progreso!

After his first bout of love for Augusta, the diarist Manolo Infante makes a remark that sums up Galdós's ideas in our Group I novels on the ideal relationship between the individual nineteenth-century Spaniard and his historical context, ideas which, ironically, are being seriously questioned in our Group II novels: "No tardé . . . en notar lo inconveniente de que se rompa la relación armónica que cada individuo debe guardar con su época" (V, 703). Neither Don Carlos nor Federico Viera, with his Golden Age notions of honour, corresponds to that ideal: the former reckons that the latter is in fact a citizen of the twenty-first century. The saintly Orozco is also ill at ease in the materialistic nineteenth century. On a minor scale, other characters in the Orozco *tertulia* continue the bewildering political representativeness. The Madrid-born cosmopolitan Malibrán curses Spain and Spaniards when he is abroad, and for this behaviour he is rewarded with a place in the Government! La de San Salomó reckons that she understands politics but we are told that "de sus explicaderas no puedes colegir si es carlistona furibunda o anarquista frenética" (V, 716). And for his constantly changing political loyalties Villalonga is now seeking a life senatorship. Where do these pillars of society stand in the question of politics? The answer that Galdós is now advancing is that political ideas and affiliations are as much an enigma as acts like Viera's suicide or Orozco's charitable deeds, or indeed the respective personalities of his characters. It is a perplexing world into which Manolo Infante steps when he arrives in Madrid from Orbajosa; but then country-town Orbajosa with its selfish expectation of preferential treatment from the Madrid government will offer Manolo a surprise too at the end of *La incógnita*.

CHAPTER 2

THE HISTORICAL DYE FADES:
THE *TORQUEMADA* TETRALOGY (1889-1895)

Because of their interlocking nature, the four novels on the life and times of the miser Torquemada have to be considered as a single unit. Like Carlos Cisneros in *La incógnita*, Torquemada is presented as an individual whose political behaviour is representative of the times and whose character portrayal is deepened by reference to the historical data and framework of the period. In the first two novels of the tetralogy, the references are precise in nature; in the last two, of a much more generalized kind. Moreover, the historical material is now used as a reference point against which to assess the important inner transformation of the protagonist, rather than as protruding landmarks in a subterranean allegory of historical events.

a) *Torquemada en la hoguera* (1889)

The narrator's opening paragraph returns to the style of the majority of our Group I novels: he confesses to an intimate acquaintance, probably shared by the reader, with the miser Torquemada. The story of the latter's punishment through the death of his son Valentín is now offered as a lesson for the reader, as a "caso patético, caso muy ejemplar, señores, digno de contarse para enseñanza de todos, aviso de condenados y escarmiento de inquisidores" (V, 906). However, the traditional moralizing tone of the narrator's remarks suggests that in this particular fictional lesson, there is no longer any need for the individual to harmonize his actions with the true meaning of contemporary history, as was the case in our Group I novels, but rather to loosen his bonds with the contemporary predicament in order to find his true self.

At the beginning of his fictional life Torquemada is presented as the epitome of his times. A vital cog in capitalist society, he is a creation of the historical events despite the timeless, archetypal nature of his professional figure:

> ... no pudo eximirse de la influencia de esta segunda mitad del siglo XIX, que casi ha hecho una religión de las materialidades decorosas de la existencia. Aquellos avaros de antiguo cuño, que afanaban riquezas y vivían como mendigos y se morían como perros en un camastro lleno de pulgas ... eran los místicos o metafísicos de la usura ... Viviendo el *Peor* en una época que arranca de la desamortización, sufrió, sin comprenderlo, la metamorfosis que ha desnaturalizado la usura metafísica, convirtiéndolo en positivista.
>
> (V, 908)

More precisely, Torquemada's career is plotted against certain political landmarks. His years of apprenticeship are from 1851 to 1868. In the year of *La Gloriosa* he made his first house purchase, "una casa de corredor" in the Calle de San Blas. At a time when the country was repeatedly torn asunder by civil disorder or war, he was able to increase his personal fortune, doubling his capital by 1875. The "radical cambio político" of the Restoration "proporcionóle bonitos préstamos y anticipos. Situación nueva, nómina fresca, pagas saneadas, negocio limpio" (V, 907). The new appointments to the Congreso and the Civil Service naturally needed new clothes and accommodation but could not afford to pay for them, and the same situation obtained with successive alternations of Liberals and Conservatives during the 1870s and 1880s:

> Toda la época de los conservadores fue regularcita, como que éstos le daban juego con las esplendideces propias de la dominación, y los liberales también, con sus ansias y necesidades no satisfechas. Al entrar en el Gobierno, en 1881, los que tanto tiempo estuvieron sin catarlo, otra vez Torquemada en alza: préstamos de lo fino, adelantos de lo gordo, y vamos viviendo.
>
> (V, 907)

And because of the rigorously present time frame of the novel, the contemporary reader is to assume that the situation still continues to the present, to 1889, when Sagasta's Liberal government, besieged on all sides, was finally to resign. Torquemada, whose personal fortune is dependent on the political upheavals, also shapes historical circumstances. All of Spanish society (soldiers, politicians, government bureaucrats) needs him: "Pues todos éstos, el bueno y el malo, el desgraciado y el pillo, cada uno por su arte propio, pero siempre con su sangre y sus huesos, le amasaron al sucio de Torquemada una fortunita que ya la quisieran muchos que se dan lustre en Madrid, muy estirados de guantes" (V, 906). In a sense Torquemada is the King of Madrid or Spanish society. The parallelism of historical and private changes is even reflected in the transformation in his domestic habits. When his beloved wife and partner, Silvia, dies, his daughter Rufina takes charge of running the family house and introduces new domestic methods:

A reinados nuevos, principios nuevos. Comparando lo pequeño con lo grande y lo privado con lo público, diré que aquello se me parecía a la entrada de los liberales, con su poquito de sentido revolucionario en lo que hacen y dicen. Torquemada representaba la idea conservadora; pero transigía, ¡pues no había de transigir!, doblegándose a la lógica de los tiempos. Apechugó con la camisa limpia cada media semana.

(my italics; V, 909)

Yet this figure of history will be forced by the illness and death of his son, Valentín, to break out of the historical mould into which he has been cast, and will have to consider the possibility of an after-life beyond the historical moment, as propounded by the Catholic Church. Believing that Valentín is being taken away from him by God as punishment for his cruel money-lending practices, Torquemada attempts to curry favour with the Divinity and thereby secure the boy's recovery, by embarking on a number of charitable expeditions to clients and beggars around Madrid, some of which are invested with an appropriately religious air.[1]

In this very tentative, unconscious search for a new set of spiritual, rather than positivistic, values, Torquemada is unfortunately instructed by the preposterous ex-cleric, Bailón, whose career is presented, at certain levels, as a grotesque caricature of his own. If he benefited from the momentous political events of the period 1868-1888 without participating directly in them, then Bailón participated directly, without benefiting. In Málaga in 1869 Bailón abandoned the priesthood, devoting his energies now to attacking his former colleagues: "Lo primero que hizo el condenado fué dejarse crecer las barbas, despotricarse en los clubs, escribir tremendas catilinarias contra los de su oficio, y, por fin, operando *verbo et gladio*, se lanzó a las barricadas con un trabuco naranjero que tenía la boca lo mismo que una trompeta" (V, 912). After a brief spell with some Protestants, he returned to the political scene in 1873 and published political pamphlets composed in

[1] See my "Sallies and encounters in *Torquemada en la hoguera*: patterns of significance", *AG*, 13 (1978), 23-31.

an absurd mixture of political and ecclesiastical styles. With the 1875 Restoration of the Bourbons, he fled abroad only to return to Spain and prison in 1877, completely disillusioned with politics and the grasping, exploitive nature of politicians. Now dedicated to the study of transcendental existence, to "sondear el grande y temerario problema de nuestro destino total" (V, 913), he seems to prefigure the change from the historical to the spiritual mould that Torquemada must now undergo. But clearly the absurd nature of Bailón's conversion must cast a parodic light upon Torquemada's experiment which, of course, ends in failure.

With more precise historical facts given in *Torquemada en la hoguera* than in *La incógnita*, there may appear initial reason for including it in our Group I, perhaps after *Miau*. Whilst our group divisions are not meant to be hermetic and some inevitable overlapping is to be expected, there is, none the less, a notable difference in the respective application of those precise historical details in *Miau* and *Torquemada en la hoguera* which should warn us of the dangers of judging the importance of the historical material included in any novel only by quantity. In the delineation of both the Villaamil family in *Miau* and Torquemada in *Torquemada en la hoguera* there is obviously an attempt to convert the respective characters into representative figures of the national history of the period, but there is one important difference which justifies our inclusion of the two novels in different groups: in Torquemada's case, the precise data of the references serves as a backdrop against which his spiritual development can be gauged. This was not the case in *Miau*. In the second and later novels of the tetralogy the national representativeness of Torquemada and his attempts to shake off this historical mould increase, but with general allusions to the socio-political hierarchies replacing precise historical references.

b) *Torquemada en la cruz* (1893)

Carrying out the deathbed wishes of his partner Doña Lupe, Torquemada visits the Aguila family and is immediately spell-bound by Cruz's aristocratic manners. From this point onwards he is determined to improve his social graces and position: "Lo que digo, no tengo política [i.e. good social manners] ..., y hay que gastar política para ponerse a la altura que corresponde" (V, 943). It is highly significant that the commencement and termination of this process of personal redirection are marked by the ambiguous use of words loaded with political connotations. Torquemada's famous last word "conversión" leaves everyone perplexed as we shall soon see, because it is never learnt whether the miser was thinking of his own conversion to a more Christian attitude or the conversion of the country's National Debt. The ambiguity of these two words, besides clearly implying that Torquemada's reassessment cannot be evaluated fully and with accuracy, continues that national frame which has already been established in *Torquemada en la hoguera* by the exact recording of historical details. Politics, the first meaning of the word "política", are the root cause of the Aguila family's present impecunious state and, thus, of the urgent need for either Cruz or Fidela to marry Torquemada: the Spanish Government not only took away their lands in La Rioja, but also defaulted on payment for fodder supplied by their grandfather in the First Carlist War. During negociations with the intermediary, Donoso, Torquemada offers to pay for the family's lawsuit. Significantly, Donoso, an influential figure in political circles, accepts the offer as they pass in front of the Congreso building (V, 969). It is Donoso, the irreproachably honest retired civil servant, who points out the national obligation Torquemada has of improving his social position and marrying into the Aguila family: "La riqueza impone deberes, señor mío: ser pudiente, y no figurar como tal en el cuadro social, es yerro grave ... Las personas de posición constituyen lo que llamamos *clases directoras* de la sociedad" (V, 958-9). This is the same argument that Cruz will later employ to make him submit to her demands for a proper social status for the family. The hierarchy of the Spanish social system depends on the contribution of the wealthy like Torquemada. To overcome his own innate reluctance to make this change, the usurer draws consolation from the example of the country's current political system: "¡Y a fe que estaban los tiempos para reparillos y melindres! ... *Sin ir más lejos*, véase a la Monarquía transigiendo con la Democracia, y echando juntos un piscolabis en el bodegón de la política representativa. Y este ejemplo, ¿no valía?" (V, 972). Not inappropriately, his wedding to Fidela, representing the union of the old and new aristocracies of Spanish society (the former, of birth, the latter, of wealth), takes place on the "víspera o antevíspera (que esto no lo determinan bien las historias) de la festividad de Santiago, patrón de las Españas" (V, 1011), as if the event were of national historical importance, as it surely was if we continue to view Torquemada as a representative type of the historical moment.

More precise historical references are used to characterize Torquemada and his relationship with the Aguila family. The events recalled are not rigorously contemporaneous, but rather are taken from the intermediate past and refer to an "episodio nacional" not hitherto recorded in the *serie contemporánea*: the 1860 African campaign of O'Donnell almost thirty years before the action of *Torquemada en la cruz*.[2] The military appearance of Torquemada, self-proclaimed descendant of the Grand Inquisitor, now takes on the more modern identity of General O'Donnell; ". . . y desde que me quité la perilla, que parecía un rabo de conejo, tengo mejor ver. Dice *Rumalda* [his servant woman] que me parezco algo a O'Donnell cuando volvía del Africa" (V, 968). His overcoat is of the same vintage, "un gabán de cuello algo seboso, contemporáneo de la entrada de nuestras valientes tropas en Tetuán" (V, 964). There also appears to exist some similarity between the leadership qualities of the fictional and military heroes. According to the old African campaigner Hipólito, O'Donnell had "aquel disponer las cosas tan a punto, y aquella *comprensión de cabeza*, que era la maravilla del Universo" (V, 990). Though Torquemada's qualities are in the sphere of finance, they are equally undisputed and marvellous, so we are told in *Torquemada en el purgatorio*:

> . . . veían en él un magistral golpe de vista para los negocios, un tino segurísimo que le daba incontestable autoridad, de suerte que teniéndose todos por gente de más valía en la vida general, en aquella rama especialísima del *toma y daca* bajaban la cabeza ante el bárbaro, y le oían como a un padre de la iglesia . . . crematística.
>
> (V, 1022)

Historical material is further interwoven into the fiction when the narrator makes a direct comparison between the battles of the 1860 African campaign and the manoeuvres in which Cruz is engaged in order to engineer Fidela's marriage to Torquemada:

> Mientras con tanta fiereza desalojaban los nuestros al agareno de sus terribles posiciones [in Hipólito and Rafael's reminiscing], en la puerta de la casa [significantly situated in La carretera de Tetuán], sentadas una frente a otra con familiar llaneza, Cruz y Bernardina platicaban sobre combates menos ruidosos, de los cuales *ningún historiador grande ni chico ha de decir jamás una palabra*.
>
> (my italics; V, 991)

Here Torquemada is no longer equated with the victorious Spanish leader but with the vanquished Moors. The parallel thus casts an ironic light on his entry into the Aguila family.

---

[2] In articles for *La Prensa* written almost at the same time as *Torquemada en la cruz* (see Shoemaker, pp.489-518), Galdós comments in great detail on another outbreak of hostilities in Spain's North African possessions.

This African War material also puts into relief the escapism of Rafael, Torquemada's opponent within the Aguila family. Talking with his sister Fidela he declares: "Déjame, déjame que me aparte de este mundo y me vuelva al mío, al otro, al pasado" (V, 998). He proudly recalls the heroic deeds of his mother's family: "Es una familia que honra a la patria española y a la Humanidad. Desde nuestro bisabuelo, muerto en el combate naval del cabo San Vincente, hasta el primo Feliciano de la Torre-Auñón, que pereció con gloria en los Castillejos, no verás más que páginas de virtud y de cumplimiento estricto del deber" (V, 998).[3] Hipólito's war anecdotes only serve to maintain Rafael's outdated sense of family honour and his desire to escape the present disgrace of a union with such a parvenu as Torquemada:

> Para Rafael, en el aislamiento que le imponía su ceguera, incapaz de desempeñar en el mundo ningún papel airoso conforme a los impulsos de su corazón hidalgo y de su temple caballeresco, era un consuelo y un solaz irreemplazables oír relatar aventuras heroicas, empeños sublimes de nuestro Ejército, batallas sangrientas en que las vidas se inmolaban por el honor.
>
> (V, 990)

The power and the glory, the externals of the "episodio nacional" of the 1860 African campaign absorb his attention as his selective memory jumps back a few decades to the last resounding military victory of the Spanish army abroad. He chooses to ignore all the bloody internal events which were the disgraceful and tragic sequel to 1860 and which Galdós recaptured in brief but frequent pictures in our Group I of the *serie contemporánea*. These same events were the immediate cause of Torquemada's rise to increased wealth and subsequent marriage into the Aguila family. In despising the O'Donnell-like Torquemada, the symbol of his age and a creation of the historical events, Rafael is inevitably criticizing some of the results of that 1860 military campaign. As in his markedly opposite feelings for his mother and father, Rafael prefers to embrace only the romantic, noble aspects of life and history.

Like Manolo Infante or Don Carlos in *La incógnita*, the old army veteran, Hipólito, is guilty of distortion or embellishment in his recollections:

... en boca del propio héroe de ellas [las hazañas], resultaban tan

---

[3] The reference to the 1797 sea-battle between English ships and a French-Spanish flotilla reminds the reader of the parameters of Galdós's reconstruction of nineteenth-century Spanish history in the *episodios nacionales*. A passing reference thus serves to join the historical world of the *serie contemporánea* with that of his more traditional historical novels.

fabulosas como si fuera el mismísimo Ariosto quien las cantase. Si se llevara cuenta de los moros que mandó al otro mundo en los Castillejos, en Monte Negrón, en el llano de Tetuán y en Wad-Ras, no debía quedar ya sobre la Tierra ni un solo sectario de Mahoma para muestra de la raza.

(V, 989)

Thus the actor in the nation's most momentous achievements can no longer record the historical reality with the complete fidelity that an Estupiñá might claim. The final layer of ridicule placed on this excursion into the past by two escapist characters is provided by Cándido's expressed intention to construct a firework display of the events of Spanish history!

In short, then, the particular story of Francisco Torquemada's marriage to Fidela Aguila is firmly related to national history; but whilst the references to the 1860 campaign underline Rafael's romantic escapism, or bring out the military-like nature of Cruz's war to win over Torquemada, there is hardly any reversible transfer of meaning from the fictional to the historical strand, as was the case in our Group I novels. It is conceivable that Galdós may be suggesting that behind O'Donnell's overseas campaign of military glory against an old enemy lurked the darker intention of securing financial advantage for a bankrupt, ruined country; but this mention of the Africa War is isolated within this particular novel in the tetralogy, unrelated to the material given even in *Torquemada en la hoguera*. The emphasis in the parallel is surely on the illustration of the fictional personages' character. National history — still concretely of the intermediate past — is recalled, but not permanently "aligned" with the fictional material it illuminates still in a meaningful way.

c) *Torquemada en el purgatorio* (1894)

In a novel that witnesses Torquemada's accession to public position and fame, firstly as a financial adviser to the Government, then as a member of the Senate, precise historical/political references continue to be employed but they are of a less precise nature and on a much more reduced scale than those in the two earlier novels of the tetralogy. The miser's motives for accepting public position appear genuine enough:

Pues acepto la ínsula. Iremos al Senado, *vulgo Cámara Alta*, y si me pinchan, diré cuatro verdades al país . . . Yo me comprometía a arreglar la Hacienda en dos semanas; pero para ello exigiría un plan radicalísimo de economías.

(V, 1067)

None the less, his participation is not totally disinterested, for this involvement in the world of government finance brings lucrative reward as the success of the tobacco franchise illustrates: His vanity is also encouraged by the attention and respect accorded him. Moreover, his political activity is strictly limited to financial matters. At last the wishes and hopes of the Stock Exchange investors of *Lo prohibido* or the Finance Ministry bureaucrats in *Miau* have been realized. Spain is now under the effective — if still indirect — control of its financial experts. In his famous banquet speech, Torquemada contemptuously dismisses the professional politicians:

> De política nada os digo. (*Voces: "Sí, sí".*) No, no, señores. No he llegado a saber todavía qué partidos tenemos, ni para qué nos sirven. (*Risas.*) Yo no he de *ser Poder*, ni he de repartir credenciales . . ., no, no . . . Veo que *pululan* los empleados, y que no hay nadie que se decida a *castigar* el presupuesto.
>
> (V, 1101)

Yet the irony is that this speech is typical of the anodyne public oratory heard so often in the Senate or Congreso, as Rafael reminds his brother-in-law. Moroever, Torquemada is guilty of the same faults that he criticizes in the politicians, for his services as adviser to the State are equally exploitive.

Now an addicted reader of *Don Quijote* and the *Historia de España*, Don Francisco is regarded by the common masses as the uncrowned King of Spain, and he is duly greeted by the Prime Minister as one of "las personas . . . que representaban dignamente al país" (V, 1073). All sections of the Spanish Establishment (apart from the King) attend his Epiphany ball, come to congratulate him on his banquet speech, commiserate with him on the death of his wife, and send their sympathies on his illness. As the king of a new dynasty, he has to occupy his palace, and this is why Cruz goads him into buying the Gravelinas palace: "Finca tan hermosa y señoril no podía ser más que del Estado o de algún príncipe" (V, 1104). Comparisons with the Spanish Royal Family of the time are invidious; one cannot really say that Galdós is drawing a political parallel between the Torquemadas and Queen Cristina and her infant son, Alfonso XIII. Galdós expressed strong support for the Queen Regent in his *La Prensa* articles, having been a member of the Parliamentary deputation which attended the Royal Palace on the birth of the heir in 1886, two to three years before the action of the Torquemada series.[4] Here again we can see very clearly

[4] See *OI*, III, 248-49.

the difference between the use of historical parallels in our Groups I and II novels of the *serie contemporánea*. In the former there were enough precise references to pinpoint the parallels, and to construct an historical allegory of the period. In our Group II we are witnessing the gradual whittling away of that precision. Simultaneously, we notice that the emphasis in the parallel between fiction and history has shifted towards the fictional component. Torquemada is still a national symbol of his age, but the identification with exact historical periods of *Torquemada en la hoguera* has given way to a vague, generalized national outline. None the less, that frame still is Spanish, not foreign or abstract; Galdós's message is still directed towards Spain and the contemporary Spaniard.

d) *Torquemada y San Pedro* (1895)

As the Marqués de San Eloy, Francisco Torquemada buys the Gravelinas property and ends his days there. The restorer of a crumbling class, he has reached the summit of society. However, the opening description of the palace in the last novel of the series suggests that the true interpretation of that social ascent must centre on its negative aspects. The palace, which for Torquemada was "un *fiel trasunto* de las oficinas del Estado" (V, 1125), is now overcome with anarchy and disorder. One of the head servants grumbles: "¡Dios, que ésta es la de todos los días, y aquí no hay gobierno, ni *ministración*, ni orden público!" (V, 1113). The dawn light slowly filters over the armour, paintings and manuscripts, suggesting that these historical possessions are vain, antiquated symbols that deserve the present-day ravages of the mice. Like the hollow suits of armour, Torquemada the marquis and nominal King of Spain is an empty man now, a person who has not found satisfaction in his public role. The greater the ascent, the greater is his frustration and annoyance as he allows himself to be pushed into a position of public symbol which he cannot really accept as a private person.

The whole trajectory that Torquemada has been made to travel is masterfully summed up in the closing days of the miser's life. First, he is commanded by Cruz to leave to the Church a bequest of a third of his wealth in order to reverse the losses suffered as a result of Mendizábal's measures of disentailment in 1836-1837. So even at the end of his earthly existence Torquemada still finds himself enmeshed in the net of nineteenth-century Spanish history. Furthermore, this proposed deathbed gesture is described with the loaded word "rasgo", which immediately recalls the historical antecedent, discussed in our chapter

on *La de Bringas*, of Isabel's famous *rasgo* of 1865, which led to a
sequence of disastrous events that in turn brought about the pheno-
menal rise in Torquemada's personal fortune. The wheel of history has
indeed come full circle. The historical overtones of the miser's last
moments are stressed even more by his plan to convert the country's
External Debt into an Internal Debt, another *rasgo* designed to help the
State's finances. In Torquemada's current situation the proposal is
absurd, especially as he makes it on the condition that Gamborena
assure him his place in heaven, and the priest has to point out to the re-
calcitrant materialist that heaven is not "un Ministerio al cual se dirigen
memoriales para alcanzar un destino" (V, 1158).[5] In one superlative
climax Galdós has captured the whole development of his historical
material so far in the *serie contemporánea*: the precise reconstruction
of an historical period which he had more or less consistently maintained
in the novels of our Group I has now gradually been replaced in our
Group II by generalized historical echoes which are used as backdrops
on which to project the attempt and ultimate failure of the individual
character (and in the case of Torquemada, a very historically-moulded
character, a creation of the tragic events of nineteenth-century history)
to escape the pull of history and realize a more independent existence.
Angel Guerra will now make the same impossible attempt, but in a
more self-conscious manner.

----

[5] Presented as a warrior type of missionary-priest who is more at home in colonial Africa than Restoration Madrid, Gamborena is a man who is out of step with
modern society and is not the best spiritual adviser for the hesitant Torquemada.

CHAPTER 3

THE CONSCIOUS ABANDONMENT
OF HISTORY:
ANGEL GUERRA (1890-1891)

Angel Guerra continues the argument initiated in *Torquemada en la hoguera* about the possibility of the individual's escape from contemporary society and history by a search for spiritual values. The conclusion now advanced, surpassing that of the three subsequently-written novels of the *Torquemada* tetralogy, is that the experiment in change can now be consciously undertaken by the individual. Exact, documented historical allusions are used as in the first two novels of the *Torquemada* series more to plot the spiritual development of the individual protagonist than to paint an allegory of the historical period. Even the very substantial authorial aside on the nature of history, the first to appear in the *serie contemporánea* since the composition of *El amigo Manso* seventeen years previously, has a definite bearing on the question of Angel's transformation of character.

The chronology of the historical period covered is presented with a tantalizing vagueness, the narrator going to deliberate lengths to obfuscate the reader. No precise dating is given and inferences have to be made from the other information supplied. Angel is twelve or thirteen years old in 1866 and is thirty during the period of the novel's action which, therefore, must take place around 1883 or 1884. Precise chronicling of Mancebo's ecclesiastical offices is not carried up to the contemporary period: "Niño de coro en 1822 ...; en 1840, órdenes ...; sacristán mayor ... en 1843 ...; en 1860, auxiliar contador en la oficina de Obra y Fábrica, donde continuaba y continuaría hasta su muerte" (V, 1322). Catalina Babel talks of going to relate her family history to King Alfonso XII and the Queen who "a renglón seguido tirará de la campanilla para llamar a Sagasta" (V, 1288). Since Alfonso's death occurred in November 1885 just after Sagasta had started his second term of office, the action of the novel must take place in the previous two years. There is no historical evidence for the attempted coup directed by the fictional character, Brigadier Campón, although there were some serious military revolts in the early autumn of 1883 at Badajoz, Santo Domingo de Calzada and in the Seo de Urgel which were quickly put down by Sagasta's government. It seems likely that in Campón's abortive coup Galdós is representing the string of coup attempts in the 1880s, especially that of General Valcampo in 1886.[1]

Because of the direction of Angel Guerra's change from political activism to religious spiritualism, the majority of allusions to contemporary political history occur in the first part of the novel. Galdós is at last including in his gallery of public types the political revolutionary, yet this figure was really becoming an anachronism in the Spain of the late 1880s and Angel's transformation into mystic guru is more in keeping with the times.

Angel's participation in the attempted coup is skilfully presented so that a number of barriers distance the reality from the reader, the clear intention being to cast doubt on the real nature of the protagonist's involvement and motives. The novel opens with Dulcenombre waiting anxiously for Angel's return and his eventual appearance is presented as if it were a common nightly occurrence, not the exceptional flight from the loyalist forces that it is:

> Amanecía ya cuando la infeliz mujer, que había pasado en claro toda la noche *esperándole*, sintió en la puerta los porrazos con que *el incorregible trasnochador* [my italics] acostumbraba llamar, por haberse roto, días antes, la cadena de la campanilla . . . ¡Ay, gracias a Dios! El momento aquel, los golpes en la puerta, a punto que la aurora se asomaba risueña por los vidrios del balcón, anularon súbitamente toda la tristeza de la angustiosa y larguísima noche.
>
> (V, 1200)

The initial impression is that Angel is either an inveterate gambler or a womanizer who abandons his wife for most of the night. The prosaic image for his wound ("trozo de res desprendido de los garfios de una carnicería" [V, 1201]), the incessant buzzing of the bee that Dulce finally manages to catch, the arsenic used for his wound and originally intended for a lame dog, are all details which control the angle from

---

[1] For his comments on this incident, see his article in *La Prensa* of September 25, 1886 (*OI*, III, 213-20).

which Angel's subsequent relation of his exploits is to be viewed. It will be an extremely fragmented relation disclosing his bitterness at the failure of the coup, which he now blames on others, and at the dashing of his chances of personal glory.

Before Angel gives his version of events, the reader knows that there is widespread confusion in the city as to what has actually happened. Some of Dulce's neighbours reckon that the cavalry garrison has revolted in favour of a Republic. Other neighbours claim that the Royal Palace is burning out of control or that seventeen generals have revolted. Dulce wonders: "¿Es verdad eso? Pues luego cada persona que llegaba a la casa traía una papa muy gorda" (V, 1204). Subsequent newspaper accounts are equally mystifying. Can anyone, then, pontificate with certainty about what did happen? Pintado, the old veteran, appears to put the coup in its proper historical perspective, as Dulcenombre reports to Angel:

> . . . me contó que . . . el cincuenta y tantos y el no sé cuántos, él solo con cuatro amigos cortó la comunicación de la Cava Baja con la calle de Toledo, y que la tropa tuvo que romper por dentro de las casas. En fin, te mueres de risa si le oyes ponderar lo héroe que es . . . con ínfulas de maestro, os criticaba, porque en vez de encallejonaros en la estación de Atocha, debisteis iros a la Puerta del Sol y apoderaros del Principal.
>
> (V, 1204)

However, Dulce's reaction is a warning that Pintado is not to be taken seriously. His military assessment may be correct, as Angel admits, but, like Estupiñá and the other amateur political historians of our Group I novels, he is concerned only with general tactics and movements and overlooks the deeper significance of the event.

When the episode is recounted, it is noticeable that Galdós is now focussing on the effects of public events on the psychology of the individual rather than on the twinning of fiction and history. The essentially tragi-comic tone in which the episode is presented is louder than that first sounded in *La desheredada* and approaching the level of the later *episodios nacionales*. The ingredient of tragedy, the shooting of the artillery officer, brings retribution to Angel with his mother's fatal heart attack, which to a great extent is the result of her anger at his reported involvement in the killing. However, the incident also has its touches of comedy: Angel receives a grazing from Mediavilla's revolver shot, whilst another participant, Montero, sprains his ankle!

Galdós again raises the question of the reliability of the narration. As a participant in the incident, Angel believes himself to be in a position to give a definitive account of the proceedings: "Cuando un hombre ha presenciado sucesos que pasan a la Historia, aunque sea de contrabando, y que acaloran la opinión, *natural es que sienta el prurito de contarlos, de rectificar errores y de poner cada cosa y cada persona en su lugar*" (my italics; V, 1206-7). Yet how can we be sure that the events occurred as he remembers or even witnessed them? It is clear from his feverish state and his erroneous belief at times that he is talking, not to Dulce, but to a "trinca del Círculo Propagandista Reivindicador", that this claim of complete truth is far from being acceptable. "Yo te aseguro, como si lo hubiera visto" (V, 1207), he declares, with the same confidence that Estupiñá had shown in *Fortunata y Jacinta*, but Dulce's reaction provides the proper corrective to that assertion: "Pero dime . . . ¿estabas tú en todas partes para saber lo que en todas partes pasaba?" (V, 1207). As if not to lose sight of the true sense of this scene, Galdós adds an authorial aside: "En Guerra hablaban aquella noche *el orgullo* del testigo que sabe lo que los oyentes ignoran, *el amor propio* del narrador bien informado y *el coraje* del revolucionario sin éxito" (my italics; V, 1207). The emphasis on Angel's emotional state at this point suggests that any historical account will be heavily coloured by this gamut of subjective feelings. Quite apart from these personal interferences, the complete accuracy of his account can never be fully guaranteed because the participant himself is unable to remember exactly the details of the event after its occurrence. When asked about the identity of the person responsible for the artillery officer's death, Angel is genuinely bewildered:

> ¿Yo? No sé decir que sí ni que no. Admitamos que sí . . . Recuerdo haber hecho fuego con un revólver que pusieron en mi mano . . . *El delirio en que estábamos no nos permitía ver la atrocidad del hecho* . . . No quiero decir que yo disculpe . . . ¿Acaso puedo decir que fuera yo? Mi conciencia oscila . . . Realmente, no fuí yo solo, y aunque lo hubiera sido . . . *Aun ahora no me doy cuenta de cómo fué.* Yo estaba ciego de coraje.
>
> (my italics; V, 1210)

Thus the events of history are shrouded in uncertainty, even for those who participate in it.

Galdós also extends his ambiguous vision to the serious remarks on the philosophy of history that the narrator and Angel make in the first chapter of the novel. Returning to the open expression of theoretical ideas on the meaning of history that he had initiated in *El amigo Manso*, he shows that the historical detail in *Angel Guerra* (and by inference, in the whole *serie contemporánea*) is related to a serious theoretical base. Angel now philosophizes on the significance of armed conflict and violence in war:

> El pueblo se engrandece o se degrada a los ojos de la Historia según las circunstancias. Antes de empezar, nunca sabe si va a ser pueblo o populacho. De un solo material, la colectividad, movida de una pasión o de una idea, salen heroicidades cuando menos se piensa, o las más viles acciones. Las consecuencias y los tiempos bautizan los hechos haciéndolos infames o sublimes. *Rara vez se invoca el cristianismo ni el sentimiento humano* [my italics]. Si los tiempos dicen *interés nacional*, la fecha es bendita y se llama *Dos de Mayo.* ¿Qué importa reventar a un francés en medio de la calle? ¿Qué importa que agonice pataleando, lejos de su patria y de los suyos? . . . Si los tiempos dicen *política, guerra civil*, la fecha será maldita y se llama *diecinueve de septiembre* [the 1868 Revolution]. *Considera que, en el fondo, todo es lo mismo* [my italics].
>
> (V, 1210)

Here Angel is perhaps expressing Galdós's very bitter disillusionment with all forms of armed conflict by Spaniards against foreigners or fellow Spaniards, the traditional stuff of national history and the basis of the traditional historical novel and of his own first two series of *episodios nacionales.*[2] The reference to the lack of Christian charity or humanitarian feelings in the assessment of what is proper national history is vitally important, for it shows that Galdós, through his protagonist, is now considering that the individual's relation to fellow individuals is superior in significance to the collectivity's military heroics. The last phrase of the quotation, "todo es lo mismo", captures his conviction of the arbitrary selectiveness of what is usually called official history, and also his exasperation and weariness with this state of affairs.

Galdós ensures that Angel's words of wisdom are not ignored by prefiguring them with a long passage of authorial comment on the nature of true history:

> ¡Ay! La pobre Dulce, mujer sencilla y casera, no comprendía *el interés de la Historia, la filosofía de los hechos graves que afectan a la colectividad, interés a que no puede sustraerse el hombre de estudio, máxime si ha intervenido en tales hechos.* Dulce creía que era más importante para la Humanidad repasar con esmero una

---

[2] In a penetrating remark in one of his articles for *La Prensa*, Galdós even conceded that violence had been responsible for the brief successes of Liberalism in nineteenth-century Spain: "Por desgracia del pueblo español, todos los triunfos del principio liberal sobre la reacción han sido ganados por la fuerza, casi siempre militar" (*OI*, III, 215).

> pieza de ropa, o freír bien una tortilla, que averiguar las causas determinantes de los éxitos y fracasos en la labor instintiva y fatal de la colectividad por mejorar modificándose. Y, *bien mirado el asunto, las ideas de Guerra sobre la supremacía de la Historia no excluían las de Dulce sobre la importancia de las menudencias domésticas, pues todo es necesario; de unas y otras cosas se forma la armonía total, y aún no sabemos si lo que parece pequeño tiene por finalidad lo que parece grande, o al revés. La Humanidad no sabe aún qué es lo que precede ni qué es lo que sigue, cuáles fuerzas engendran y cuáles conciben. Rompecabezas inmenso: ¿el pan se amasa para las revoluciones o por ellas?*
>
> (my italics; V, 1209)

This famous passage repeats a basic premise of the *episodios nacionales* and the *serie contemporánea*: that individual lives are intimately inter-connected with the events and deeds of the collectivity. But what sounds new in this repetition of an old refrain is his anguished inability to determine the exact nature of that relationship, the respective importance of public and private affairs. Here Galdós seems to be straining at the leash, chafing at the pull of political history and its demands on his fiction. Yet he cannot bring himself to make the final break. For he considers himself an "hombre de estudio", a serious student who thinks deeply about the meaning of political and public events, trying to rationalize his feelings and reactions into "la filosofía de los hechos graves que afectan a la colectividad", and as an intellectual and an artist, he cannot reject this public world out of hand as his protagonist is now ready to do and as perhaps he himself would like to. Angel's abandonment of political activities thus represents an impossible dream for Galdós, whose intellectual honesty is such that, despite his re-pugnance towards the insane tragedy of Spanish political life, he knows he must continue recording it. None the less, the conflict of attitudes which this passage brings out into the open was one which was to persist into the later *episodios nacionales*, which Galdós was to start writing three years later.

Another aspect of this rich authorial admission of feeling is the statement that it is, above all, the intellectual who has been involved in public events who is unable to escape this fascination of history. It is almost as if Galdós is revealing something of his inner self, part of the psychological factors behind his own enthusiasm for history, for the historical event that he selects to illustrate this point in the life of Angel Guerra is the barbarous execution in July 1866 of the sixty-six sergeants of the San Gil barracks in Madrid who had unsuccessfully tried to revolt against their superiors and were punished by O'Donnell's government. This episode, witnessed by the fictional Angel Guerra, was also one of the bloody disorders which Galdós personally witnessed in his first few years in Madrid after his arrival from the Canary Islands. The grisly horrendous description he provides in *Angel Guerra* is repeated in the companion *episodio nacional* of the fifth series, *La de los tristes destinos* (1907), and in his own autobiography *Memorias de un desmemoriado* (1915).[3] The mental scar which the executions left on Angel and on Galdós himself is objectified in the crazed appearance of another spectator: "La cabeza de aquel hombre era como un escobillón; su rostro, una máscara griega contraída por la mueca del espanto . . . De su cuadrada boca salió, más que humana voz, un fiero rugido que decía: '¡Esto es una infamia, esto es una infamia . . .!' " (V, 1239). The memory of that "terrible página histórica" (V, 1239) always reappears in times of great stress for Angel Guerra, his mind filled by the images of the frenzied stranger and the "sargentos pataleando entre charcos de sangre". Indeed that experience and other unspecified "episodios nacionales" are the primary reason for his political activism.

The observer of history now becomes an actor of history in the botched-up coup, an episode which Galdós presents almost as the comic inversion of the historical tragedy. If the San Gil sergeants of 1866 had failed to involve their officers, the plotters (officer types, one supposes) now fail to enlist the support of the artillery sergeants at an unidentified Madrid barracks. If the plotters of 1866 had been punished by the severest penalty possible for rebellion, their fictional counterparts of 1883-1884 escape scot free. The "fusilamientos, sangre y escenas de destrucción y venganza, el castigo y las represalias del pronunciamiento vencido" (V, 1212) that Dulce anguishedly foresees do not materialize. Executions appear a thing of the past, as even the coup leader, Campón, is released, and Angel is not arrested because a family friend, the Marqués de Taramundi, succeeds in getting the Government to turn a blind eye. Yet if the 1883 fictional *putsch* is a parody of its historical predecessor, it contains a similar element of tragedy in the shooting of the artillery officer. Thus the lesson offered by the 1866 execution — the inhumanity of man to man, or more specifically, the inhumanity of nineteenth-century Spaniard to nineteenth-century Spaniard — is reinforced by Angel's experience as a political activist. This lesson persistently forces itself on him in the form of a recurrent nightmare.

[3] See José María Jover Zamora, "Benito Pérez Galdós: *La de los tristes destinos* (caps I y II)", in *El comentario de textos, 2: De Galdós a García Márquez* (Madrid, 1974), pp.15-110, for a discussion of Galdós's presentation of the executions in the companion *episodio nacional*.

Significantly, the first occurrence of that nightmare in the novel precedes the conflict with his mother which will result in her death, and it also anticipates the later conflict with the Babel family which will lead to his own death. The lesson which history repeatedly thrusts before him is one which Angel chooses to ignore.

Disillusioned with the farce of public history, Angel rejects politics to search for a different set of values, and under the spell of Leré's forceful personality and her Tolstoyan sermons on non-violence, he withdraws to Toledo and the surrounding countryside. The political world of Madrid seems very distant: "En aquel rincón de paz y silencio, ¿qué le importaba que el Estado se llamara República o Monarquía, ni que el Gobierno fuese de esta o de la otra manera? Tales problemas no eran ya para él más importantes que el trajín y las idas y venidas de las hormigas arrastrando hacia su agujero la pata de un escarabajo" (V, 1338). Imperial Toledo is the perfect refuge from nineteenth-century Spain and contemporary history, and he can now identify with the religious spirit of timeless Spain through an aesthetic appreciation of the city's beautiful architecture: "No le resultaba aquello ciudad del occidente europeo, sino más bien de regiones y edades remotísimas, costra calcárea de una sociedad totalmente apartada de la nuestra" (V, 1317). But even this romantic retreat does not insulate him from the threat of violence from his fellow human beings, an eternal truth that the 1866 historical event and his own abortive 1883 coup had presented clearly for his instruction. Two voices of reason remind him of the inherent absurdity of his switch from politics to religion. First, Dulce chides him: "¡Ay, hijo! No has caído en la cuenta de que es cosa muy ridícula pasar de lo revolucionario a lo eclesiástico" (V, 1297). The priest Casado also speaks the truth directly to his face: "Por mucho que se modifique externamente, entusiasmándose con el simbolismo católico y volviéndose tarumba con la poesía cristiana, detrás de todos estos fililíes está el temperamento de siempre, el hombre único, siempre igual a sí mismo" (V, 1515). Angel may have changed his aims and be working for a religious revolution, but it is with the same rebellious temperament that drove him into politics and he cannot change his basic character, however hard he tries.

Angel's serious, if defective, attempt at spiritual regeneration within the confines of Toledo might have succeeded in its principal aims but for the fateful reappearance of the Babel family with whom he first came into contact during his days of political activism. The tentacles of nineteenth-century Spanish political life continue to stretch out to embrace him even in this religious hide-out, and he cannot shake off the past. The presence of the Babels in the novel is also important because of the varying attitudes towards contemporary political events that they exhibit, attitudes which are really ironic inversions of some of those previously held by Angel. In many ways they are also an anticipation of the bizarre Ansúrez family whose different members stand as a symbol of a diseased and divided Spain in the fourth and fifth series of the *episodios nacionales*.

The parents, Catalina and Simón, illustrate the two types of approach to history recorded in *Angel Guerra*. Catalina's absurd pretensions about her royal ancestry (both English and Spanish) offer a grotesque parody of the past history of Toledo and its churches which plays an important part in Angel's religious conversion. Her centuries-old dynasty, she asserts, is superior to that of the families currently occupying or claiming the Spanish throne: "Dijo que ella no reclama la corona de España porque no quiere chocar, pero que su dinastía es la legítima, así, así, y que don Carlos y Alfonso son unos usurpadores" (V, 1424-5). Such ridiculous pretensions are matched by the government service and contemporary political interest of her husband, Simón, whose transition from revolutionary plotter to government functionary, with promotion at the end to the Ministry, coincides with Angel's move to Toledo. The hilarious commotion that he and the other drunken amateur plotters, Pito and Bailón, create during heady oratory sessions is a parody of Angel's plotting activities and their failure recorded in the opening chapter of the novel. Simón has a "bigote militar prolongado, como el del general León" (V, 1216),[4] and boasts stupidly of engineering national events: "Si no es por mí, no llama la reina a O'Donnell el cincuenta y seis . . ., porque, verán ustedes . . . Estábamos Escosura y yo en Gobernación, cuando . . ." (V, 1217).[5] When he fawns over the generous Angel, he uses the events of history, and in particular those of 1868 — that cardinal event in Galdós's life and career[6] —, to justify his newly acquired conservatism:

> El sesenta y ocho, hasta las clases pudientes nos alegrábamos de que hubiese jaleo; pero los tiempos han cambiado, y ya miramos mal al elemento levantisco. Lo que me decía don Juan Prim cuando la Constituyente: "Desengáñese usted, amigo Babel: el país lo que quiere es trabajar." Vengan tratados de comercio,

---

[4] Diego de León (1807-1841) won a famous victory at Belascoaín against Carlist forces in the First Carlist War (1838). He was executed for his attempt to abduct Queen Isabel to the Basque Country.

[5] Patricio de la Escosura (1807-1878), writer and politician (first, a *moderado*, then, a *progresista*), served as Ministro de Gobernación under Espartero in 1854.

[6] See my "Galdós, the Madrid Royal Palace . . .".

vengan ferrocarriles y venga moralidad administrativa. Cierto que
no faltará el día menos pensado una revolucioncita, porque la
sociedad no anda bien; pero vendrá en tiempo maduro, y cuando
las clases conservadoras la pidamos ... A propósito, querido
Angel, hoy estuvo a verme aquel buen Argüelles que se interesa
por mí en el Ministerio, y me dijo que el ministro desea mis ser-
vicios en la Inspección del Timbre.

(V, 1287)

These absurd claims to have hob-nobbed with the great figures of the
past, reminiscent of José Izquierdo's anecdotes in *Fortunata y Jacinta*,
reveal the emptiness of Simón's political ideas and his total concern for
his own economic survival through political patronage, thus providing
an ironic counterpoint to Angel's involvement with national history.

Simón's brother, the crippled mariner Pito, is also used in a
similarly reflective function, though not from the political standpoint.
A veteran of overseas heroics, he is given to exaggeration when narrating
his adventures. Land-locked in Madrid and Toledo, Pito can only return
to the vastness of the open sea in alcohol-fuelled stupors. Like Angel he
feels happiest in the wild solitude of the *cigarral* and philosophizes
about the emptiness of life. Yet his tragic sense of life can be quickly
dispelled by carnal delights, alimentary or sexual. Violence is also a
resort that comes quickly to his mind. Pito is, then, another lesson for
Angel to read, mark and inwardly digest, as he ponders his own religious retreat.

Dulcenombre, the most sympathetic member of the Babel
family, professes disregard for the whole political process. Drawn into
the revolutionary maelstrom through her association with Angel, she
readily admits that her only preoccupation in life is her love for him:
"Debo alegrarme de que las revoluciones salgan mal y de que eso que
llaman la cosa pública te ponga la cara fea, para que te guste más la
mía. Yo, como no tengo nada que ver con la cosa pública ni me importa, te quiero y te querré siempre lo mismo" (V, 1213); "Mientras te
tenga a ti, ¿qué me importa que al país se lo lleven los demonios? Bien
mirado, es tontería apurarse por esa entidad oscura y vaga que llamamos
el país, y que no se cuida de los que se sacrifican por él" (V, 1214).[7] As
with Fortunata and the heroines in the later *episodios nacionales*, love
becomes an antidote and not a complement to political activism. Yet it
is also as self-deceiving and possessive as political activism because the
individual ego dominates all other considerations.

---

[7] Leré too shows a lack of interest in Angel's political confession as she sews.
Both she and Dulce are compared by Angel to historical figures, but of the distant
past.

Angel Guerra is typical of many characters in both of our Groups I and II of the *serie contemporánea* who, wittingly or unwittingly, exploit politics for their own ends, whether those ends be altruistic or materialistic. He tries to progress to a more spiritual code of values and away from an absorption in the world of historical/political processes to a greater, more conscious extent than characters such as Fortunata, Villaamil, Carlos Cisneros and Torquemada. And in this attempt he could be said to reflect the same yearning of Galdós himself, a yearning which, however, is still inevitably controlled and curtailed by his sense of the historical moment and his inevitable involvement with it. Unlike the fictional character, the author cannot yet jettison that part of his experience. But Angel's attempts to do so prove a failure because he does not comprehend the dominance of the ego in his own and other people's actions. He fails to realize that association with others in some kind of miniature society will only repeat the conflicts of will between competing egos that characterize traditional society. The historical lessons provided for Angel by the tragic events of the real "episodio nacional" of 1866 – the executions of the sergeants – and of its fictional duplication in the abortive coup of 1883 are not absorbed by Angel in the correct way because his wounded pride is too much of an obstacle. Surely the lesson of the historical episode of 1866 for Galdós is the essential inhumanity of man to his fellow human beings, of one Spaniard to another. It is this tragic outlook which retains Galdós's residual interest in the march of public events, the nasty jolt of real history which will always hold his attention, while the inane droll of parliamentary speeches, political wheeling-and-dealing and public oratory will be happily abandoned.[8] His attitude to the last category of national historical event has been consistently contemptuous throughout the *serie contemporánea*. In Angel's excruciating recollections of the San Gil executions and the narrator's independent comments on official history we are almost returning to the anguish of José Relimpio in the first novel of the series. However, in *Angel Guerra* Galdós is not using the 1866 incident as a base for the reconstruction of an historical period as in *La desheredada*, but is applying it as a pertinent measuring stick by which to gauge an individual character's reaction and motivation, and also as an escape-valve for his own conflicting views. The

---

[8] In his *Memorias de un desmemoriado* (1915), almost fifty years after the event, Galdós could still eloquently and movingly express his eternal abhorrence of the 1866 executions: "Como espectáculo tristísimo, el más trágico y siniestro que he visto en mi vida, mencionaré el paso de los sargentos de Artillería llevados al patíbulo en coche, de dos en dos, por la calle de Alcalá arriba, para fusilarlos en las tapias de la antigua Plaza de Toros" (VI, 1672).

paradox of Angel's experience is that now we have a fictional character traumatically affected by an historical event, but who, despite the lingering, indelible traces of that experience, fails to absorb the correct lessons because of an obstructive ego.

PART III

MINIMAL VESTIGES

a) *Tristana* (1892)

Sandwiched between, and in contrast to, *Angel Guerra* and the last three novels of the *Torquemada* tetralogy, *Tristana* records only a minimum of historical references, thereby entitling it to be considered alongside the later *Nazarín* (1895), *Halma* (1895) and *Misericordia* (1897) in our Group III of the *serie contemporánea*.

In *Tristana* the historical material reveals no overall pattern of relevance for the total meaning of the novel as was the case in our Groups I and II. This indifference to the political/historical frame of contemporary society is all the more surprising in a novel where, in the well-known world of the Madrid suburb of Chamberí, and at a time more or less contemporaneous with that of the narration, the contentious social problem of women's rights and careers is dominant. The mention of national politics occurs only briefly when Tristana and the servant Saturna are reviewing the professions open to women. For the latter politics are a closed shop to women, but Tristana energetically asserts that she could make as good a politician as any man:

> Pues yo te digo ... que hasta para eso del Gobierno y la política me parece a mí que había de servir yo. No te rías. Sé pronunciar discursos. Es cosa muy fácil. Con leer un poquitín de las sesiones de Cortes, en seguida te enjareto lo bastante para llenar medio periódico.
>
> (V, 1550)

Don Lope will, of course, brook no such female emancipation. He is a figure of the Golden Age past, with an exaggerated sense of honour which, although prompting laudable acts of generosity to Tristana's father and to Tristana herself, alienates him from contemporary society. He abhors all the official organs of the modern state — the police, the law courts, the tax office, the Church and the army —, and anachronistically believes that the modern army should be organized

on the lines of the medieval orders of chivalry! More seriously, like
Feijoo in *Fortunata y Jacinta*, he considers that man is subject to no
law of society in matters of love: "Sostenía que en las relaciones de
hombre y mujer no hay más ley que la anarquía, si la anarquía es ley;
que el soberano amor no debe sujetarse más que a su propio canon in-
trínseco, y que las limitaciones externas de su soberanía no sirven más
que para desmedrar la raza" (V, 1547). Tristana's love for Horacio
upsets these egotistical ideas, and though in the end he takes sole
possession of his woman, it is in conformity with the laws of society,
marrying the crippled and distracted Tristana in church: ". . . unas
breves fórmulas hiciéronla [Tristana] legítima esposa de Garrido, en-
casillándola en un hueco honroso de la sociedad" (V, 1611). Their
anarchical tendencies overcome, both end up good bourgeois pillars
of society.

Given the novel's dialectic – from potential disorder to questionable order, it is surprising that Galdós does not choose to pencil in
precise parallels with recent Spanish history, as he had done in *Angel
Guerra*. It is as if the counterpoint of precise contemporary history no
longer interests him because he is now placing all his attention on the
ultimately futile struggle of the individual to surmount and obliterate
the socio-political frame. If the latter is now accorded any vestigial
mention in general, odd, fleeting allusions, it is because it is the supreme
obstacle to which his protagonists will eventually and reluctantly suc-
cumb. The "femlibbism" of Tristana like the *donjuanismo* of Don Lope
is eventually controlled and diverted into the proper channels by
society. The same fate will befall Nazarín's evangelical crusade.

b) *Nazarín* (1895)

Nazarín likes to consider himself as a person who does not
belong to his age. Wishing to recreate the world of Jesus, he rejects the
historical social frame of the present in favour of a return to a past
mystical age. This profound anti-historicism governs his ideological
repudiation of any form of printed word, including the novel and the
history book:

> Ya verá entonces el que lo viere el caso que hace la Humanidad
> de tanto poema, de tanta novela mentirosa, de tanta historia que
> nos refiere hechos cuyo interés se desgasta con el tiempo y aca-
> bará por perderse en absoluto. La memoria humana es ya pajar
> chico para tanto fárrago de Historia.
>
> (V, 1686)

It also determines his journey into the countryside. The decision to practise a form of evangelical Christian charity is presented, however, as an act of social rebellion, an escape from the proper demands of society's law officers, although Nazarín himself tries — unsuccessfully — to gloss over its social significance. Nazarín does perform charitable works, but he has ignored the reasonable claims of the Law to enquire about his involvement in the fire in the Madrid tenement house, and the police are justified in interpreting his flight to the country as evidence of his guilt.

It is interesting to note that his first encounter after escaping the confines of Madrid is with a group of soldiers. His first impression is one of alarm: he believes that a real battle is being fought. This obvious misinterpretation receives the proper corrective from the ocular expression of the roadside dog that attached himself to him:

> ...“No se asuste, señor amo mío, que esto es todo de mentiri-jillas, y así se están todo el año los de tropa, tirando tiros y corriendo unos en pos de otros. Por lo demás, si nos acercamos a la hora en que meriendan, crea que algo nos ha de tocar, que ésta es gente muy liberal y amiga de los pobres.”
> Un ratito estuvo Nazarín contemplando aquel lindo juego y viendo cómo se deshacían en el aire los humos de los fogonazos.
>
> (V, 1710)

Nazarín fails to appreciate the lesson that reality is offering here in the form of these military manoeuvres. Even in the country society needs to make its presence felt and its guardians need to remain ever vigilant against its enemies, who could well include him. For the reporter in Part I finds his ideas on evangelical charity socially dangerous, and society's administrative role is indeed subverted by his precipitate aid to the villages of Villamanta and Villamantilla before the arrival of the government doctors.

Nazarín's contempt for the structures of existing society takes its bitterest form in his condemnation of politics:

> ... la política es agua pasada. Cumplió su misión, y los que se llamaban problemas políticos, tocantes a libertad, derechos etc., están ya resueltos, sin que por eso la Humanidad haya descubierto el nuevo paraíso terrenal.
>
> (V, 1726)

Politics cannot solve today's problems and he is tired of the empty rhetoric and the absurd posturings of political nonentities. Here Nazarín could almost be voicing Galdós's own constant complaint about the political system. Does that mean that the latter can go as far as his protagonist and reject it totally? In *Angel Guerra* he had fantasized somewhat through the fictional adventure of Angel's religious order about such a possibility, but he had finally rejected the experiment as impossible. Angel could not escape the pull of the national past, as his nightmare of the 1866 executions proved. In *Nazarín* Galdós again allows his fictional protagonist to wander down the road of idealistic experiment, whilst he, as author-narrator, retains a more balanced and realistic perspective, not now from the angle of the historical past, but from an awareness of society's political structures. The puffed-up ignoramuses whom Nazarín abhors so much do control his life and actions when they perceive him to be a threat to the system.

No such lack of awareness is shown by those marginal misfits, the beggars whom Nazarín meets in the countryside. They are very eager to know who is in control in Madrid because political attitudes and policies implemented by the forces of law and order directly affect them. Such an interest and the mention of politicians' names on the beggars' lips sound quite a paradox; society's rulers and outcasts are joined in one grotesque association, which is given visual form at the beginning of the novel when one of the characters celebrating Carnival at *Chanfaina*'s boarding house carries a mask of the Prime Minister (V, 1680). Likewise, the old man who accompanies Nazarín in the chain-gang back to Madrid at the end of the novel absurdly claims that he has lost his place in the Civil Service because Cánovas gave up the premiership at an inopportune time: ". . . derribaron al Gobierno para evitar mi reposición" (V, 1754). It is a preposterous claim, of course, but not too dissimilar in tone and general content to those uttered on occasion by Tomás Rufete in *La desheredada* and Ramón Villaamil in *Miau*. Nazarín is, of course, uninterested in this political talk just as earlier he had been unable to confirm to one of the tramps whether Sagasta had resigned or not from the premiership. Yet it is to the reality of the Sagastan regime that he is led back at the end. He now has to learn how to preserve his evangelical ideals within the straitjacket of organized Restoration society run by the professional politicians. This is the same lesson that his pupil Halma will eventually learn, to her final advantage, in the sequel that bears her name.

c) *Halma* (1895)

Nazarín's forced return to Madrid (to await trial) and the realities of contemporary society is accompanied in *Halma* by a number of assertions which stress the authenticity of the narration in an apparent reversal of the conclusions forcefully established in *Nazarín* about the impossibility of expressing the paradoxes of reality. *Halma* has a sure source for its account, the "archivo nazarista", and the narrator now considers himself "un historiador de conciencia" (V, 1772). However, Nazarín continues to be a curious enigma to be pawed over by all sections of society including the country's political leaders, and even Cánovas, presumably at this time Opposition Leader, is opposed to giving Nazarín a stiff sentence.[1] This fascination with the itinerant priest is the latest fad of Madrid society, just as at other times it will be "una moda de exaltaciones democráticas" (V, 1788). The threat which Nazarín's universal evangelism poses for the vital notion of national unity and patriotism is inversely represented by a reporter who compares his prison cell to a Minister's antechamber.

Nazarín's formidable ideological opponent is Feramor, brother of Halma and the only resident in Madrid who is not interested in Nazarín or *nazarismo*. A member of the Senate and a great administrator, he would be capable of putting order into the accounts of the Finance Ministry, according to the priest Flores. He is a great admirer of the English parliamentary system and is hailed as a saviour of Spain because of his practical sense of economics. One of the old landed aristocracy, he devotes his life and energies to serving the modern State in a way that seems to realize the hopes cherished by Cristóbal Medina in *Lo prohibido*. Yet this paragon of patriotic service does nothing more than make a few boring speeches in the Cortes, and arranging usurious loans seems to attract his greater interest. In short, Feramor is the typical hypocritical paladin of Restoration society and its empty materialistic values. Consequently, he is totally opposed to his sister's desire to use her inheritance to set up a religious commune at Pedralba.

For Halma's intentions are clearly as rebellious as Nazarín's had been: she wants to make a total break with the bourgeois capitalist society represented by her brother and his associates, "aquellas cabezas atiborradas de política, de falsa piedad y de una moral compuesta y bonita para uso de las familias elegantes" (V, 1862). In accordance with her democratic ideas, Halma tries to establish at Pedralba the notion of social equality as well as religious fundamentalism. However, her small band of followers still persists in calling her by her aristocratic title, even exaggerating her rank: ". . . la doña Catalina es reina, sí, señor, una reina o emperadora de los extranjis de allá muy lejos, y . . . hubo una

---

[1] He again replaced Sagasta as Prime Minister in March 1895: so the novel's chronology is very contemporary, 1892-1895.

rigolución por donde la echaron del trono, y el Papa Santísimo la mandó acá en son de penitencia" (V, 1833). The reference is hyperbolic but it does serve to underline the revolutionary nature of Halma's plans which are unconsciously aimed at the subversion of traditional society. The Queen of a new order should be a person like Halma, but normal society will not allow her to set up a rival hierarchy and structure. The representatives of the pillars of the Spanish Establishment − Remigio (Church), Laínez (State) and Amador (Science) − come to Pedralba, disunited and squabbling, to inform her of the claims of the traditional order to which she must now conform. Halma finally recognizes this interdependence of the microcosm and the macrocosm of the State: ". . . no somos libres . . . dependemos de una autoridad" (V, 1863). Forced to return to Madrid, Halma and Urrea, like Nazarín before them, must co-exist with and within the traditional hierarchies. This they manage to do, but at the same time they preserve their independence as a joint unit: "Esto no es ya un instituto religioso ni benéfico, ni aquí hay ordenanzas ni reglamentos, ni más ley que la de una familia cristiana, que vive en su propiedad. *Nosotros nos gobernamos solos, y gobernamos nuestra cara ínsula*" (my italics; V, 1874).

As if to emphasize the debasement of the outer traditional structures, Galdós allows Urrea to resolve the two outstanding problems (his marriage to Halma and Nazarín's discharge by the authorities) through a manipulation of the old political system. Urrea uses Severiano Rodríguez's antipathy towards Feramor to secure Remigio's transfer to a Madrid parish, and the news of this appointment produces from Remigio the hilarious announcement that Nazarín's sanity will be easily certified. The socio-political structure remains unchanged in the lives of contemporary Spaniards but for the more spiritually aware fictional characters it no longer represents a source of anguish and despair because it has ceased to interest: for them the collectivity is not worth changing, for only the individual can change in the company of those whom he or she loves and is loved by, although that love is still sexually based. Galdós's continuing study of the rightful place of the individual within contemporary society and the nature of that relationship may not need the precise corroboration of recent national events, but it can never jettison the general outline of the socio-political entity whose functioning, through precise historical events, does influence and finally control individual destinies.[2]

---

[2] G.G. Minter, "*Halma* and the writings of St. Augustine", *AG*, 13 (1978), pp.86-89, puts forward an interesting, if ultimately unconvincing, suggestion that the novel can be viewed as a commentary on the great nineteenth-century polemic over the separation of the temporal and spiritual powers of the Papacy.

d) *Misericordia* (1897)

It has generally been recognized that in Benina Galdós achieves the definitive crystallization of a positive reaction to a corrupt society. Her charitable Christian spirit, free of the complications of sexual lust and egotism, puts her above the pettiness of the contemporary world, allowing her to be unaffected by the capricious turns of fate. Her final serenity of spirit is also achieved within Restoration Spain and in the knowledge that all civilized society is basically the same and that, therefore, there is no point in escaping to distant parts as Almudena suggests from time to time and as Nazarín, Angel Guerra and Halma had vainly attempted. Galdós's definitive statement on the whole question of the relationship of the individual to contemporary society is formulated by Benina towards the end of the novel:

> . . . en dondequiera que vivan los hombres, o verbigracia, mujeres, habrá ingratitud, egoísmo y unos que manden a los otros y les cojan la voluntad. Por lo que debemos hacer lo que nos manda la conciencia y dejar que se peleen aquéllos por un hueso, como los perros; los otros por un juguete, como los niños, o éstos por mangonear, como los mayores, y no reñir con nadie, y tomar lo que Dios nos ponga delante, como los pájaros.
>
> (V, 1988)

Benina's firm incorporation within organized society is emphasized from the beginning. The band of beggars which besieges the worshippers at the church of San Sebastián has a well-defined hierarchy: Casiana and Pulido are its leaders and *La Burlada* its persistent rebel, while Benina occupies the lowest position. *La Burlada* makes ironical political references in her argument with the *Caporala*: "¡Ay hija . . ., ni que *fuas* Cánovas!" (V, 1881); ". . . señora presidenta de ministros . . . Vuestra eminencia ilustrísima" (V, 1886). Surrounding the church like an army, this "cuadrilla de miseria" wages a war "por la pícara existencia" on a battlefield which is covered, not with blood, but with bugs and insects. Moreover, this miniature society, with its major and minor capitalists, is one of many in Madrid. The beggars who gather around the church of San Andrés have a similar, if less tyrannical, organization. Indeed, according to the priest Romualdo, the whole of Spain is filled with beggars and paupers, and the country will soon become the largest workhouse in Europe.

As in the preceding novels of our Group III, the marginal characters who live outside the social order but reflect its structure in their own organization, perform the task of sketching in the few precise political references there are. The beggars maintain that the poor times for their profession are the result of the political situation. Thus Pintado laments:

> ¡Quién se acuerda del San José del primer año de Amadeo! ... Pero ya ni los santos del cielo son como es debido ... Todo es por tanto pillo como hay en la política *pulpitante*, y el aquel de las suscripciones para las *vítimas* ... Limosna hay, buenas almas hay; pero liberales por un lado, el *Congrieso* dichoso, y por otro las *congriogaciones*, los *metingos* y *discursiones* y tantas cosas de imprenta, quitan la voluntad a los más cristianos.
>
> (V, 1878)

He also prophesies that a revolution is imminent because "los *artistas* [artesanos?] pedían *las ocho horas* y los *amos* no querían darlas" (V, 1915). Martínez Palacio's suggestion that these beggars are a grotesque parody of the empty pompous world of Restoration Spain is entirely correct and acceptable.[3] By concentrating his attention on the lowest members of society Galdós shows that the values and attitudes of the Establishment permeate all classes and that there is no escape from the effects of the political system. Spanish society is, by association, then, a group of beggars. Symbol and reality meet when the beggars of San Sebastián harass the guests at a high-society wedding, falling upon the wedding party in such mad confusion that the guests are stampeded into throwing money to the jostling crowd: "Era como un motín vencido por su propio cansancio. Los últimos disparos eran: '*Tú cogiste más ..., me han quitado lo mío ..., aquí no hay decencia ..., cuánto pillo ...*' " (V, 1929). In materialistic Restoration Spain, the "episodio nacional" is no longer a feat of arms, or parliamentary manoeuvring even, but a grotesque attack by the outcasts on the columns of normal, established citizenry.

The real revolution that the country needs is a spiritual one which will follow the lead of Benina's charitable behaviour towards others, the culmination of an experiment which Galdós had conducted in earlier novels with such characters as Camila, Fortunata, Villaamil, Nazarín and Halma. Benina does not need to flee to Jerusalem with Almudena, for she can live within the confines of Restoration Spain oblivious of its hierarchies, whether they be imposed by Juliana or by the beggars. In his final assessment of her character, Galdós significantly makes use of the same military terminology with which he had described her colleagues in the band of beggars:

---

3 See Javier Martínez Palacio, "Miseria y parodia galdosiana de la restauración", *Insula*, 26, no. 291 (February 1971), pp.4-5.

... su conciencia le dió inefables consuelos: miró la vida desde la altura en que su desprecio de la humana vanidad la ponía; vió en ridícula pequeñez a los seres que la rodeaban, y su espíritu se hizo fuerte y grande. Había alcanzado glorioso triunfo; sentíase victoriosa, después de haber perdido la batalla en el terreno material.
(V, 1986)

Benina surpasses her colleagues because she is a figure for all seasons and all times. Her dissociation from the flow of contemporary history is dramatically captured when she and Almudena sit at the base of Mendizábal's statue, appropriately situated in the Plaza del Progreso, and try to unravel their grave financial problems: "... quedóse un rato en meditación dolorosa, mirando al suelo y después al cielo y a la estatua de Mendizábal, aquel verdinegro señor de bronce que ella no sabía quién era ni por qué le habían puesto allí" (V, 1887). This sentence resumes very accurately Galdós's anguished, almost total anti-historicism at this stage in his career. The unfulfilled promise of Mendizábal's national economic reforms of 1836-1837 is poignantly recalled in his rusting statue looking down on Spain fifty years or more after his death, a Spain still troubled by fundamental economic problems. Mendizábal's *desamortización* had benefited only a small sector of the country, the bourgeoisie, thereby encouraging their selfish tendencies. The missing factor in his equation for the economic revival of Spain was Christian charity, so manifestly practised by the old woman sitting beneath his statue; if that brotherly love had existed in Mendizábal's day, then the course of nineteenth-century Spanish history would have been vastly different. Talking with Paca, she explains that the market fruit-stalls, the Bank of Spain, the houses in the city, all belong to God, who is her King; Benina overcomes nationalism and patriotism by the greater strength of her religious faith.

The sterile pull of the historical past is represented in *Misericordia* by Frasquito Ponte Delgado, who lives off the memories of his past social glory. A profusion of precise historical data chronicles the exact stages of his social eclipse:

Su decadencia no empezó a manifestarse de un modo notorio hasta el 59: se defendió heroicamente hasta el 68, y al llegar este año, marcado en la tabla de su destino con trazo muy negro, desplomóse el desdichado galán en los abismos de la miseria para no levantarse más ... El destino que con grandes fatigas pudo conseguir de González Bravo, se lo quitó despiadadamente la revolución [i.e. of 1868]; no gozaba cesantía, no había sabido ahorrar.
(V, 1918-9)

His manners, customs, clothes and memories all date from before *La Gloriosa*: his top hat was fashionable in the 1820s, his hair-style in the 1850s, and his shoes were already worn out the year Prim was assassinated. This last detail can serve as a good example of how Galdós's attitude to the incorporation of precise historical data has changed during the course of his writing of the *serie contemporánea*. In *La desheredada* the memory of Prim's tragic death had been the cornerstone of the historical allegory. Sixteen years later in *Misericordia* the same event is presented merely as one of a number of precise one-line historical references to characterize the old-fashioned ways of Ponte before his electrifying encounter with Benina. The allusion to the assassination of Prim has become a faint, off-stage echo which Galdós himself can no longer declare of relevance for his own or any other individual Spaniard's life. Long gone are the days when Galdós felt that he could arouse his compatriots' interest in the relevance of the historical events of the recent past for the contemporary present.[4]

4 In *El abuelo*, written the same year as *Misericordia*, there are a number of statements deriding the value of history: "La verdad es que la Historia nos trae acá mil chismes y enredos que no nos importan nada" (VI, 19); "Tan mentira es una [la Historia] como otra [la Mitología]" (VI, 47). On the topic of history in *El abuelo*, see John Beverley, "Seeing history: reflections on Galdós' *El abuelo*", *AG*, 10 (1975), pp.55-60.

PART IV

THE BRIEF RETURN OF ALLEGORY

The period 1881-1897 was one of continuous novel-writing for Galdós and thus we are justified to some extent in our attempts to trace a coherent development in his treatment of contemporary historical material from *La desheredada* to *Misericordia*. It is true that in 1892 he turned to writing plays for the stage but he did not stop the composition of what he later labelled the *serie contemporánea*. After 1897, the picture changes somewhat: in 1898, under the pressure of financial trouble with his publisher, he resumed work on the *episodios nacionales*, abruptly halted in 1879. The hectic publication of twenty-six *episodios nacionales* in the next fourteen years, along with failing eyesight, left him little time to write contemporary novels. Only three more titles were to be added to the series: *Casandra* (1905), *El caballero encantado* (1909) and *La razón de la sinrazón* (1915). Separated from the mainstream, they can hardly be said to contain any significant body of historical references to the recent past. Nevertheless, in the last two novels at least, Galdós does continue his interest in the general problem of history and its role in individual destinies, now at an abstract allegorical level.

a) *Casandra* (1905)

The first novel of our Group IV really seems a continuation of the style of our Group III novels, with the odd precise fact inserted as mere background information or explanation. The details are suitably associated with the oldest character, Doña Juana, and with her dead husband, Don Hilario, who amassed a fortune "en los aciagos años del 73 al 76, cuando vino el desastre de la Hacienda, cuando el consolidado se plantó en 17, y de allí no subía ni a tiros; cuando la nación no tenía con qué pagar los cañones Krupp, ni con qué dar un rancho el Ejército" (VI, 128). Paradoxically, Doña Juana despises the *nouveaux riches* who have profited from Mendizábal's *desamortización* and she is determined, when she dies, to leave all her money to the Church and not to her host of relatives. The rumour of this intention, in turn, motivates the fatal attack by Casandra and the latter's consequent imprisonment, with Juana's money reverting to the overjoyed relatives. Clementina may utter political names in her epileptic attacks, and Insúa and Cebrían may have served in the Carlist court, but these facts are not given any prominence, the main theme of the novel being centered on the hypocrisy of the bourgeoisie who use religion for material gain. There is no suggestion either that the individual is struggling against the socio-political structure. None the less, historical events are at the root of Doña Juana's attitude towards her relations, and are thus the starting point for the plot.

b) *El caballero encantado* (1909)

The penultimate novel in the series can be considered Galdós's most politically committed novel.[1] Written when he was actively engaged in national politics as the leader of the Socialist-Republican coalition, it deals with concrete socio-political problems affecting contemporary Spain. Whilst most of the other novels in the series dwelt on the hollowness of national politics in the capital, *El caballero encantado* deals with the pernicious effects of Government measures and policies as experienced in the countryside. The two worlds are joined in contrast by the fantastic experiences of Tarsis, a Madrid *señorito* who is magically transformed into a country labourer with the name of Gil. Before his metamorphosis he is shown to possess a cynical disregard for the empty values of Restoration society:

> ¿Pues por qué sostengo que tampoco hay aquí política? Porque la que tenemos se ha hecho aristocrática. Fijaos en el pisto que nos damos los diputados, en la vanidad de los ministros, que ocupan ancho espacio en la sociedad por el viento de que están inflados. ¿Hay aquí un político que tenga algo en la cabeza? Ninguno.
> (VI, 233)

He also laments the absence of any decent agricultural system, justice, industry or banking in Spain. He thus has a basis on which a spiritual reform can be undertaken, and this is precisely the purpose of his

[1] See Joseph Schraibman, "Galdós y 'el estilo de la vejez' ", *Homenaje a Rodríguez-Moñino* (Madrid, 1966), II, pp.165-75; Julio Rodríguez-Puértolas, *Galdós: burguesía y revolución* (Madrid, 1975), pp.93-176.

voyage of fantasy through the Spanish countryside. He now witnesses at first hand the problems of tenant farming and land tenure, the terrible poverty of the ghost town of Boñices and the abysmal level of State education in the country schools. Finally he suffers the tyranny of the *caciques* in his jobs as shepherd, miner and archaeological digger.

During this voyage of discovery of the nation's social ills, he is accompanied and instructed at various times by the allegorical figure of La Madre, a personification of Spain's history since the dawn of time. She is clearly a sister to a similarly allegorical figure, Mariclío, who is a prominent figure in the last series of the *episodios nacionales* which Galdós had interrupted to write *El caballero encantado*.[2] However, La Madre's historical lessons are confined to the distant past, and there is very little mention in the novel of nineteenth-century events. These crop up in the account of the past life of Celedonia Recajo, who married when Fernando VII was still King and can recall Espartero's victory parade in Madrid in 1854. There is no mention whatsoever of the events which rocked Spain during the composition of *El caballero encantado*: the *semana trágica* in Barcelona, when protests against the renewed war in Morocco led to bloody street clashes and the internationally condemned execution of Francisco Ferrer. The only allusion is very indirect, La Madre commenting that "toda guerra que mis hijos traben con gente mora me parece guerra civil" (VI, 294).

For an active political leader of the day, Galdós's stony silence about contemporary events is understandable; but not so his reluctance to include documented events of earlier nineteenth-century history . . . unless he had an ulterior motive. The escapist, nostalgic nature of this historical spirit incarnated in La Madre is underlined by the figure of Becerro, the antiquarian and digger at the ruins of Numancia. It is he who is responsible for Tarsis's voyage of self-discovery in the Spanish countryside and the *señorito*'s important meetings with La Madre. Becerro is always her most obedient servant, championing the supreme value of "la historia alta, . . . la que nos cuenta las virtudes máximas" (VI, 277). However, once he loses his job at Numancia, he changes his tune and in spite rejects Tarsis's definition of La Madre as "alma de la raza, triunfadora del tiempo y de las calamidades públicas; la que al mismo tiempo es tradición inmutable y revolución continua":

> . . . las Madres pasaron, las Hermanas también . . . No hay historia de lo presente. Lo presente no es más que espuma, fermentación, podredumbre. Lo mejor será que nos muramos todos

---

[2] See Hinterhäuser, pp.113-14.

prontito. Después, el caos . . ., un caos delicioso.

(VI, 323)

The *volte-face* is very significant as Galdós now seems to be placing in doubt the utility of an identification with the spirit of the country's history, when in the Group I novels this was the ideal goal to be strived after.

When they return to the twentieth-century normality of Madrid society after their magical tour, Tarsis and his wife, Pascual (-Cintia), propose to implement La Madre's ideal of total social regeneration achieved by a social harmony based on a synthesis of all classes. As I have argued elsewhere, Galdós seems to place the feasibility of this utopian dream in doubt.[3] As the young couple listen to a Beethoven symphony at the mansion of one of their aristocratic friends, they enunciate to themselves the main points of their reform plans: they will drain the swamps around Boñices and build a new town upon the same land; they will construct twenty thousand schools in the whole of Spain and their son will become a teacher of teachers; Becerro will become National Archivist and a statue will be erected to the eccentric Don Alquiborontifosio, the pupil-less schoolmaster of Boñices. Finally the *caciques* will be sent to sweep the roads and distribute the newspapers! Feeling very happy with each other, they slip home to make love! Once more, it seems, Galdós's fictional and historical characters fail to measure up to the situation. They cannot absorb the true lesson which La Madre gives them: that she is their creation and that only they — Tarsis-Gil and Pascuala-Cintia or all individual Spaniards, whom the couple represent — are responsible for the course of Spanish history. The future prosperity of all Spain lies in the selfless, harmonious *convivencia* of her children, she insists, repeating the note that had echoed behind the tragedy of historical and fictional events in *La desheredada* and all the other novels of the *serie contemporánea*. Yet she also indicates to Tarsis that any change in the nature of the individual Spaniard is impossible for her or anyone else to achieve. She may continually hope for glory and power once more, but she more or less denies the possibility of that dream by accepting the fundamental corruption of Spaniards, jesting: "Te asombras, hijo, de que teniendo tu Madre un poquito de virtud sobrenatural, sazonada . . ., con unas gotas de humorismo sepa trastornar de vez en cuando las leyes de la Naturaleza y no acierte a corregir o atenuar siquiera la condición aviesa de los

---

[3] See my "Sex, egotism and social regeneration in Galdós' *El caballero encantado*", *Hispania*, 62 (1979), pp.20-29.

hombres?" (VI, 332-3). The vengeful nature of the lovers' programme proclaimed during the Beethoven concert, the lack of realism in most of the proposals and the artificiality of the physical surroundings in which the plan is expounded, all point towards the absence of change in their condition: they are still self-centred aristocrats. The importance of La Madre's revelation of the limitation of her powers cannot be underestimated. Here we have the Spirit of Spanish History confessing the cause of her weakness, the source of all her tragedies, to be the corrupt nature of individual Spaniards. This has been Galdós's conclusion throughout all the other novels in the *serie contemporánea*. In the penultimate novel of the series the faulty moral condition of man is related to the whole sweep of Spanish history, for he still cannot conceive of isolating the individual Spaniard from his national historical context.

c) *La razón de la sinrazón* (1915)

Another apparently optimistic solution to the problem of the individual's place in society is advanced in the last novel of the *serie contemporánea*. General allusions to the power structure, rather than precise references, are the norm: Alejandro becomes a Government Minister, but detests the patronage and corruption of his leaders, Dióscoro and Pánfilo. Wanting to serve his country in a more noble way, he decides to introduce drastic new agrarian laws. However, his intention to divide up the *latifundios* meets with stiff opposition and he is forced to retire from politics to a life of married bliss in the Campo de Vera with his beloved Atenaida. There they practise "la verdadera santidad, que consiste en cultivar la tierra para extraer de ella los elementos de vida, y cultivar los cerebros vírgenes, plantel de las inteligencias que en su madurez han de ser redentoras" (VI, 393). The novel closes with an important proclamation by Atenaida, similar to the lovers' programme in *El caballero encantado*:

ATENAIDA — (*Avanzando con solemne arrogancia como personificación de una idea sublime.*) Ved en esta mujer humilde el símbolo de la Razón triunfante. (*Alejandro y el Cura la contemplan extáticos; y ella, soberanamente hermosa, pronuncia las últimas palabras.*) Somos los creadores del bienestar humano. El raudal de la vida nace en nuestras manos fresco y cristalino; no estamos subordinados a los que, lejos de aquí, lo enturbian. Somos el manantial que salta bullicioso; ellos, la laguna dormida. (*El rostro de Atenaida aparece coronado de estrellas.*)
(VI, 395)

These are fine words, but the fantastic nature of the novel raises doubts about Galdós's unqualified faith in this ideal of an idyllic country retreat far from the maddening political crowd. He may still allow himself the luxury of such an escapist dream, but, ever the realist, he is prompted by his fifth column of reason to surround that wild dream with fictional constraints. Thirty-five years before, he opened his *serie contemporánea* with another escapist scene in which the individual (Tomás Rufete) dreamed of closing down the Spanish Parliament to get some personal peace from the harassing politicians. The dream is lovely, Galdós seems to be saying, especially when, as he has shown in all the novels of the *serie contemporánea*, that political system is nauseatingly corrupt; but the sad reality is another story. Dreams remain unrealized and unrealizable in Restoration Spain.

CONCLUSION

The principal aim of our study was to determine whether the novels of the *serie contemporánea* constitute a special kind of historical novel. At a basic level all of the novels of the series consciously and deliberately reproduce the fundamental relationship of individual Spaniard to Spanish society in the nineteenth century and are therefore historical. Galdós may vary his presentation, preferring now a densely detailed idiom, now a more vague or generalized colouring, but he always presents his characters and their stories within the historical parameters of contemporary Spanish political society as he knew it. Even so, it could be objected that by this basic definition any novel could be called "historical", and that the passages of historical/political material in the *serie contemporánea* are relatively few and brief and are not regularly alternated with fictional developments as is normal in the traditional historical novel and in Galdós's own *episodios nacionales*. Indeed, if quantity is the yardstick for measuring the importance of such passages, we are obliged to accept the conventional notion that by including these historical references Galdós is merely "authenticating" his pictures of contemporary Spanish life, making them more or less plausible by placing them within recognizable historical frames. However, such a viewpoint ignores the consistency and subtlety with which Galdós inserts historical details throughout the series, often at strategically important places and in such a way as to form an integrated and meaningful pattern.

The majority of the factually precise references to nineteenth-century Spanish history occur in the first of the four groups into which we have divided the *serie contemporánea*. In the remaining three groups, they gradually decrease, with isolated passages in Group II, the odd reference in Group III, and practically nothing in Group IV.

In Groups I and II the range of the references seems particularly comprehensive. The major events of the period 1860 to 1890 are covered: the 1860 African campaign (*Torquemada en la cruz*); the pre-revolutionary period, 1863-1868 (*El doctor Centeno*, *Tormento* and *Angel Guerra*); the 1868 *Septembrina* (*La de Bringas*); Amadeo's short-lived reign, the Second Carlist War, the First Republic and the Restoration of the Bourbon dynasty (1870-1875) (*La desheredada* and *Fortunata y Jacinta*). The latter novel is also noteworthy for the amount of historical detail about earlier periods of Spanish history. None the less, the limits are still the nineteenth century, as they are in the *episodios nacionales*. When Galdós strays into other centuries of Spanish history (as in *El doctor Centeno*, *Tristana*, *Angel Guerra* and *Halma*), historical detail is used as a contrastive device to offset the attitudes of characters towards contemporary society. In short, there is a certain homogeneity about the historical details in the novels of Groups I and II. Through these fragmented snatches Galdós is constructing a mosaic of recent national history.

The manner in which these specifically mentioned events are covered varies considerably. Galdós can be very meticulous in his chronicling: for example, individual incidents of the Second Carlist War are faithfully recorded in *La desheredada*, as are those of the 1860 African campaign in *Torquemada en la cruz*. Over other periods, like the pre-revolutionary years of 1863-1868, he prefers to skate rather rapidly, only highlighting salient events like the 1866 execution of the San Gil sergeants (*Angel Guerra*) or the *Noche de San Daniel* revolt (*Fortunata y Jacinta*). The relative absence of any significant post-1875 coverage is due not only to the relative calm of the Restoration period, but also to the change in Galdós's use of historical matter after 1888.

In Group I, above all, Galdós turns his gaze back a number of years, but at the same time he relates the past to the contemporary period of the novel's composition. In so doing he is suggesting a) that there is a very important continuum in nineteenth-century history; b) that the Spain of the Restoration from which he was writing is intimately linked, as it surely was, to those periods between 1860 and 1875 which he treats separately in his novels of Groups I and II; and c) that not much has changed or will change in Restoration Spain since those days of yester-year. Galdós could not have enjoyed a better vantage point to make this observation than his Cortes seat in Sagasta's *Parlamento largo* of 1885-1890. If we have no political speeches at this time with which to corroborate this conclusion, the record contained in the articles he wrote for the Buenos Aires newspaper, *La Prensa*, is singularly helpful.

This ability and desire to see the never-ending parallelisms in nineteenth-century Spanish history had been evident in the first words Galdós published, the preamble to the historical novel *La Fontana de Oro* (1870), where he claimed that there could be a "relación . . . entre muchos sucesos aquí referidos [1820-1823] y algo de lo que aquí pasa [December 1870]" (III, 10). Galdós possessed the mind of an historian, perceiving a pattern in the chaotic succession of political events over the years. In Group I, however, he is not writing as a professional historian, but cultivating what Deegan calls the "novel of the historical imagination". His brief, indirect presentation of the data merely records events and does not permit any exploration of their cause or implications. Instead, he relies upon the strength of his fictional story, with its profound study of human behaviour and motivation, to suggest to the reader the possible human reasons behind the historical events. By joining the threads of history and fiction at important strategic points in the novels, he is able to encourage the reader to apply the behaviouristic analysis to the historical elements, transferring some of his discoveries on the fictional plane to the historical and vice-versa. This is, indeed, a very economical style of making the historical point without interrupting the flow of the narrative to switch from one strand to another.

This subtle allegorical style is used with notable success in *La desheredada*, *Fortunata y Jacinta* and *La de Bringas*, the last-named being perhaps the most consistently developed allegory or novel of the historical imagination, precisely because the characters and their respective actions on both the fictional and historical levels are correlated in time and space with such exactitude and frequency. In *El doctor Centeno*, *Tormento* and *Miau* the parallelisms are not so strongly forged, but a general similarity of development between fiction and history is maintained, so that the novels still remain allegories of the period.

In the Group II novels, the life of the main protagonist alone (not of a number of characters, as in Group I) is linked to the national scene, with precise and general political statements, but what appears at first to be an allegory of an historical period (in *Torquemada en la hoguera*, *La incógnita* and *Angel Guerra*) gradually becomes a measuring stick by which the character developments of these nationally representative protagonists can be plotted. The novels of Group III contain only the barest of references, with Galdós dropping all allegorical intentions as he zones in on individual attempts to escape Spanish society. In the Group IV novels, however, historical allegory returns briefly, now in abstract proportions, to represent once more the individual Spaniard's relationship with the forces of national history. Thus, three of our four groups of novels go beyond the merely casual authentication of the historical dimensions of their stories in their endeavour to represent the dynamic of the relationship between individual and historical society by means of different shades of allegory.

This immediately raises the question of why Galdós chose this indirect allegorical format instead of composing a more traditional historical novel. The first obvious answer is that, generally speaking, episodes, characters, developments and repercussions of recent national history would be familiar to his reading public. In these novels of the historical imagination even an abstract word like "rasgo" could be full of fruitful political/historical connotations for the reader, as we saw in *La de Bringas*, *Fortunata y Jacinta* and *Angel Guerra*. On other occasions, reticence about certain details is more effective, as in the description of the anti-Amadeo protest in *La desheredada*.

In the novels of our Group I historical events are presented from a distance, when at times a close-up of the reality in question would have been possible and even appropriate. The result is that these historical events are distorted, given a generally farcical tone, only occasionally pierced by discordant tragic notes (Prim's assassination in *La desheredada*, the postscript to General Pavía's 1874 take-over of the Congreso in *Fortunata y Jacinta* and the 1866 execution of the rebellious sergeants of the San Gil barracks in *Angel Guerra*). The relation of these events through the actions, words or emotions of the fictional characters "downgrades" the historical event to some extent, but it is a method of humanization which Galdós pointedly applied in his *episodios nacionales* in the belief that behind the facts, plans and movements of official history there were always persons at play, and that as human beings, they were blessed with the same virtues or afflicted with the same vices as lesser mortals. This is obviously a very simplistic way of looking at often complicated matters and may justify some critics' disregard of the novels of the *serie contemporánea* as valid accounts of history. However, it is a mistake to make excessive demands of a genre which cannot be expected to provide as perfect a record as the history primer, and we would do well to recall Amado Alonso's observation that "la novela histórica fracasa irremediablemente como historia".[1] None the less, Galdós still has a statement to make on the historical events as he perceives and interprets them, and in reducing the complexity of

---

[1] Amado Alonso, *Ensayos sobre la novela histórica* (Buenos Aires, 1942), p.99.

historical developments to a single motivation (basically egotistical materialism, in various shades and measures) he is not doing a disservice to nineteenth-century Spanish history, but pointing out the basic truth that in the last analysis political history is shaped by people of flesh and blood and that the reader himself is capable of shaping public history.

The second reason for Galdós's choice of this indirect method is surely that he wanted to turn his attention to more recent national history, instead of the intermediate past he had so admirably treated in the *episodios nacionales*. He wanted, in other words, to be the historical novelist of a period which had directly affected his own life, but which still could not be regarded as "historical" in the accepted sense because it was so recent. Above all, he thought about contemporary Spanish history and its relation to the nineteenth-century Spaniard. In the *serie contemporánea* there is a philosophy of history – the acid test of a true historical novel for Fleishman[2] – which is expounded briefly and sporadically in *Fortunata y Jacinta* and *La incógnita* and more extensively and emotionally in *El amigo Manso*, *La de Bringas* and *Angel Guerra*. This is proof that Galdós did not turn off the tap of the philosophy of history in 1879 with the end of the second series of the *episodios nacionales*, and leave it turned off till 1898, when he launched into the third series.

Apart from these icebergs of philosophical thought, the whole *serie contemporánea* is a visible confirmation that Galdós was vitally concerned with the question of the role of contemporary public history in the lives of ordinary individuals. In our Group I, amidst the self-seeking politicians, civil servants, and uninterested female figures, there is a small group of individuals who show varying degrees of interest in national political history: Relimpio (*La desheredada*), Florencio Morales (*El doctor Centeno*), Estupiñá (*Fortunata y Jacinta*), Villaamil and Mendizábal (*Miau*). But vanity about their historical role (Morales, Estupiñá, Villaamil) or sexual lust (Relimpio) nullify the potential advantages of the lessons to be derived from their awareness.

This didactic intent is underlined in *La desheredada*, *El amigo Manso*, *El doctor Centeno*, *Fortunata y Jacinta* and *Miau* by the appearance of juvenile or untutored characters who are educated in life's wider lesson by elder guide figures. Inversely, in *La de Bringas* and *Lo prohibido*, the unreliable narrators no longer want to instruct the contemporary reader. If there is any positive attitude advanced to

2 See Fleishman, p.15.

counteract the pull of cynicism or political opportunism, it is the vibrant force of love, first tentatively suggested in *Lo prohibido* in the relationship of Camila and Constantino. Fortunata's fate in *Fortunata y Jacinta* is that she cannot find a suitable lover with whom to develop properly her redemptive ahistorical energies. Dulcenombre in *Angel Guerra* in our Group II is in the same mould, but likewise suffers rejection by her lover, Angel. In our Group III, love, like religious evangelism, has to be purged of its egotistical element before, in *Misericordia*, the humanitarian non-sexual love of Benina for all men and women can be triumphantly opposed in Galdós's one optimistic denouement to the values of those characters who live in normal society and by its rules. In the last two novels of our Group IV, love, albeit sexually based and even egotistical, and political regenerationism are combined, apparently with success, although Galdós's allegorical formulation here creates doubts about the practicability of such perfection in the real world.

In conclusion, then, the theme of contemporary history in the *serie contemporánea*, though one of many, is vitally important for a correct interpretation of Galdós's intentions and achievements in these novels. Because that theme is consistently treated in a meaningful way, all of the novels of the series can be regarded as special types of historical novel, as historical allegories or novels of the historical imagination. History is never bluntly slapped down on the page in blotches; rather fine details are sketched in here and there to suggest wider horizons for the alert reader. Though a separate division in Galdós's fictional writing, the *serie contemporánea* provides an important link, not hitherto recognized, between the first two and the last three series of *episodios nacionales*. There is a continuum in Galdós's writing on Spanish nineteenth-century history, an interest he could never forsake although he was clear-sighted about its depressing negativity. His shorthand, suggestive style in the *serie contemporánea* allowed him to maintain that interest while developing others. The consequence is that the novels of the series are enriched in a manner unequalled by anything written by his immediate predecessors or contemporaries in Spain. What novels prior to *La desheredada* (other than the traditional historical novel) go beyond the mere background chronology of landmark events? Certainly works like Fernán Caballero's *La Gaviota* (1849), Juan Valera's *Pepita Jiménez* (1874) or Pedro Antonio de Alarcón's *El sombrero de tres picos* (1874) give only superficial attention, if any, to the contemporary political reality. To his great credit, Benito Pérez Galdós could not ignore that reality, however depressing for him, and when writing novels where such material could so easily have been omitted.

APPENDIX

FIFTY YEARS OF SPANISH HISTORY
An outline of the historical period 1860-1910

The year 1860 marks the high-water point of one of the few stable political regimes in nineteenth-century Spain: the Unión Liberal government (1856-1863) of Leopoldo O'Donnell, which was a mixture of splinter groups from the two major nineteenth-century political parties, the *moderados* (Centre Conservatives) and the *progresistas* (Liberal Democrats). At this mid-term point, foreign investment and the construction of a railway system had lifted Spain's economy to a new prosperity. Her army had also achieved a notable victory over the Sultan of Morocco's forces with the capture of Tetuán in the short-lived African campaign of 1860. However, further overseas adventures in Santo Domingo (1861), Mexico (1862), Chile and Peru (1865-1866) were not so successful, only serving to assuage temporarily the smouldering discontent at home. By 1863 the Unión Liberal had collapsed, the two parties unable to agree on a common platform, and when the Queen failed to summon them to form a government, the *progresistas* began plotting with the more radical *demócratas*. Surrounded by obscurantist advisers such as Sor Patrocinio and Padre Claret, the frivolous and superstitious Queen Isabel II had to rely increasingly on the personal government of her trusted favourites, Generals O'Donnell and Narváez. Two tragic blunders by an O'Donnell government – the 1865 *Noche de San Daniel* attack against student protesters in Madrid, and the 1866 execution of sixty-six mutinous sergeants from the Madrid barracks of San Gil – aroused the public's indignation. Furthermore, the economic bubble had burst by 1867 with a sharp drop in railway construction and a crisis in the cotton industry as a result of the American Civil War. By April 1868, with O'Donnell and Narváez both dead, Isabel II could turn only to the unscrupulous González Bravo for help to prop up her tottering regime. His rash banishment in June of disaffected Unión Liberal generals and the Queen's ambitious brother-in-law, the Duque de Montpensier, to the Canary Islands and Portugal respectively, was the decisive move that assured the success of a revolutionary coalition of Prim's *progresistas*, Ruiz Zorrilla's *demócratas* and the *moderados*.

The September 1868 Revolution, *La Gloriosa* or *La Septembrina*, as it is alternatively called, launched in Cádiz when Prim's secret arrival from England coincided with the return of the exiled generals, was an immediate success. A brief bloody battle at Alcolea near Córdoba was the only obstacle in the revolutionaries' march on Madrid. Within a week they were in control of the country, with the Queen and her latest lover, Marfori, taking the train of exile to France whither González Bravo had scampered at the first news of the revolution. Although the word "revolution" is a misnomer to describe the little that actually happened in September 1868, there can be no doubt that 1868 is an important watershed in nineteenth-century Spanish history and things would never be quite the same again. General Serrano, an Unión Liberal general and one-time lover of the Queen, was named Head of State, with Juan Prim, hero of the battle of Castillejos in the 1860 African campaign and of the 1862 Mexican expedition and the leading spirit behind *progresista* plots in the sixties, becoming Prime Minister. The task of keeping the disparate groups in the Revolutionary coalition together was a test of Prim's political skill. If the *demócratas* gained male universal suffrage in the very radical 1869 Constitution, Prim's *progresistas* and the Unión Liberal *moderados* were able to secure the retention of the monarchy as the country's political form. With the Bourbons beyond the pale, Prim scoured Europe for a suitable occupant for the Spanish throne, managing in the process to ignite the Franco-Prussian War of 1870, before the Italian prince, Amadeo of Savoy, agreed to take the position. His arrival in Cartagena in the final days of 1870 was preceded by the severest blow yet dealt the Revolution: the assassination in Madrid of the charismatic Prim. Had he survived, the history of Spain in succeeding years would surely have taken a different course.

Amadeo tried to play the role of constitutional monarch or impartial referee between the warring political parties. By February 1873, after barely two years of frustrated rule, he abdicated and left the country to its own devices. The main partners in the 1868 Revolution (the *progresistas* under their new leader, Sagasta, and the *demócratas* of

Ruiz Zorrilla) were no longer willing to co-operate in the parliamentary game. The beneficiaries of this political vacuum were the Republicans whose fortunes had increased dramatically.

However, the First Republic was beset with difficulties from the start: the Second Carlist War had broken out in the north in 1872 and now, with disorder spreading to Madrid and the rest of the country, that war intensified. Unable to wait for the establishment of a Federalist Republic, some cities in the south (especially Cartagena and Murcia) proclaimed themselves independent cantons opposed to the central authority of Madrid. Moreover the Republic could not count on the firm authority of a strong president: within ten months Figueras, Pi y Margall, Salmerón and Castelar had taken supreme control of the country only to relinquish it after a short period. Men of intelligence and probity, they could not control the wilder extremists within their ranks or counter the plots of the army and the monarchist supporters of the Bourbons.

By January 3, 1874, the disorder of the Republican governments had been halted by a conservative backlash: General Pavía's storming of Parliament marked the return to a more authoritarian government, this time under the direction of the indispensable General Serrano. However, when he was unable to terminate the festering Carlist War in the north, the *alfonsista* party, ably led by the astute Cánovas, managed, through the decisive intervention of General Martínez Campos's proclamation at Sagunto in December 1874, to bring back a Bourbon, the young Alfonso XII, to the Spanish throne.

This ironical return of the Bourbons seven years after they had been bundled unceremoniously out of the country can only be explained by the widespread desire, especially amongst the growing middle class, for peace and order after the anarchy of the First Republic. Now at another important turning-point in its turbulent nineteenth-century history, Spain was lucky to be able to count on the wisdom of the monarchist leader, Antonio Cánovas del Castillo, who realized that eternal confrontation between parliamentary groups was fruitless. Architect of the so-called *turno pacífico* system, he was able to give the country an important period of stability as he and his Conservative party alternated in power with Práxedes Mateo Sagasta and his Liberals. By prior agreement, when one party had enjoyed sufficient power or had run short of ideas, it allowed the other to take its place. This system, indeed, was a far cry from the intransigence of previous eras when the army had felt compelled to intervene in the form of *pronunciamientos* to preserve the State. The Restoration system, as it was called, (1875-1931), was to be one of the most stable and prosperous periods in modern Spanish history. The succession of governments in the first fifteen years (1875-1881: Cánovas; 1881-1884: Sagasta; 1884-1885: Cánovas; 1885-1890: Sagasta) contrasts markedly with the endless string of months-old, even days-old, governments in pre-1875 Spain.

The country was also fortunate at this time to have an energetic, popular young King, Alfonso XII, who personally participated in the victory over the Carlists in 1876. His tragic death in 1885 from typhoid fever, though universally mourned, did not really arrest the growing prosperity and stability of the Restoration. The wise and decorous statesmanship of his second wife, María Cristina (his first wife, the popular María de las Mercedes, had died tragically in 1887, five months after their marriage) ensured the continuation of the *turno pacífico* and the consolidation of the new monarchy. The degree of compromise achieved by this new system can be gauged by the fact that if the Conservatives were able to ensure the supremacy of the Catholic Church in the realm of public worship and education, the Liberals were able to introduce universal suffrage in 1888. In the circumstances, it is not surprising that the Spanish economy recovered from the slump of the sixties, with increased foreign investment leading to increased production of metals, cotton and wine and more railway construction. However, by 1886-1887 the economic bubble had once again burst and the country's industries, especially the Catalan textile trade, needed high tariffs to protect them against foreign competition.

If by the end of the 1880s Republican plots against the monarchy had petered out, the omnipotence of the *caciques* (local political bosses in the country areas), upon whom the leaders of the two main parties in Madrid depended, was becoming an ever increasing threat to the stability of Spanish democracy. The loss of Spain's troublesome overseas possessions (Cuba, Puerto Rico and the Philippines) in the 1898 war with the United States led to increased instability and periods of morbid self-examination and soul-searching. However, all attempts to regenerate the by now anchylosed political system, whether by politicians such as Maura, Silvela and Canalejas or by the thinkers and writers of the Generation of '98, proved futile. Moreover, the bourgeois *turno pacífico* offered no place for the expanding proletarian parties. The Socialist party had been founded in 1874 and along with its union, the UGT (founded in 1882), was strong in Madrid and the industrial regions of the Basque Country and Asturias. In Cataluña, Aragón and Andalucía, Anarchist revolutionaries had made their demands known in a terrifying fashion right from 1868 with bomb attacks and arson. In Cataluña this mixture of dangerous ingredients was compounded by the renaissance of Catalan culture and the formation of separatist political parties. The fuse that ignited this powder keg was the infamous *Semana trágica* of July 1909 when the Madrid Government, in trying to put down an armed protest against another African campaign, succeeded only in alienating regionalist opinion. The carnage and church-burning, followed by the execution of the scapegoat, Francisco Ferrer, signalled the beginning of the end for the Restoration system of alternating governments, an end that would be reached in 1923 with General Primo de Rivera's coup.

BIBLIOGRAPHY

1. THE HISTORICAL PERIOD

Aguado Bleye, Pedro, and Alcázar Molina, Cayetano, *Manual de historia de España*, 3 vols. (Madrid, 1954-1956)

Beck, Earl R., *A Time of Triumph and of Sorrow: Spanish Politics During the Reign of Alfonso XII, 1874-1885* (Carbondale, Illinois, 1979)

Bleiberg, Germán, *Diccionario de historia de España*, 2nd ed., 3 vols. (Madrid, 1968)

Carr, Raymond, *Spain 1808-1939* (Oxford, 1966)

Clarke, H. Butler, *Modern Spain 1815-1898* (Cambridge, 1906)

Fernández Almagro, Melchor, *Historia política de la España contemporánea*, 3 vols. (Madrid, 1969)

Ferrandis, Manuel, and Beirao, Caetano, *Historia contemporánea de España y Portugal* (Barcelona, 1966)

Gribble, Francis, *The Tragedy of Isabella II* (London, 1913)

La Rosa, Tristán, *España contemporánea: siglo XIX* (Barcelona, 1972)

Olivar Bertrand, Rafael, *Así cayó Isabel II: siglo de pasión política* (Barcelona, 1955)

Palacio Atard, Vicente, *La España del siglo XIX, 1808-1898: introducción a la España contemporánea* (Madrid, 1978)

Ramos Oliveira, A., *Politics, Economics and Men of Modern Spain 1808-1946*, trans. Teener Hall (London, 1946)

Tuñón de Lara, Manuel, *La España del siglo XIX*, 2 vols. (Barcelona, 1976)

Vicens Vives, Jaime, *Manual de historia económica de España*, 3rd ed. (Barcelona, 1959)

2. THE HISTORICAL NOVEL

Alonso, Amado, *Ensayos sobre la novela histórica* (Buenos Aires, 1942)

Azorín (Martínez Ruiz, José), "La novela histórica", in his *Clásicos y modernos* (Madrid, 1919), pp.189-94

Butterfield, Herbert, *The Historical Novel: An Essay* (Cambridge, 1924)
Deegan, Thomas, "George Eliot's novels of the historical imagination", *Clio*, 1, No. 3 (1972), 21-33
Fleishman, Avrom, *The English Historical Novel: Walter Scott to Virginia Woolf* (Baltimore, 1971)
Gogorza Fletcher, Madeleine de, *The Spanish Historical Novel: 1870-1970* (London, 1974)
Lukács, Georg, *The Historical Novel*, trans. Hannah and Stanley Mitchell (Harmondsworth, 1976)
Matthews, James Brander, *The Historical Novel and Other Essays* (New York, 1901)

3. GALDOS: BIBLIOGRAPHIES

García Lorenzo, Luciano E., "Bibliografía galdosiana", *CHA*, 84 (1970-1971), 758-97
Hernández Suárez, Manuel, "Bibliografía", *AG*, 3 (1968), 191-212; 4 (1969), 127-52; 6 (1971), 139-63; 7 (1972), 144-65; 9 (1974), 175-206
Sackett, Theodore A., *Pérez Galdós: an Annotated Bibliography* (Albuquerque, 1968)
Varey, J.E., "Galdós in the light of recent criticism", *Galdós Studies*, ed. J.E. Varey (London, 1970), pp.1-35
Woodbridge, Hensley C., *Benito Pérez Galdós: a Selective Annotated Bibliography* (Metuchen, New Jersey, 1975)

4. GALDOS: SELECTED CRITICAL STUDIES

Amorós, Andrés, "El ambiente de *La de Bringas*", *Reales Sitios*, 6 (1965), 61-68
Anon., "Five years in Madrid", *TLS*, 12 October 1973, pp.1227-28
Blanco Aguinaga, Carlos, *La historia y el texto literario: tres novelas de Galdós* (Madrid, 1978)
—, "On 'The birth of Fortunata' ", *AG*, 3 (1968), 13-24
Bly, Peter A., *Benito Pérez Galdós: La de Bringas*, Critical Guides to Spanish Texts, 20 (London, 1981)
—, "Fortunata and No 11, Cava de San Miguel", *Hispanófila*, 20, No. 59 (1976-1977), 31-48
—, "Galdós, the Madrid Royal Palace and the September 1868 Revolution", *Revista Canadiense de Estudios Hispánicos*, 5 (1980), 1-17
—, "The use of distance in Galdós's *La de Bringas*", *Modern Language Review*, 69 (1974), 88-97
—, "Sallies and encounters in *Torquemada en la hoguera*: patterns of significance", *AG*, 13 (1978), 23-31
—, "Sex, egotism and social regeneration in Galdós' *El caballero encantado* ", *Hispania*, 62 (1979), 20-29

Casalduero, Joaquín, *Vida y obra de Galdós (1843-1920)*, 3rd ed. (Madrid, 1970)

Davies, G.A., "Galdós' *El amigo Manso*: an experiment in didactic method", *BHS*, 39 (1962), 16-30

Dendle, Brian J., *Galdós: the Mature Thought* (Lexington, Kentucky, 1980)

Gilman, Stephen, "The birth of Fortunata", *AG*, 1 (1966), 71-83

—, "The consciousness of Fortunata", *AG*, 5 (1970), 55-66

—, "Novel and society: *Doña Perfecta*", *AG*, 11 (1976), 15-27

Gullón, Ricardo, "Cuestiones galdosianas", *CHA*, 34 (1958), 237-54

—, *Técnicas de Galdós* (Madrid, 1970)

Hinterhäuser, Hans, *Los "Episodios nacionales" de Benito Pérez Galdós*, trans. José Escobar (Madrid, 1963)

Kirsner, Robert, "Sobre *El amigo Manso* de Galdós", *Cuadernos de Literatura*, 8 (1950), 189-99

Lambert, A.F., "Galdós and the anti-bureaucratic tradition", *BHS*, 53 (1976), 35-49

Lowe, Jennifer, "Galdós's use of time in *La de Bringas*", *AG*, 15 (1980), 83-88

Montesinos, José F., *Galdós*, 3 vols. (Madrid, 1968-1973)

Nimetz, Michael, *Humor in Galdós: a Study of the "Novelas Contemporáneas"*, (New Haven, Connecticut, 1968)

Ortiz Armengol, Pedro, "Tres apuntes hacia temas de *Fortunata y Jacinta*", *Letras de Deusto*, 4 (1974), 241-59

Pattison, Walter T., *Benito Pérez Galdós* (Boston, 1975)

Regalado García, Antonio, *Benito Pérez Galdós y la novela histórica española 1868-1912* (Madrid, 1966)

Ribbans, Geoffrey, "Contemporary history in the structure and characterization of *Fortunata y Jacinta*", *Galdós Studies*, ed. J.E. Varey (London, 1970), pp.90-113

—, "*Historia novelada* and *novela histórica*: the use of historical incidents from the reign of Isabella II in Galdós's *episodios* and *novelas contemporáneas*", *Hispanic Studies in Honour of Frank Pierce*, ed. John England (Sheffield, 1980), pp.133-47

Ricard, Robert, *Aspects de Galdós* (Paris, 1963)

—, *Galdós et ses romans* (Paris, 1961)

Rodgers, Eamonn, "The appearance-reality contrast in Galdós' *Tormento*", *Forum for Modern Language Studies*, 6 (1970), 382-98

—, "Realismo y mito en *El amigo Manso*", *CHA*, 84 (1970-71), 430-44

—, *Pérez Galdós: Miau*, Critical Guides to Spanish Texts, 23 (London, 1978)

Rodríguez, Alfredo, *Aspectos de la novela de Galdós* (Almería, 1967)

—, *An Introduction to the "Episodios Nacionales" of Galdós* (New York, 1967)

Rodríguez-Puértolas, Julio, *Galdós: burguesía y revolución* (Madrid, 1975)

Ruiz Salvador, Antonio, "La función del trasfondo histórico en *La desheredada*", *AG*, 1 (1966), 53-62

Sánchez, Roberto G., "The function of dates and deadlines in Galdós' *La de Bringas*", *Hispanic Review*, 46 (1978), 299-311

Scanlon, Geraldine M., "*El doctor Centeno*: a study in obsolescent values", *BHS*, 55 (1978), 245-53

Schraibman, Joseph, "Galdós y 'el estilo de la vejez' ", *Homenaje a Rodríguez-Moñino* (Madrid, 1966), II, pp.165-75

Sinnigen, John H., "Individual, class and society in *Fortunata y Jacinta*", *Galdós Studies II*, ed. Robert J. Weber (London, 1974), pp.49-68

Sobejano, Gonzalo, "Forma literaria y sensibilidad social en *La incógnita y Realidad* de Galdós", *Revista Hispánica Moderna*, 30 (1964), 89-107

Terry, Arthur, "*Lo prohibido*: unreliable narrator and untruthful narrative", *Galdós Studies*, ed. J.E. Varey (London, 1970), pp.62-89

Varey, J.E., "Francisco Bringas: *nuestro buen Thiers*", *AG*, 1 (1966), 63-69

Weber, Robert J., *The Miau Manuscript of Benito Pérez Galdós: a Critical Study*, University of California Publications in Modern Philology, 72 (Berkeley, 1964)

Wright, Chad C., "The representational qualities of Isidora Rufete's house and her son Riquín in Benito Pérez Galdós's novel *La desheredada*", *Romanische Forschungen*, 83 (1971), 230-45

—, "Imagery of light and darkness in *La de Bringas*", *AG*, 13 (1978), 5-12

Zahareas, Anthony N., "El sentido de la tragedia en *Fortunata y Jacinta*", *AG*, 3 (1968), 25-34

LIVERPOOL MONOGRAPHS IN HISPANIC STUDIES

General Editor: James Higgins
Assistant Editors: Ann Mackenzie, Roger Wright

1. THE POET IN PERU. Alienation and the Quest for a
    super-reality.   JAMES HIGGINS
    x+166pp. ISBN 0 905205 10 3. 1982.

In this first full-length study of a wide range of modern Peruvian
poetry, Dr. Higgins offers readings of the work of six poets — Eguren,
Vallejo, Belli, Cisneros, Moro, Adán. His study shows that, although
these writers differ widely from one another, they share a common
dilemma — how to reconcile the dichotomies of their society — and a
common artistic stance — the poet is a man outcast from society, but
able because of this to apprehend a greater reality in a visionary world.

Dr. Higgins is Senior Lecturer in Latin-American Studies in the
School of Hispanic Studies, University of Liverpool.

". . . the interpretations of all the poets are provocative and will
provide a basis for further discussion of this important area of Spanish-
American literature." *Bulletin of Hispanic Studies*

2. GALDOS'S NOVEL OF THE HISTORICAL
    IMAGINATION. A Study of the Contemporary Novels.
                                                    PETER A. BLY
    xii+195pp. ISBN 0 905205 14 6. 1983.

*   *   *   *   *

OTHER VOLUMES IN PREPARATION